'It is a delight to see Marshall-Andrews's mischievous mind at work … a witty and indiscreet book that is a bitter denunciation of "the cynical abuse of power which was the stock-in-trade of Blair's government"' *Times Literary Supplement*

'His disloyalty to the New Labour apparat is principled, but expressed with a light heart and a clear conscience – lighter and clearer, probably, than those of more obedient MPs.' *Spectator*

'It is difficult to think of a single MP in the current Parliament who matches his wit and his ability to pick a fight with his own government … It ought to be required reading for anyone considering a political career.' Iain Dale, *Total Politics*

'The author is the sort of politician, regarded as a maverick troublemaker by party managers, who is needed to protect our civil liberties from unprincipled assault.' Chris Patten, *Financial Times*

'Subversive and funny' *Oldie*

'The author's well-balanced critique of the shortcomings of the present British parliamentary system is juxtaposed with an inescapable sense of gratitude and admiration for the Labour party, making this memoir a fine, captivating and greatly inspiring read.' *Good Book Guide*

'One of the most scathing yet incisive analyses of the Blair era … a delight … a heartfelt, partisan and refreshingly honest account by a decent man who saw his party taken over and perverted by a gang of power-hungry politicians and flim-flam merchants.' *Contemporary Review*

'Brilliant, witty and excoriating, the answer to all the self-serving autobiographies written by New Labour's yesterday men. Too political and principled for contemporary politics, Bob Marshall Andrews was the attorney general we should have had – civil liberties would have been preserved, Iraq would not have been invaded and companies taking bribes would have been prosecuted. Alas.' Helena Kennedy, QC

f a single ks been so wittily dissent, Bob e for character, dehouse.' Peter

BOB MARSHALL-ANDREWS joined the Labour Party in 1971. He entered Parliament as the member for Medway in 1997 and quickly gained a reputation on the libertarian left by repeated rebellions against the government, especially on issues relating to civil liberty. He is widely respected in the Westminster media-circuit, a frequent panellist on the satirical news quiz *Have I Got News For You*, a regular contributor to the national press, and the founder and trustee of the George Adamson Wildlife Trust. He has written two published novels *The Palace of Wisdom* and *A Man Without Guilt.* A barrister, he was appointed QC in 1987, and has prosecuted and defended most forms of serious crime and many serious criminals, specialising in fraud.

OFF MESSAGE

The complete antidote to political humbug

Bob Marshall-Andrews

P

PROFILE BOOKS

This paperback edition published in 2012

First published in Great Britain in 2011 by
PROFILE BOOKS LTD
3A Exmouth House
Pine Street
London ECIR OJH
www.profilebooks.com

1 3 5 7 9 10 8 6 4 2

Typeset in Garamond by MacGuru Ltd
info@macguru.org.uk
Printed and bound in Great Britain by
CPI Group (UK) Ltd, Croydon, CRO 4YY

A CIP catalogue record for this book is available from the British Library.

ISBN 978 1 84668 442 5
eISBN 978 1 84765 465 6

CONTENTS

FOREWORD

At school I was, briefly, the goalkeeper for the Second XI Hockey. In those days the protective clothing worn by hockey goalkeepers was mainly metal. Starting at the feet, huge iron casts were clamped on to the boots; above these, the thigh-length pads were strongly braced with steel; then came the comparatively light whalebone chest protector; and above it all, a Darth Vader/Hannibal Lecter metal mask through the visor of which one peered into the North London drizzle. The Second XI pitch was a lamentable affair, used for a number of other sports, and thus, by February, had become a sea of mud, particularly in the area of the goal mouth. However much I tried to remain mobile, the weight of the defensive costume assured that after about ten minutes I sank uncontrollably into the mire and became wholly and completely stuck in the middle of the goal. This position was not as hopeless as it sounds. Not infrequently, opposing forwards would break through the outer defence preparing to smash the ball into the net. They, of course, expected the goalkeeper to move swiftly towards them to close the angle and narrow the range of fire. In fact, they were confronted by a totally immobile and heavily armoured opponent, gesticulating wildly from the waist up, but otherwise breaking all the elementary rules of hockey defence. Frequently, this completely threw them. Suspecting some kind of elaborate feint, they often shot wide or, more frequently, shot the ball directly at me, anticipating some form of late movement. This caused injury or concussion but also saved the goal, for which I received wholly undeserved acclaim as I was carried from the field.

I often thought of this analogy as I sank into the metaphoric Westminster mud, contemplating, as I did so, the reason for my existence. However, one has no idea how many goals one may have saved simply by being threateningly inactive. In a valedictory piece on the *PM* programme, the splendid Eddie Mair asked me this self-same question: 'Do you think, in your time at Westminster, you have achieved anything?' I attempted to give him a short faltering list but added, I hope legitimately, that one had no idea what contribution I and my fellow band of dissidents had made, simply by our immobile presence.

On one occasion, I remember approaching a senior Home Office minister and asking whether it was the Government's intention, yet again, to attempt to remove the right of trial by jury for those charged with serious fraud offences. The Government minister rolled his eyes to the ceiling and back again, and indicated that the present intention of the Home Office was to dispense with the legislation altogether. When I enquired as to the reason for this unusual volte-face, he replied that 'it wasn't worth the trouble you buggers would cause'. Thus, by comparative inaction but a suitably threatening posture, we had, in all probability, saved a considerable Commons battle and defeated the legislation before it was struck at the goal mouth. As I reflected many years ago, they also serve who only stand in mud.

CHAPTER 1

OF BEGINNINGS

In which we reflect on the motivations of politicians and the sublime happiness of being without ambition – Recount the disastrous consequences of a joke told at the River Café – Reflect on the abuse of power and patronage – Consider the enduring influence of a wonderful woman – Recall an interesting confrontation with the Militant Tendency, and finally arrive at the Mother of Parliaments at a difficult and venerable age.

People enter politics, I believe, for one of two broad reasons. The first is to achieve power; the second is to control it. Both may be honourable, but the first is obviously likely to attract far more rogues than the second. It is a division that may arguably separate the most famous revolutionary double acts of history and of literature. Robespierre, for all his initial purity and vision, was seduced and demented by power to deadly and terrible effect. Danton, his fellow rebel, wished only to control it and died as its victim on the guillotine. Lenin forged the greatest and bloodiest revolution in history in order to achieve power – which he did – and having done so presided over the murderous death of millions. Trotsky, for all his ruthless acts, abhorred power and ended his life in exile and with an ice pick in his head. Fidel Castro, whilst loathing the corrupt regime of Cuba, desired to replace it and to rule – which he did – as the longest standing dictator of the twentieth and twenty-first centuries. Che Guevara, his golf partner and comrade-in-arms, was gunned down in the jungles of Bolivia surrounded by a small group of followers.

Shakespeare himself recognised the dialectic. Cassius, 'lean and hungry' for power, fully justified Caesar's reservations as to his dangerous attraction. Brutus, poor, decent, honourable Brutus, friend and murderer, loathed power and, indeed, was seduced by Cassius on precisely that basis. Brutus, noblest Roman of them all, died on his own sword at the Battle of Philippi.

In my short time in British politics I never aspired to power or office – which was lucky, as there was never the faintest chance of my achieving or retaining it. The only office to which I felt any ambition was that of Attorney General. That would not have lasted long and, indeed, would barely have survived New Labour's first assault on the principle of trial by jury. The only reason why, in moments of fantasy, I regret never achieving that historic role is the effect that it might have had on Britain's part in the Iraq conflict – but that is indeed mere fantasy. The absence of ambition, whether in the British parliamentary system or any other, and relative old age (fifty-three is now positively geriatric in terms of joining Parliament), at least provides a measure of detachment. This memoir is not intended to be a treatise of the shortcomings (dire as they are) of the present British parliamentary system. Great works have already been produced which distil this unhappy state of affairs. I would direct the reader to Christopher Foster's luminous book *The British Constitution in Crisis*, and I have no doubt that my good friend Peter Hennessey will soon produce his own weighty lamentation on the death of the Cabinet system of which he has so long been a powerful and vocal advocate.

This is intended to be a small political odyssey. The Cyclops' cave will be more in evidence than the Sirens but, nonetheless, I hope that it will have a sub-Homeric capacity to amuse. No such book, however, would be complete without some reflection on the perilous state of the British political system and the fact that we have evolved a dangerous presidential form of government without any of the essential checks and balances recognisable from Montesquieu to Tom Paine. This failing has had consequences in the nature of the legislation that we have passed, the capacity of Government to drift into authoritarian control and, of course, in the awful consequences of the Iraq War into which we were led not only by duplicity and deceit, but also by a system that allowed a single dishonesty to dominate the decisions which were taken across the political spectrum.

It did not start well. Some four weeks before the General Election of 1997, Helena Kennedy and Charlie Falconer (both shortly destined for the House of Lords) organised a fundraising dinner at the River Café. It was very smart and was intended only for lawyers, at a cost of £500 a plate. Richard and Ruth Rogers, who were also members of the high priesthood, were to provide an exceptional River Café meal at a remarkable price in order to enable the excess payments to swell the already bulging coffers of the Labour election machine. As a candidate, I thought that my time (and possibly my money) would be better employed in attempting to persuade the electorate of Medway, whose affinity with the River Café is, to say the least, tenuous. Unhappily, as it turned out, this was not to be. John Mortimer had been booked to make the speech at this great event, which was to be attended by the Blairs themselves and other members of their close entourage, including (fatally as it transpired) the putative Lord Chancellor, Derry Irvine. John Mortimer was indisposed, which resulted in Helena phoning me on the day before the dinner. Would I fill the gap and make the after-dinner speech? With a little reluctance I agreed, and Helena finished our conversation with the observation that it wouldn't do me any harm.

I don't suppose she has ever been so inaccurate in a long and distinguished career at the Bar and in politics.

The party was very grand. Labour was approximately twenty points ahead in the opinion polls, steering straight for a glorious victory and (perhaps because of this fact) the dinner was attended by 250 lawyers, many of whom had not previously been conspicuous in the vanguard of leftish politics. It was, indeed, a jolly event and the food, as predicted, was excellent. The Blairs held court at one end of the room, sitting together with Helena and Derry Irvine. I was placed at the far end. The time came to make the speech. I had only been given a limited time in which to prepare this important address (that, at least, is my principal mitigation). I rose and began with some welcomes to the group and expressed the not unreasonable view that never in the history of the Labour Party had Georgio Armani been so well represented. That didn't go down badly, and I forged on.

Part way through the speech I had settled on a pleasantry about Derry Irvine. I had met him only once briefly at the Bar when he and I had appeared for some ten minutes at consecutive Master's applications. The immediate distinction between us was the number of books that I was carrying (many) and the number that he was carrying (none) as behind him was an entourage of young men employed for this very purpose. I did not remind him of this meeting, but we had a number of mutual friends and I was aware (as were many others) of his more famous characteristics. I therefore embarked on a small pleasantry.

'Many things,' I said, 'are going to change under New Labour, but there is one thing that looks as if it will remain exactly the same and that is the character of the Lord Chancellor. It looks as though we are in for another Presbyterian, ascetic, teetotal Scot – well, a Scot anyway.'

For many in the room this gentle gibe appeared to be well received. It was, of course, a reference to Derry's reputation as a singular trencherman and, in particular, a lover of fine wine.

Indeed, a lover of much fine wine. At the end of the evening I said my farewells and disappeared back to Richmond. The following day I received a telephone call from a friend who told me she had been phoned by Helena Kennedy, and that Helena had informed her that Derry had phoned her at six thirty in the morning 'speechless with rage'. He was, said Helena, demanding an apology to the Blairs. I was a little mystified.

'To the Blairs?' I asked.

'Yes, to the Blairs,' she replied.

I still find this difficult. Whilst I have made many apologies for ill-advised pleasantries, it was the first time I had ever been asked to apologise to A for something I had said, as a joke, about B's drinking. Having politely declined the invitation, I got on with attempting to be elected by the constituents of Medway, who remained totally ignorant of the grotesque political faux pas committed by their future Labour member.

I remained ignorant of any likely consequences until I arrived at the House of Commons, partly expectedly, on 2 May 1997. Shortly after my arrival I was approached by Chris Mullin, whom I had known in the Labour Party for many years, and with whom I shared a number of interests, including scribbling the odd novel (two each) and attempting to mitigate the worst effects of the miscarriages of justice within the British legal system.

After welcoming me to Parliament, Chris asked whether I would be prepared to serve on the Home Office Select Committee, a committee he expected (rightly, as it transpired) to chair. I told him, of course, that I would be delighted to serve under his chairmanship and he said he would put me on his list to be suggested to the Whips. We parted on our usual good terms. It was a not altogether unsurprising invitation. The Labour Party was singularly bereft of QCs (I was the only one) or Recorders of the Crown Court (likewise). I felt I had something to bring to the party and looked forward to making a contribution on the legal and civil libertarian issues that were bound to be part of the committee's deliberations in the coming years. I felt a sense of quiet satisfaction. I would now have a reasonably constructive job to do in Parliament without being a member of the Government which I did not aspire to join. There was a slight disadvantage in that I had already decided to leave my practice at the Bar if I was appointed to a Select Committee, in order that I could give my full time to what I, even then, regarded as a singularly important parliamentary task.

This self-satisfaction was brief. A week later I met Chris at a party being held by Clare Short at Lancaster House.

'I wonder, Bob,' he said, 'if I could have a quick word?'

'Of course,' I said, and we took our drinks to a quiet corner of the garden.

'It's about the Select Committee,' he said.

'Ah,' I replied, 'I have no problem at all, Chris. I would be delighted to serve under your chairmanship.'

Unusually, he appeared a little discomfited.

'Yes,' he said. 'Well, I'm sorry to say you've been taken off.'

'Taken off?' I said. 'Taken off what?'

'Yes, I'm afraid you've been taken off the committee. I put you down as one of my starred members but you have been taken off.'

'Who exactly by?' I enquired. Even then, I thought it was very early in my political career (six days) to have made any powerful enemies.

'Well,' said Chris, 'I'm afraid it is at the highest level.'

'No. 10?' I said, both startled and a little alarmed. 'I don't know anyone in No. 10.'

Chris ignored the obvious inaccuracy and then said: 'Bob, did you make a speech during the election campaign about the Blairs?'

To which I replied, entirely accurately, 'No', and we parted.

It was only moments later that I realized the speech to which he must have been referring, as I had made no public utterances outside my constituency in the whole of the election campaign. I reflected on this and, as I did so, was aware of a mounting sense of anger. As to my own predicament I was almost indifferent. There would be some advantages of not sitting upon a Select Committee and, no doubt, there would be other opportunities within Parliament. However, even then, I was aware of a strong aversion to the intervention of the Executive in the selection of a body which was designed specifically and principally to control that very Executive. At that time I had, as far as I was aware, had no contact with either of the Blairs whether in a political or a legal circumstance. Nor did I know any of the essential power-brokers in No. 10.

The more I reflected on this unhappy state of affairs, the more concerned I became; so I asked for a meeting with the Chief Whip, Nick Brown. It was our first meeting and one which I remember well. In the coming years I got to know and like Nick Brown. He was a dedicated Brownite and on a number of occasions we made common cause, covertly and otherwise, to remove the incumbent Prime Minister. I was invited to sit down in the Chief Whip's office. It was the first of many such sittings.

'What,' said Nick, 'can I do for you?'

I explained the problem. I did not mention the full conversation at Lancaster House but I told the Chief Whip that I had been asked to sit on the Select Committee but I had now been told by Chris Mullin that I had been removed from the list. I was anxious to know why this was. Nick Brown was, at first, dismissive. Many people, he said, go on and off Select Committees, so it may be that the committee was just over-subscribed. I told him that I didn't think so. However immodestly, I pointed out that my qualifications for sitting on this committee were pretty good. At that point he disappeared behind his large desk and re-emerged with a folder. He opened and studied it. He then said,

'Did you make a speech in the election campaign?'

'I made many speeches during the election campaign,' I replied.

'Ah,' he said. 'It can't be that then,' and put the file away. 'Don't worry,' he added, 'I'm sure this will be a minor setback.'

This was, as it transpired, a glorious understatement.

I cannot deny that I had the beginnings of a sour, acrid taste in my mouth. It contributed also to a growing sense of alarm at the cynical abuse of personal power which was the stock-in-trade of Blair's government and which did much in the coming years to corrode and corrupt Westminster politics. In its small and utterly insignificant way, it demonstrates one of the major vices of our political system; namely patronage.

Our Cabinet system of Government, much lauded by the great constitutional Victorian writers such as Dicey and Bagehot, relies entirely on the capacity of the legislature (the Commons in particular) to control the Executive and, in particular, the Prime Minister. Without this essential check and balance, Cabinet Government is immensely dangerous as it is dominated by the Prime Minister who ultimately has the power to appoint and sack his colleagues from the very legislature which is exercising the control. The conflict is immediately apparent, but throughout the history of Parliament until the twentieth century was concealed by a number of factors, not least the nature and character of those who served in the legislature itself. Although many, of course, sought office, many certainly did not. On the Tory benches the squirearchy did not generally aspire to Government but exercised an informal social power over their Prime Minister in the grey-suited corridors of the Carlton Club.

When Labour achieved a mass vote and became a major parliamentary party, the class warriors of the trade union movement fell together easily and, occasionally, uneasily with the intellectuals of the Bloomsbury group. Again, the concept of the 'professional' politician was very different. All that changed in the second half of the twentieth century and we now live entirely with the ascendancy of the professional politician who has no other aim (not, in itself, illaudable) than that of achieving a position in Government. In order to achieve that aim, they must obtain the favour of the Prime Minister; and in order to obtain that favour, they must, of course, conform to the dictates of the Executive. This problem has become steadily and implacably worse. It is far greater than the procedural deficiencies which undoubtedly exist within the Commons' rules which favour the Executive. It is part of a political culture which is now firmly embedded in what has become a presidential system and which lacks the checks and balances necessary in such a form of democratic government. My own small story is simply a part of that wider context.

When I became a Member of Parliament I did not aspire to be or to become either a minister or a maverick. Without consciously contemplating either, I understood that I was too old for both. By modern political standards I was a borderline blanket case. I had been a moderately successful barrister and QC, and had written one reasonably successful novel. All of which begged the obvious question which was proposed to me by Philip Howard, in the course of a kind and agreeable interview, shortly after my election, 'Why did you do it?' The question, of course, had both a personal and political dimension. The political aspect was easier to answer. I wanted to be a professional backbencher which, I believed naively, was still an essential part of the English constitution and the political landscape. I wanted to be a modest and constructive curb on the Executive should the Government abuse the massive real power with which our constitution endows it. I also wished to lend constructive support to what I believed could be an historic administration and possibly one of the most important in British history. I foresaw a lengthy period of Labour rule which would address the serious problems of the British constitution, buttress parliamentary power, entrench historic civil liberties which had been threatened by the Thatcher administration, and address the twin problems of poverty and inequality through fiscal reform and the handmaiden of public service. Poor innocent fool, as I now realise.

The personal answer to Philip Howard's question 'Why did you do it?' is a little more complex. It will be of marginally greater interest to students of psychology than politics, although what makes any politician become one evokes its own elemental curiosity. I will do my best to abbreviate my own primrose path to Parliament whilst acknowledging it to be a minor self-indulgence and taking not the least offence if the reader in search of political rather than personal revelations should move directly to Chapter 2.

I was not a natural socialist and came from a working-class Tory culture. My father became a Fleet Street compositor after seven years' apprenticeship. My mother's family were originally from County Cork and she herself was born in the Irish county of Edgware which, for over a hundred years, had traditionally formed a refuge from famine. The fifth of seven children (five survived to become adults), she was fortunate to obtain a scholarship to a grammar school which she (rather than her equally qualified siblings) was able to attend. The family fortunes by that stage no longer required every child to enter the workplace at the age of fourteen. She became a fearsomely good primary school-teacher and the memory of the number of pupils who attended her funeral is still capable of pricking my eyes. My maternal grandmother 'did for' wealthy people in north-west London and, it subsequently and ironically transpired, assiduously scrubbed the steps of one branch of the Bates family, which was, eventually, to produce my wonderful wife Gillian. My maternal grandfather was a baker's assistant with whom I spent a considerable amount of my very early years, as he read from a vast and eclectic range of books. He was immensely well read, totally self-taught and a chronic alcoholic. So wide-ranging was the choice of literature that my opened mind began to see most intellectual discipline as a shifting kaleidoscope and my mother records two occasions when she heard my grandfather saying sternly to me on his lap, 'No, that has nothing to do with how Nelson lost his eye'. I have, to this day, retained a penchant for the non sequitur.

At the age of eleven, I was immensely fortunate to achieve a County Award (later known as an Assisted Places Scheme) to Mill Hill School, the middle-range public school in north-west London which shares with Harrow the distinction of being one of the only two public schools that can see each other across the Thames Valley. Many years later, in Parliament, I was to oppose the continuation of the Assisted Places Scheme. I did so with a heavy heart and a nagging sense of guilt. I still believe that the existence of such startling benefits to the few has a deleterious effect on the many, and I remain wholly opposed to selective education. However, at the age of eleven, I was quite incapable of such political niceties and, after living on the North Circular Road, I found the environment and stimulation of the great school a joy beyond telling. It was an interesting and salutary fact that County Award boys (they formed approximately a quarter of the school) either thrived or found the system extremely difficult. I thrived but I was a difficult boy and was frequently beaten. When I finally became a monitor myself I declined to beat anybody until I was, on one occasion, positively ordered to do so by the House Master and I applied the slipper with such force that the object of the punishment was quite astonished to be told that it was over. I played all manner of sport but mainly rugby and, through the wonders of the parliamentary style debating society and inspired teachers, fell immoderately in love with my own language.

But I remained a Tory. Ironically, in the 1950s most schoolmasters (particularly at non-conformist public schools) were quite fiercely left wing. Such debating skills as I possess were rough hewn in long (and I suspect, for them, tiresome) dialectics on the subject of Marx, the Medicis, money and pre-Raphael-ites, subjects about which I spoke a lot and knew embarrass-ingly little. I had an ambition to become an actor and, partly to avoid the delay and uncertainty of obtaining an Oxbridge place (I was not, as they would have said, 'in the first rank'), I went to Bristol University, where I continued the delights of acting, debating and playing rugby; an indulgent life now immeasurably enhanced by the discovery of women and very large quantities of subsidised liquor. It has been said many times to the point of exhaustion (and it is undoubtedly true), that we were (and are) the most fortunate and well-starred generation that has probably ever existed at any time or anywhere on the planet. The exhaus-tion of war had led to welfare but also, as part of the process, to the indulgence (some would say gross indulgence) of the entire peacetime generation. We had it all. Not only did a grateful nation (to which we had contributed precisely nothing) provide us with free education, free teaching, free tutorials, apparatus and accommodation but had, for good measure, added a grant by way of pocket money which in today's terms amounted to approximately £10,000 a year. We collectively argued and fought endlessly about politics. Political debate became an increasingly important part of my life and, in due course, I was fortunate enough to win the Observer Mace debating tournament almost entirely thanks to the skill of my partner, David (now Lord) Hunt, who was destined to become Chairman of the Conserva-tive Party.

And I was still a Tory. I was proud of my working-class roots, such as they were, but I was still a Tory. By the end of my time at university I had met and fallen in love with Gill Elliott, who was to become, and still thankfully is, my wife. We shared then (and to a certain extent still do) a great many dissimilarities. One of the chief among them was class. Gill was the daugh-ter of a naval captain, granddaughter of an admiral, Hampshire born and bred, brilliant sportswoman in the Joan Hunter Dunne mould, a former debutante and, even then, a fierce and active socialist. It is quite remarkable what strong physical attraction will do for the mind. As a result of two years of dialectical attrition I was, by the time we left university, far less of a Tory than I had been. But I was still a Tory. We then parted. I was bound for America. One of the rewards for winning the Observer Mace tournament was to be assigned by the English Speaking Union to a debating tour of American universities (thirty-six in all) for a period of three months. For her part, Gill was bound for Botswana to spend nearly a year teaching in one of the poorest of African schools in the bush at Serowe. Self-evidently, our experiences were very different. For my part, the experience was a wild mixture of discovery and sybaritism. The Vietnam War was at its height. Everywhere in the universities we attended, students were burning draft cards and the war was the most frequent topic of our debates, understandably, full of a political urgency which I had never experienced. In accordance with the great debating tradition, my travelling partner Inigo Bing (now His Honour Judge Inigo Bing) and I took alternate sides. This may have been in the great tradition of platonic debate but it was an intellectual exercise pushed to its outer limits in the face of real conflict on a massive and serious scale. It was my lot to debate in favour of the American commitment in Vietnam in both Berkeley and Wisconsin universities, the two epicentres of student revolt. Both assembled audiences of well over a thousand students. As a forensic and rhetorical test I have never experienced its like, either in the Old Bailey or in the House of Commons, no matter how heinous the crime by either individual or government.

I returned to England physically (though enjoyably) shattered and emotionally drained. Gill, for her part, taught African children in Botswana under the hegemony and leadership of Patrick van Rensberg. She returned with the foundations of her socialism firmly in place, just as I returned with my former adherence to market capitalism in a dangerous state of collapse. For months we argued incessantly, but the outcome was never in doubt. I became a convert with all the zealous enthusiasm that entails and much to the surprise of my rugby-playing colleagues. Socialist politics became, if not an obsession, at least a necessity. We joined the Labour Party (of course) and in 1974, I fought a gruelling but entirely enjoyable parliamentary campaign (for Labour) in the hopeless seat of Richmond, which is where we lived.

It was a rock solid Tory seat and my campaign enjoyed a large measure of freedom from central control. This was admittedly pushed to the limit when a group of rugby players from Wales came to dinner at my house on the evening of the Welsh International at Twickenham. While I was obtaining monstrous quantities of Indian food, they hijacked my car, equipped as it then was with a loudspeaker for use in the campaign. They toured several of the more exclusive and wealthy areas of Richmond broadcasting as the Labour candidate and exhorting the residents to give away all their wealth to the poor.

Notwithstanding this small setback I achieved a creditable result and, thereafter, in the mid 1970s, trailed my coat around the outer London constituencies attempting to find a parliamentary berth. My attempts could hardly have been made at a less auspicious moment. At precisely this time the Labour Party, and in particular the London Labour Party, was energetically infiltrated by the Trotskyite left, who fought an extraordinary, and, at times, brilliant, campaign of infiltration. It was based upon total commitment, Herculean labour and a capacity to induce a terminal state of boredom in the fragile institutions of the democratic Labour Party, then based on the gentle traditions of British utilitarian socialism rather than the credos of bloody revolution. I subsequently read Trotsky in first translation and was amazed to find how accessible, persuasive and, at times, intellectually entertaining his work could be. It appeared to bear no resemblance whatsoever to the interminable procedural devices and mental torture which were the stock-in-trade of the adherents of the Militant Tendency.

I had a grudging respect for Trots and confidently expected their politics to mature, which, of course, it did. Unhappily, in the case of many, it matured into support for the New Labour Project which possessed similar humourless, authoritarian and unprincipled intolerance to the more juvenile philosophy they had previously embraced. There were also individuals in the tendency for whom, despite their professed loyalty to the Labour cause, it was difficult to find any affection. One such young man confronted me during a rare shortlisting meeting in the constituency of Battersea South. This occurred in 1976. I had applied for selection as the Labour candidate in this solid Labour seat. I was, by then, somewhat surprised to receive a nomination and, indeed, to be shortlisted and asked to attend at the final selection to address the constituency Labour Party. In the event, I made what I considered to be a moderately left-wing speech concentrating on the failure of the (then) Labour Government to deliver a socialist paradise to the country in general or to the citizens of Battersea South in particular. It wasn't particularly badly received and I waited with some confidence for the inevitable questions. The first interlocutor, called from the back of the room, had a Che Guevara moustache (I believe I had one myself at the time) but otherwise did not appear particularly fearsome. His first question was at least short.

'What,' he said dismissively, 'does a middle-class wanker like you think you can do for Battersea South?'

This sort of question is famously disallowed in court proceedings, being the type normally characterised as 'when did you stop beating your wife?' The first premise is subsumed into the question, thereby making it impossible to answer without reconstructing the query itself. In this particular case there were, of course, two premises. The question assumed both 'middle-class' and 'wanker' before it was possible to hold forth on future plans for the constituents of Battersea. I received no assistance from the chairman and, indeed, sensed from him – and also from the majority of the audience – a certain sympathy with both the nature of the question and the way in which it had been formulated. I can't remember exactly what my answer was, but I did my best in a short peroration to refute both allegations of class betrayal and the sin of Onan and to express my vision for the future of south London, both of which were received with almost complete indifference. It was at that point I decided to relinquish my political aspirations and to concentrate on the criminal bar.

Ironically, the Trotskyite period left an indelible mark on the radical wing of the Party and became the idle stock-in-trade label used by the politically illiterate. On one occasion, long after my election to Parliament, I was dining with Tim (Lord Razzall) in the Peers' Dining Room in the House of Lords. He was approached by Lord Levy, Tony Blair's appointee into the House of Lords, tennis partner and general fixer and fundraiser. In terms of fundraising, Tim occupied a similar place in the Liberal Democrats and so the two of them had become well known to each other. Tim indicated me as his dinner guest and said:

'Of course, you know Bob Marshall-Andrews.'

Lord Levy frowned slightly and indicated that he did not. A little surprised by his response, Tim added by way of explanation:

'You must know Bob. He's the Labour member for Medway and,' he added (smiling to indicate the irony), 'a good friend of Tony Blair.'

Three days later Tim approached me and said he had a good story to tell. Levy had apparently come up to him that morning in a state of some consternation.

'Can I have a word?' he had said and, leading Tim into the corner of a corridor, spoke darkly.

'Your friend, you know he's a Trot. Did you realise that?'

It has occurred to me since, that I might tell Lord Levy that the conventional Trot view of me was as a middle-class wanker, but have, on reflection, restrained myself, as I suspect he would himself fall into much the same category and I would not want to promote any affinity between us.

After my rejection by Battersea South and others, I remained a solid member of the Labour Party and, on occasions, subscribed to elections and where necessary worked the streets. Otherwise I remained dormant. My return to active politics was occasioned by Neil Kinnock, who had become a friend during the 1974 campaign. We met at a rugby match in 1987 and shared a beer. He asked me where I had been. I told him that I had tired of fighting Trots into the early hours of the morning and had been attempting to make a modest living at the criminal bar.

'Come back,' he said. 'We are winning this battle and the Party is changing fast.'

It was enough of an encouragement. I had just taken silk and the idea of returning to active politics was attractive. With my background, any chance of a safe seat was, of course, unthinkable – as was the prospect of Tory marginals within the Greater London area. In the event, I was lucky enough to be chosen as the candidate for Medway, where a fine stalwart Labour Party was full of committed members, apparently oblivious to the status with which I had been endowed by their comrades in Battersea South. I was proud to be selected and still am. Together we fought four campaigns, three of them successful.

I soon discovered that there was an entirely understandable although ulterior motive for my selection as a candidate. The Medway Towns had, at that time, a Conservative council of quite extraordinary unpleasantness. I have many good Tory friends, both inside and outside politics (see Chapter 4: Of Friendship) and I am well aware that local government occasionally throws together dreadful councils of whatever political persuasion. This particular administration was dire to an extent that I came only slowly to believe. Many of its members were steeped in property development. The conduct of its committees resembled Kazakhstan rather than Medway, and it embraced a culture of total secrecy that was, ironically, to be its undoing. I was subsequently informed by a number of the leaders of the local Labour Party that my status as a QC had been an important aspect of my selection. It was fondly hoped that this legal status would in some way act as a counterbalance and counterweight to the prevailing lawlessness of that local government. And so, surprisingly, it proved. Shortly after my selection, a document was leaked to me from a senior council source. It revealed that the council was proposing to sell the entire council housing stock at a price markedly less than that which had been advised by the appointed surveyors, Savills. Ironically there was nothing necessarily dishonest in this decision and it could probably have been justified on a number of grounds. However, so great was the culture of secrecy which had surrounded the council that the Savills' report was simply buried. All criminal lawyers know that there is nothing so powerful as a concealed document; and so it transpired. Questions were asked in Parliament. The council's record was placed under intense local scrutiny and, against the political run of play, the Tory administration fell. It was a fortuitous political victory, entirely deserved but, in truth, little to do with me. Nonetheless, it welded me to the local Party and, largely as a result, I was re-selected to fight the 1997 election and, on 6 May 1997, arrived, slightly breathless, at the Palace of Westminster, where I remained as a member for thirteen years.

To weary and mix the conventional political metaphors, I failed spectacularly to climb the greasy pole, but managed to clamber up the rough learning curve of a system incomprehensible to anyone who has not undergone the unique experience of inhabiting the Mother of Parliaments.

resist the Government's implementation of schemes that were positively detrimental to the interests of his constituency such as the positioning of an airport on large acres of natural beauty. In addition, if his constituency contained institutions of particular note, size or value, such as a naval dockyard or industrial complexes, it was the 'job' of a Member of Parliament to pay particular attention to the safeguarding and promotion of such enterprises at a national level. Except in so far as they touched upon these matters of national interest, the individual problems and peccadilloes of constituents were, by common consent, the preserve of local councillors, the social services, local government departments or the myriad of other voluntary or semi-voluntary agencies which evolved in order to assist the citizen through the increasingly complex demands of a modern society. To employ an old adage, Members of Parliament represented their constituency in Parliament and not Parliament in their constituencies.

All this changed in the 1960s at the behest of the Liberals, as they then called themselves. Desperate to find a new form of politics in order to arrest their seemingly inevitable total decline, they happened upon the idea of 'community' politics. This has many derisory terms such as 'pavement politics' (associated with their reputation for inspecting paving stones for inconvenient or possibly dangerous cracks). They embraced with enthusiasm the concept of the parliamentary surgery, and lost no opportunity to heap criticism and opprobrium on those Members of Parliament who failed to hold weekly or fortnightly events to which their constituents could bring a vast and unregulated quantity of problems. Thus the surgery swiftly became a part of the British political establishment. Woe indeed to the Member of Parliament who did not hold such regular conclaves in order to deal with many problems which he had neither the power, knowledge or influence to solve. Inevitably, however, Members of Parliament began to develop some expertise in areas previously thought to be outside or beyond their political sphere.

As with many Members of Parliament, I was much blessed with my constituency staff. My PA, Jill Fennell, was, and is, in biblical terms, a treasure beyond rubies. Beyond her many gifts as a secretary, typist, administrator and gloriously funny companion, was an encyclopaedic knowledge of the benefits system. This knowledge came from an unhappy period on the poverty line caused by the terminal illness of her husband. By the 1990s, social policy had evolved a ghastly cat's cradle of benefits, means-tested, non means-tested, temporary, long-term, mobility-related and otherwise. As a commercial fraud lawyer I was unfamiliar with any of these forms of assistance, but it rapidly became clear that all my knowledge of commercial banking was totally inadequate in helping me to understand the labyrinth of entitlement, much of it centred on disability. I was also appalled at the level of real poverty that existed in 1997 in the Medway Towns. I was aware, of course, of the statistics, many of which had been carefully massaged in the dying part of the Tory administration. I was wholly unprepared for the breadline existence on which many of my constituents existed, overwhelmingly because of some form of disability within the family.

I was also fortunate to have the services of my constituency researcher, Stephen Hubbard, a giant Welshman and former lock-forward who was able to deal with the (mercifully few) violent arrivals who infiltrated themselves among the increasing ranks of the sad, mad, bad and harmlessly eccentric, who saw advice surgeries as a form of refuge and group therapy. Apart from the benefit system and associated problems, failings of the NHS and, rarely, serious cases of mass fraud or public misfeasance, we did, in truth, have remarkably little power or influence over the many assorted and eclectic problems that came through our surgery door.

The term 'surgery' gave rise to a common misconception that we had some form of medical training, experience or expertise. As a result, over the years, an extraordinary number of appliances were revealed in my consulting room and, on occasions, placed on my desk. These included various forms of prosthesis and attachments normally associated with private bodily functions. On two occasions, apparently deficient eyes were produced, gazing sadly out of their protective boxes at the Labour Party posters on the walls. A number of gallstones were proudly exhibited, as were several sets of apparently defective teeth. The teeth problem generally concerned the refusal or unwillingness of dentists or the regional hospital to replace or re-form uncomfortable sets of gnashers. On more than one occasion we encountered a problem which must be well known to dentists, namely that, after the removal of the sets of false teeth, the explanation of the complaint became incomprehensible. One can only nod sympathetically when a constituent has thrust a set of false molars under your nose with the explanation, 'Id odlu uncupatible id den bock ad por edding.'

One interminable complaint centred on the refusal of the hospital to provide metal bridgework rather than the cheaper plastic alternative. Once as a gesture of sympathy, and in order to bring the consultation to a speedy conclusion, I removed my own rather deficient bridgework (the result of several confrontations in the front row of the scrum), in order to demonstrate a measure of solidarity. I am indeed fortunate to have such accommodating staff.

My fondest memories concern the eccentric. One Saturday morning a charming gentleman attended with the tearful news that Alice and John had been forcibly taken away by the council. He had cared for them for some years following the death of their mother in a boating accident. Jill, my wonderful PA, is a widowed mother and always finds such stories distressing. I could sense her beginning to reach for the Kleenex before 'family' photographs revealed Alice and John to be alligators, happily residing in a pool excavated in the living room and apparently watching the BBC. A local and national campaign followed to persuade the council to relent. Unusually, it was supported by the neighbours in addition to the National Herpetological Society who pronounced the converted home to be entirely suitable (and, of course, safe from motor boats). The campaign failed. Officials appeared to be obsessed with the possibility of escape and the destruction of fish stocks in the Medway estuary. Alice and John were moved to Faro Zoo in Portugal where they appear to be happy when regularly visited by their former guardian. We recorded this as a failure in our surgery book.

Two equally delightful ladies regularly attended to tell me in hushed tones that '*they*' had returned to the house adjacent to their own home. Early recourse to the electoral roll revealed the next door house to be unoccupied. This was hardly surprising as '*they*' were said to be extra-terrestrials (and therefore not entitled to vote). Apart from their worrying presence, '*they*' caused no trouble apart from the rearrangement of washing on the garden line. I undertook to bring this to the attention of the Home Secretary. This was one of the rare instances where I failed to honour a personal undertaking provided to my constituents.

Over the years, the number of my constituents attending surgeries as a result of grinding poverty seriously diminished and when I am asked why in the face of its appalling record on matters of civil liberty and war, I have kept the faith with the Labour Party, it is this fact more than any other. The much reviled reforms – specifically tax credits for children, working families and those suffering from disabilities – have proved mightily effective in curing a raft of quiet suffering that had been all too apparent in the late 1990s.

Some years ago, driving in my car out of the Commons' Carriage Gates entrance, I stopped to ask a lonely Scotsman whether he wanted a lift.

'Very good of yer,' said Gordon, getting into the car and directing me to his flat, then in Marsham Street. When we arrived, we spent a little while chattering about some topical and forgotten political dilemma. I ended by expressing the view just set out, as to the effect his policies had had among the chronically poor. The fact that he underwent a moment of quite genuine and gratified embarrassment has always contributed to my support of his political cause (I think to the surprise and alarm of my dissident friends).

The same improvement occurred, let it be said, in health and education. The problems that remain with education are the inequities caused by the selection process that still blight the prospects and future of so many students and children not just in my constituency in Kent, but nationally. These domestic agonies have inevitably, however, been replaced by the issues of immigration. I do not support undeserving claims for British residence or citizenship and I enquire closely into claims for asylum and the necessity for the reunion of families. Some claims are, undoubtedly, questionable, others plainly bogus. However, no one but the hardest Member of Parliament would suggest that our present system is anything other than iniquitous and, on occasions, grossly unfair. The uprooting, effective arrest and incarceration of children who have, on occasions, been born and successfully educated in this country to secondary school age, is completely indefensible in a humane and civilised country. It is yet another example of the need for elected politicians to see it as their duty to reject the pusillanimous campaigns of the popular media and to establish a parliamentary culture based on justice and humanity.

CHAPTER 3

OF PRINCES

In which we see signs of a dangerous mental condition in the Man About to Rule and the corrosive conflict at the heart of Government – Reflect on the counselling skills of Mr John Prescott – Recall the author's historical analysis to the Today *programme and a brutal encounter with the Chief Whip.*

It was on 19 October 1996 that I first formed the view (which I still hold) that Tony Blair, destined to be Prime Minister of Great Britain from 1997 to 2007, was dangerously delusional. It was at the Labour Party Conference and he was making the Leader's speech. We were looking forward to certain victory and the hall was full of a sense of glorious expectation.

It was a good speech (he can still make them). It was funny, perceptive and charmingly self-deprecatory in that way one came to know so well and loathe so much. I was unable to go and see it in the hall but I managed to secure standing room in the Press Gallery next to my friend, Jim Naughtie, the great presenter of the *Today* programme; and I got to read the press release of the speech as it was being made. As I looked around at the assembled hacks, I could see their rapt attention to the page and the universal turning of the sheets at precisely the moment the Prime Minister reached the end of another declamatory passage. I admired the forensic skill he displayed. The speech contained some fine metaphors. 'Britain is Coming Home' was the recitation and, repeated regularly, it moved the hall to a greater and greater sense of history. There came a point, however, when he departed entirely from his script. Jim turned the pages in the expectation of finding that they had been misplaced but it quickly transpired that this was simply a forensic departure in full flight. The metaphor changed. The repetition contained the words 'My covenant with the British people'. I began to feel a sense of unease. *My covenant*. No mention of ours, no mention of the movement itself. That, however, was due to come very quickly. Raising both arms in the body-hugging gesture which, again, was to become his hallmark, he said 'We all know that we can trace this great movement of ours … [in the rhetorical pause I speculated – as I am sure did many – on the precise founders that he had in mind: the Chartists, the Levellers and other great dissident heroes of British social and political history]. We all know that we can trace this great movement of ours to the Prophets of the Old Testament!' It was a profound moment. Even among the massed ranks of the Labour Party Conference, by that stage in a state of semi-tumescence, there was a distinct pause as they digested the hitherto unknown and unsuspected fact that it was Moses, Elijah, Elisha, Jehoshaphat and Co. who had founded the Labour Party, and not Keir Hardie.

They soon recovered. Many, no doubt, regarded it as a joke, and perhaps it was. What was not a joke was 'my covenant'. The confident, swaggering egotism was to be a permanent refrain that finally found its dreadful nemesis in the Iraq War.

There was a not unfortunate consequence that a number of Labour candidates gathered thereafter in the Conference Bar in order to discuss the speech. It was then that the Old Testament Prophets Lunching Club was founded and, indeed, it meets to this day. Its members are not the most loyal of Labour's back-benchers, nor, indeed, are they necessarily the most profound. However, it has, over the years, been a sounding board for constructive dissidence within the Party and has amused the many hacks who we have invited to our table.

Perhaps the Old Testament Prophets remark was a joke. I, myself, remained profoundly uneasy and still do. The clear religiosity associated directly with the presidential, quasi-Messianic fervour left me with a sense of impending danger. It has, indeed, been the source of much of the conflict inherent in New Labour and the disasters in foreign policy. Blair's total belief in his own moral rectitude and, furthermore, his capacity to reinvent both history and political undertaking has underscored many conflicts, not least that with Gordon Brown. His effortless reinvention of the leadership agreement reached between them at the Granita restaurant caused permanent destructive conflict in Government: destructive, in that it poisoned the atmosphere between the two men; and doubly destructive for what it did to the Cabinet. The process of Cabinet can only work if there is a measure of cohesion between those who are in its top rank. Where there is deep and bitter division this will, inevitably, be used and exploited by its lesser members. It also encourages the appointment of unelected *consigliores* (*pace* Alastair Campbell) to provide partisan support and perpetuate strife. It is toxic. Its effects are numerous and manifest themselves in many aspects of legislation, such as the tidal wave of authoritarian and repressive criminal justice 'reforms' that were driven, unchecked, through Parliament. It also allows the creation of cabals such as that which conspired in the iniquity of the Iraq War.

The problem, of course, extended to both men. It is impossible not to reflect on the well-known story and example given by psychology professors to their students at their first seminar. It attempts to define the difference between psychosis and neurosis. The psychotic, it is said, believes that two and two is five. The neurotic knows that two and two is four but hates it. It is a convenient template for the relationship between Blair and Brown. Brown, a decent and tortured man, knows reality only too well and in so far as it applies to domestic and global poverty, hates it. Blair's measure of reality is that which at any stage he believes to be true. Often (indeed very often) this obviously accords to his advantage. It is frequently said that Tony Blair knows nothing of history. This is not entirely true. Blair knows his history but it is his history and no one else's. In his luminous polemic 'Yo Blair', Geoffrey Wheatcroft cites Blair's speech in New York following 9/11. I can do no better than to reproduce this extraordinary passage, which does much to exemplify and distil the personality of the man:

Displaying further detachment from reality, eagerness to ingratiate himself in America, and sheer ignorance of history, he told a stricken New York: 'My father's generation knew what it was like. They went through the Blitz,' and went on, 'there was one country and one people that stood side by side with us then. That country was America, and the people were the American people.'

'The Blitz' was the name popularly given to the bombing of London and other British cities in the autumn and winter of 1940–41. At that time, many countries 'stood side by side with us': the dominions – Canada, Australia, New Zealand, South Africa – whose parliaments had voted to join the war in September 1939; hundreds of thousands of Indian volunteers; the exiled governments of Europe – Czechoslovakia, Poland, the Netherlands, Denmark, Norway and Free France – with their fighting forces; and Greece, which was as yet undefeated in an heroic struggle with the Axis. Come to think of it, apart from Soviet Russia, just about the only important country on earth which was not 'side by side with us' that winter was the United States, which was very profitably neutral.

The situation between the two men was made substantially worse by irregular attempts at peace and reconciliation made by another of New Labour's princes, the Deputy Prime Minister, John Prescott. In terms of marriage counselling, they resembled the throwing of barrels of gunpowder on to a kitchen fire.

In thirteen years I had little direct contact with Prescott. On one occasion, however, he visited my constituency to open a part of the Channel Tunnel Rail Link. The link is a triumph of transport technology of enduring economic and cultural value. It passes straight through the Medway Towns but, unhappily, fails to stop. Little direct benefit is obtained and many of my constituents were blighted by noise in previously peaceful sur-roundings. This they bore, and bear, with remarkably good grace and stoic humour, conscious of the wider good and the neces-sity of sacrifice. In a long self-regarding speech Prescott made not one mention of the ancient towns in which he stood or the burden they cheerfully carried in the national interest. Under-standably this caused resentment (not least from me) and I wrote to Prescott pointing out the error and suggesting an (albeit late) message to the citizens of Medway expressing the Government's appreciation. I received a curt and dismissive reply. To the offi-cial draft Prescott appended his own scrawl: 'Not surprised at this coming from *you*.' There are many who maintain that there lies behind Prescott's boorish and bullying exterior a fine and balanced mind. They possess powers of perception I sadly lack.

The conflict between Blair and Brown surfaced and resur-faced on many occasions and, of course, was the subject of public and political comment. We were frequently and indi-rectly warned by the Whips that it would be extremely unhelp-ful for Members of the backbench to comment on this obvious attritional warfare. Generally speaking we avoided doing so, for no better reason that it became very tedious. However, on one occasion I appeared on the *Today* programme at seven o'clock in the course of a Labour Party Conference in Bournemouth, when a particularly venomous and public passage between the two most powerful men in the country was in full flow. On the programme we were dealing, I think, with some criminal justice legislation. At the end, John Humphrys could not resist (he often can't) the temptation to ask for my views about the state of the leadership and, in particular, what my views were as to the relative status of Blair and Brown. I thought for a moment and gave an answer which I still think to be partially true. 'I think,' I said, 'that we have the best Chancellor of the Exchequer for half a century and the worst Prime Minister for a century and a half.' That was at seven a.m.

Before lunch I received a message asking me if I would be good enough to visit the Chief Whip when Parliament convened, which I duly did. Hilary Armstrong did not lose any time with pleasantries but came straight to the point.

'Bob,' she said, 'how could you, how could you possibly say Tony is the worst Prime Minister for 150 years?'

I had, of course, been expecting some question of this kind, so I was a little rehearsed when I said, 'Chief Whip, I have been thinking about that answer and, on reflection, I have come to the conclusion I was wrong. It was very early in the morning and I was unprepared for it to be put in those terms. On reflection, I think it is necessary to go back to Wellington before one can find a Prime Minister who has treated his own people with more contempt and deceit.'

The Chief Whip appeared confused, thought for several seconds and then said, 'Well, I wish you had made that clear at the time.'

CHAPTER 4

OF FRIENDSHIP

In which we lament the absence of friendship among the political classes and consider the reasons therefore – Reflect on the strange customs of the Members' Dining Room – Travel to the far north to support Mr David Davis and the cause of Liberty and am rewarded by the company of Misses Shami Chakrabarti and Rachel North – Your author is threatened with expulsion from the Labour Party by Mr Geoffrey Hoon (now unhappily suspended himself) and learns the secret of maintaining a fine cellar, drinking much fine wine and seldom buying a drop.

The creation of friendship is rare in politics. There will be those who will tell you otherwise. They are lying or very sad or both. There are perfectly good reasons for this. Firstly, Parliament is a workplace and thus is liable to all the usual antagonisms between those climbing the same emotional ladder and attempting to shin along the same greasy pole. Superimposed upon this normal, occasionally bitter, rivalry is the discord inherent in political persuasion, commitment and activity. Few things can cause such venomous animosity between human beings as sharing the same political or religious beliefs. As with religion, so in politics, the closer the apparent theology, the more venomous the personal aversion tends to become. In Labour Party politics, this is again overlaid by issues of region and class. Setting aside understandable personal aversions, I have no doubt that many of my colleagues within the Labour Party, and in particular within the ranks of New Labour, find it quite inconceivable that moderately successful professional people, particularly if they appear convivial, can possibly aspire to any form of socialism, however mild. It is easier, they might observe, for a camel to pass through the eye of a needle than one fat jolly barrister to enter the pantheon of socialist orthodoxy. But that is only the beginning. The hair shirt of bigotry worn by any association of the Left comes in many fashionable shapes and sizes. Each bears its own stamp and trademark and each will immediately attract the opprobrium or derision of those wearing a different, more or less uncomfortably fitting suit.

During my time in Parliament this state of affairs was exacerbated by the advent of New Labour's high moral tone and total lack of principle. Political comrades, however disparate their costumes or the nuances of their beliefs, are capable of operating as a coherent unit when well led. This changes when a substantial number begin to believe that the commander-in-chief is an opportunistic charlatan. None of this is improved if the second-in-command manifestly holds the same view. The Old Testament Prophets, otherwise synonymous with the 'usual suspects', were and are a fine, eclectic, independent, clever and (almost throughout our bi-annual lunches) articulate group of Labour backbenchers. They included, of course, Brian Sedgemore, a mighty rugby-playing socialist intellectual of total unbending principle who was thus guaranteed to attract the personal vilification of Tony Blair. His resignation speech (from the Labour Party and from Parliament) on the issue of Control Orders was a volcanic tour-de-force, equal to any that has been heard in the Chamber for centuries.

Friendship is also rare between members of opposing Parties. There is little fraternisation. Government and Opposition backbenchers seldom eat and drink in each other's company. Indeed, it is discouraged. When I had been in the House barely two weeks, Brian Sedgemore and I agreed to eat together in the Members' Dining Room. When we arrived, all the tables were full, with just two seats remaining at a table on the far west end of the room, traditionally reserved for Tory Members of Parliament. Sensible convention dictates that all seats in the Members' Dining Room are, at least theoretically, free to any Member. Brian and I approached the Tory table and enquired whether anyone objected to our taking the free seats. 'Yes. Bugger off,' said an unfriendly voice at the far end of the table. Such an invitation could not be lightly ignored. We immediately parked ourselves in the vacant chairs for what transpired to be a more than usually enjoyable dinner, as my neighbour was David Davis, subsequently to become the Tories' best Shadow Home Secretary and a valued ally in the endless battles for civil liberty.

(It is a matter of passing interest that the owner of the voice who instructed us to 'bugger off' was Shaun Woodward, the Tory billionaire who subsequently defected to the Labour Party and became one of its ministers.)

My collaboration with David Davis in attempting to defeat some of the most draconian and dangerous of the Government's legislation became something of a political scandal. Our alliance was based on a profound reverence for rugby football, civil liberties and wine of just about any description. We also shared an aversion to New Labour Home Secretaries and their zealous attack on the principles of British constitutional freedoms. This was particularly so in the case of David Blunkett, whose zeal to punish and imprison became his political stock in trade. Before and during these Parliamentary debates, David and I cooperated closely, assessing the strength of Labour dissent and opposition to punitive legislation (which was by no means always total or assured). As recorded in another chapter, I took little trouble to conceal this illicit cooperation. It led, however, to one confrontation with David Blunkett. It was during the passage of the 2003 Criminal Justice Act, one of the largest and worst pieces of criminal justice legislation in any century and one which has caused endless grief and injustice throughout the criminal legal system. We had reached the last stages of the Bill and in particular the clause which would have removed the right to jury trial in complex cases. Substantial numbers of Labour backbenchers had either voted against the Government or abstained. As a result, the Government's majority had been decimated and the House of Lords had announced their implacable opposition to the clause. At this point, Blunkett confronted the option of withdrawing the clause in its entirety or facing defeat on the Bill. During the debate in the Commons he had been literally spitting with rage. Much of his fury was reserved for me, whom he repeatedly referred to as 'my honourable and learned friend' which left not the slightest doubt that in the Blunkett lexicon, *learned* was a direct synonym for 'wet liberal bastard'. His position, however, had become hopeless, and he entered into negotiations with David Davis, then newly appointed as Shadow Home Secretary. While these were continuing, David and I had a drink in the Members' Smoking Room. We discussed the prospect of leaving the non-jury clause in the Bill but inserting a double lock to ensure that it could only become law by an affirmative vote of both Houses taken in full session rather than committee. We both agreed that this device would effectively kill the measure and require the Government to bring another and separate piece of legislation in order to give the clause effect. A meeting was arranged behind the Speaker's Chair – a not uncommon occurrence when horse-trading of this kind occurs. David informed me of the meeting and I attended in order to listen to the details. It was not a friendly meeting. Blunkett had lost the issue and he knew it. He conceded the amendments with ill grace and ended with the words, 'I hope then that you are satisfied' and then, without pause, thrust a finger at me and said 'I hope he is, too'. Presence observed by the blind is a common literary metaphor, employed famously by Milton, Louis Stevenson and many others. I had never seen it in action in reality and it haunts me still.

Friends may be difficult to find in politics, but enemies abound. In one sense, political opponents are, by definition, political enemies, but personal vitriol – and I have had my share – is generally the preserve of your own side and needs to be born with equanimity; there is no point in harbouring a sense of injustice. There are, indeed, Labour MPs who believe that their dissident colleagues damage the Labour Party and the Government more, say, than the invasion of Iraq, the sale of privileges or the infliction of punitive tuition fees on poor students. They are wrong but happy and fixed in their beliefs. This may lead to the odd episode of vulgar abuse on the Terrace but is otherwise contained. There was only one occasion when I was subjected to actual violence, being manhandled by a Labour MP against the statue of Lloyd George in the Members' Lobby during the debate on the Terrorism Bill 2005. Ironically, two junior Labour Whips restrained my assailant which must have been a difficult (though decent) decision for them. It was, in truth, unedifying and nasty, and bore out in a most graphic form the truth that there is no hostility so violent and implacable than that which exists in comrades engaged in the same political strife.

The friendship between David Davis and myself was to be tested following the famous Commons' vote on forty-two days detention. Some weeks previously, David had informed me of his intention to resign as Shadow Home Secretary if the vote for forty-two days was carried. He told me this over a drink in the Pugin Room, having previously left a message on my mobile that he wanted to see me 'about something important'.

What he told me came as something of a surprise, not to say a shock.

'Why would you resign?' I asked.

'In order to force a by-election on the issue of civil liberties.'

I reflected on this for a moment. 'I think,' I said carefully, 'that it's absolutely insane but I also think it's wonderful.'

'Exactly what I think,' said David and ordered another drink. Whilst it was coming I pondered the possibilities.

'What,' I said, 'if the Government declines to put up a candidate against you?'

'I've thought about that,' said David, 'but I really don't think they can possibly do that. It would look terrible if they concede a by-election on a straightforward civil libertarian vote. It would appear to be rotten and gutless at the same time.'

'Precisely,' I said. 'I think that's exactly why they are capable of doing it.'

As the drinks arrived, I distinctly remember saying: 'I will, of course, come and work for you.'

'Good,' he replied. 'It would mean that you would be expelled from your Party.'

'Exactly,' I said. 'Which is rather better than resigning on this issue, which I would in any event.'

On that happy note, we changed the subject.

In due course, the vote proposing forty-two days detention without charge came before the Commons. David led for the Tories and the debate is described elsewhere. I was reasonably confident that there were sufficient Labour rebels to beat the Government, particularly in view of an unprecedented number of abstentions and two ministerial resignations. I was particularly heartened by the growing sense of panic within the Government, which included my only personal telephone call from Gordon Brown. In the event the vote was a famous catastrophe for the Prime Minister. The Bill was passed by a majority of nine, which relied entirely on the Ulster Unionist vote. It was widely believed that extravagant promises had been made to the Unionists, who would otherwise have had little interest in the legislation. The measure would never survive the House of Lords and it was, I thought, a resounding victory. Immediately afterwards I returned to the same favoured position in the Pugin Room where David and I had conducted our previous conversation. I purchased the drinks whilst awaiting his arrival and when he sat down, I congratulated him upon a monumental victory in the Commons.

'There we are,' I said. 'We have won. You can continue on the front bench.'

'Certainly not,' he replied. 'I have just seen Cameron and tendered my resignation.'

I protested: 'We have won this debate. It will never survive the Lords. Forty-two days is dead. Dead in the water.'

'We did not win. We lost – albeit through foul play, but we lost nonetheless. It is the Commons that matters, not the Lords. If Brown thinks he has popular support he will force it through the Lords using the Parliament Act. Then we will be on the verge of a general election and Cameron will lose his nerve. We still need the civil libertarian issue to be tested in the country, and we need it now. We can't wait four years for an election.'

I had no doubts then, and I have none now, as to the absolute sincerity of his view. When his resignation became public it was widely questioned by the press on the basis that it was a quixotic, self-serving, Boys' Own gesture, designed only for self-preferment. That, in my view, says a great deal more about newspaper editors than it does about David Davis. During a long career in what David Blunkett would call the wet liberal tendency on freedom and civil liberties, I have never known anyone more passionately engaged in their defence than David. It is not simply part of his politics, it is his defining characteristic as a politician. It was too late to dissuade him and, in truth, I don't think I should or could have done so. If it transpires that he has lost his career in Government, then the country will be the poorer for it. At the time of writing that remains unknown.

Notwithstanding my faltering reservations about David's resignation, I immediately resolved that I would hold to my word and campaign on his behalf, whether or not the Government put up a candidate. In due course, as I prophesied, they did not and, in truth, they had no choice. For this Government to have fought any campaign on the single issue of civil liberties would have been political suicide. I was immediately contacted by various parts of the media who duly reported the following day that I, and in all probability, other Labour Members of Parliament, would join David Davis in his campaign. This, in turn, led to a confrontation with the Chief Whip who asked to see me on this subject. The Chief Whip at the time was Geoff Hoon, recently Secretary of State for Defence, hammer of the Iraqis and one of the perpetrators of the war

Geoff was, and is, well aware of my view that, as a result of his participation in the Iraq War, he might well be answering questions in The Hague and not in Parliament. Despite that, we have always got on well and I can confidently say that I have enjoyed better relations with Geoff than any other member of the war party.

'Is it true,' he asked, as we arranged ourselves on the Chief Whip's sofa, 'that you are going to work for David Davis in the by-election?'

'Absolutely,' I said. 'I have given him a solid undertaking that I will do so.'

'You do realise, that that's against Party rules?'

'No,' I said. 'As I understand it we have declined to put up a candidate, which,' I added, 'I regard as both gutless and wrong. Nonetheless, we have decided not to do so. In which case there is no Labour candidate I can act against. As we are not putting up a candidate, it seems necessary that at least a Labour voice should be heard.'

'Ingenious,' said the Chief Whip, 'but wrong I'm afraid.'

He then produced a copy of the Parliamentary Rule Book and referred to a marked and underlined passage.

'I was unaware of this myself,' he said, 'but it's quite clear that members of the Parliamentary Labour Party cannot support *any* candidate for *any* other party in any election whether or not the Labour Party is standing. It's quite clear.'

'What's the sanction?' I asked.

'Expulsion,' he replied promptly.

'Does that mean that if I work for the Democrats in America, the ANC in South Africa or the Save Our Local Surgery campaign in the parish elections (no Labour Party candidate standing) that I face automatic expulsion?'

'Yep,' he said, closing his eyes. 'Look, Bob. I know it's fucking rubbish, you know it's fucking rubbish, but that's the rules. What's more, there will be loads of our colleagues out there who will regard this as a heaven-sent opportunity to get rid of you.' Opening his eyes, he added: 'That, incidentally, does not include me.'

'Well,' I said, 'expulsion it is. I'll tell the parents to come and get my trunk.'

And that was it. Of course, I heard no more from the Whips' Office. I dutifully went north and campaigned for David, together with a substantial number of Tory ladies, and took the long train journey back to London with the fearless Shami Chakrabarti, and Rachel North, who was a victim of the London bombings and has campaigned ceaselessly on issues of civil liberty ever since. We managed to empty the bar of its entire stock of wine (both colours); quite one of the nicest train journeys I have ever had in the cause of liberty – or anything else for that matter. David won, of course, but, far more important, was the turnout at 37 per cent for an unopposed election. The people of Haltemprice expressed their multi-party contempt for the Government's commitment to imprisonment without trial, a victory of far greater significance than the press it received.

Until he became Mayor of London in 2007, I also enjoyed a distant, parliamentary friendship with Boris Johnson. An early trough in my relationship with the New Labour establishment was caused by an article in the *Daily Telegraph*, dated 1 December 1997, barely six months after my election. The article occupied one half of the back page, was devoted entirely to me and was written by Boris, then editor of the *Spectator* and feature writer on the *Telegraph*. It appeared under a banner headline:

THE LEADER OF LABOUR'S OWN OPPOSITION

beneath which, and sunk into the body of the article, was an interesting picture taken by the *Telegraph* photographer. The photograph depicts me in front of the House of Lords with one arm raised in the classic salute of the Marxist left. It taught me something about press photography, which I have imparted to colleagues when they arrive at the House. The first rule is beware of any press photographer who falls to his knees and changes his lens. I was, in fact, doing my imitation of Lord Healey's well-known acclamation of Parliament, both arms raised at the same time. By excising one half of the body with a low lens it produces the desired Marxist result. I rather liked it, but it had a seriously provocative effect on the Whips, who pinned it on their notice board to act as a public warning against indiscipline. This had the desired impact on a number of the more immaculately New Labour members and I vividly recollect one of my ambitious lady colleagues attempting to hide behind a statue of Disraeli when she saw me approaching down the corridor.

The interview which gave rise to the fateful piece in the *Telegraph* took place over two hours and two bottles of wine in the Atrium Restaurant at Millbank. For my part, I had no doubt that Boris was bound for greatness, and clearly recollect that he had cheerfully neglected to wear either cufflinks or buttons, which I took to be a Bullingdon eccentricity. Despite the background to our interview, there is one passage describing New Labour which I believe bears examination today. Having described me as a mixture between Rumpole and a French police chief, Boris records my saying:

> 'I am worried about the amount of power this Government has. There has been a collapse of almost all counter-vailing forces to Government in our democracy. The Tories don't exist. They wander the corridors of Westminster with victims' grins, you know, to stop people hitting them. In the Chamber there is no sense of threat. The Labour Party, which has always been a check on the Labour leadership, has conceded power to the NEC. There is a Tyranny of Enlightenment. You achieve your legitimacy directly from the people and through focus groups and phone-ins. This is dangerous, and it worries me.'

With the hindsight of thirteen years I claim a small, sad measure of prescience.

Subsequently, when Boris became a Member of Parliament, we frequently made common cause in the Chamber during debates on the more draconian aspects of the Government's terrorism legislation. We also debated against each other at a number of universities. He has a wonderful and infectious debating style, carefully combining articulate wit and salient attack within an apparent bumbledom. It is, I believe, the root of his unaccountable sex appeal.

He can also demonstrate mastery of the other great art of political debating, namely plagiarism. On one occasion when we were debating at Oxford, I began my speech with an entirely true account of my regrettable experience in a taxi immediately following the 2001 election result. I was, I said, going to Paris for the weekend. We took a taxi to Heathrow and, on the way, I noticed that the driver was looking at me quizzically from time to time in his rear mirror. As we neared the Heathrow exit, he finally opened the slide and enquired: 'Ok guv, give us a clue?'

I had been slightly prepared for this approach and so I was able modestly to dissemble. 'I'm a politician,' I replied. 'I'm just a backbencher but I'm very frequently on the television, dealing with things like war or civil liberties. I also write articles and have scribbled the odd book. I expect that's it.'

Without changing his expression, the taxi driver replied, 'Yes guv. Thanks for that. Which terminal did you want?'

I told this pleasant little story at the beginning of my Oxford speech. It went reasonably well and I noticed that Boris, on the opposition benches, was studiously writing. Some months later, I met a man at a party who was, I believe, an officer in a city livery company. He asked if I knew of Boris Johnson. 'Yes,' I said. 'I know him quite well.'

'What an enormously funny fellow he is,' said my fellow guest. 'He came to speak to us last week and told some frightfully funny stories. Do you know, he told us that, shortly after the last election, he had been in a taxi going to Heathrow and the taxi driver, after a while, had said to him, 'Alright, guv, give us a clue.'

'Really,' I said a little acidly. 'Did Boris tell the taxi driver that he was a politician and journalist? And did the taxi driver ask which terminal he was going to?'

'Exactly,' said my friend. 'That's exactly what he said. What an amusing fellow he is!'

I decided not to correct my friend at the time but to wait until I got the opportunity to write a book.

Perhaps surprisingly during my time in Parliament, I became friendly with a number of Tory grandees, many of whom demonstrated, time and again, that strange synergy between Tory knights and civil liberty which may be traced, arguably, to Magna Carta. Pre-eminent among these was Sir Peter Tapsell, affectionately known in *Private Eye* as Sir Peter Gusset. Peter is a magnificent and terrifying parliamentarian whose trenchant opposition to Blair's Wars was underpinned by his brilliance as an historian and his own army service. In the Commons he exemplified the near universal contempt among former soldiers for Blair and his addiction to warfare and the sacrifice of others. On one memorable occasion, towering above the gangway, he described Blair (then present on the front bench) as 'more steeped in blood than any Scotsman since Macbeth'. He was always also a master of the wholly inadmissible question and, on one occasion, asked the Prime Minister why he thought so many people regarded his presidency of the EU as a lamentable failure – a question the Prime Minister appeared unable to answer.

Peter also taught me how to consume a lifetime of fine wine without expense. This occurred during a *Spectator* lunch to which I had been invited by Boris Johnson and Nick Soames. It was a splendid lunch, during which I met and sat next to Rowan Pelling, then editor of the *Erotic Review* whose knowledge of her specialist subject was at least as joyous and profound as Peter's knowledge of wine. The lunch was a brainwave of Nick Soames, who was then the *Spectator*'s wine correspondent. The idea was simple. At a series of lunches, he persuaded Boris Johnson to invite the chairmen of London's great wine shippers to provide copious quantities of their product and to discuss them over the course of the meal. The attraction to the shippers was, of course, publicity in the *Spectator*. The attraction to Soames (and to his guests) was the provision of vast quantities of free and outstanding liquor. During the course of this meal, Peter Tapsell explained the basis of his consumption of fine wine. The chairman of El Vino's had been selected for the privilege of supplying the wine and, before each course, delivered a small lecture on the excellence of its provenance. After the third course, Peter Tapsell addressed him directly.

'You know,' he said, 'I don't think I have bought any fine wine for years – extraordinary but true. I drink a good deal of it, but I don't often buy any.'

'That's interesting,' said the chairman. 'How do you manage that, Peter?'

'Well,' said Peter, 'when I bought Roughton Hall I found it had a cellar, unhappily completely empty. A local wine merchant advised me to buy a few dozen cases of bonded claret and burgundy which he expected to appreciate in value. Over the years they quadrupled in value, and we had an arrangement that every time he sent me a case he sold one for me out of bond. And so it went on. Every time we drink a case it pays for itself. That's it really. I drink quite a lot of it. Never seem to buy any.'

It was a simple tale, beautifully told, but in its way it provided a lesson in economics of which Adam Smith would have been proud and reflected, no doubt, Peter's successful career as a stockbroker.

the House of Commons. The similarity with any boys' public school, major or minor, is strikingly apparent to anyone who has been anywhere near them. The Whips have their own corridors. The Chief Whip has his or her own study. Other MPs (boys) are not permitted within the Whips' offices where they lounge on sofas, occasionally throw balls of paper at each other and pin amusing notices on the wall disparaging their less fortunate colleagues. There is no overt flogging. However, the power of disgrace and punishment hangs heavily over those who are affected by it. Whips themselves have an extraordinary hierarchy. Junior Whips are pretty rough trade. Senior Whips have some authority and status. The Chief Whip has unique access to Government and the Prime Minister and, on occasion, sits within the Cabinet. To be a Whip is widely regarded as the first and essential rung on the way to ultimate preferment. Few British Prime Ministers have not, at some stage in their career, been Whips, albeit briefly. Whips (like Platoon Commanders) are placed in charge of a number of their fellow Members of Parliament, normally on a regional basis. How they succeed in controlling their platoon and reporting back to the Senior Whips on the behaviour, prospects and potential danger of their own subordinates, is regarded as an essential method of displaying their fitness for high office. I am told that one Junior Whip was immediately reduced to tears when he was informed that I was to be one of his particular cohort. Despite a certain amount of pleading by him, I remained on his roll. When I heard this, I felt sorry for him. He was (and is) a decent enough fellow, wholly unfitted for high office (or probably any office at all). In fact he did briefly attain a post as a very junior minister in one of the junior departments at the extreme end of the 2005–2010 Government when, as in the last days of Third Reich, it was necessary to promote almost anyone left standing in order to maintain the illusion of an army.

The first job of the Whips and the Whips' Office is to maintain parliamentary discipline and to ensure success at the vote.

The two are, in many ways, synonymous. The New Labour Project, and those who devised it, believed firmly that the downfall of the Labour administration which led to the rise of Thatcherite Conservatism lay almost entirely in its lack of discipline. As they looked back at Labour Party conferences of the 1970s, they collectively shuddered at the outpouring of free speech and the metaphorical blood which, on occasion, ran down the conference floor. To them, this was not the acme of political liberty and debating, it was the essential harbinger of doom. Discipline and control were, therefore, to be pre-eminent features of New Labour. While these were later to be reflected in its legislation, they first became apparent in the Parliamentary Labour Party itself.

Within the Party there are two immediate instruments of communication and control. The first is the weekly whip. This is a document with a number of enclosures. The Labour whip is pink, and bears on it the Divisions and the likely business of the week. Under the Divisions are a number of lines colloquially referred to as the 'whips'. A three-line whip demands compulsory attendance. A two-line whip indicates that attendance is desirable and preferable and, indeed, the unspoken statement is that those who adhere to it are likely to be viewed with favour for demonstrating their zeal and their graft. A one-line whip is an entirely voluntary business, allowing Members to attend or not at the various debates usually (but not always) because no vote is anticipated. In the past (so I was informed by those who had far longer careers in Parliament than my own) one- and two-line whips were frequent. The three-line whip was reserved only for those occasions when it was absolutely necessary that Members should vote. In my thirteen years in Parliament I do not recollect more than a dozen occasions when a two-line whip was placed upon the paper. In the overwhelming majority of the thousands of debates that took place in Parliament in this period, a three-line whip was imposed. In well over half of these debates no

Division was, in fact, called, so hundreds of Labour Members of Parliament dutifully sat and waited for the conflict that never came. The purpose of this exercise was not to facilitate Party business; it was to exercise control. Members who had pressing evening engagements within their constituencies, or social engagements nearer at hand, were (unless very fortunate indeed) needlessly imprisoned in the Palace of Westminster. Release from this drudgery was a matter of naked favouritism meted out in the gangmaster tradition of the Glasgow Waterfront.

The second instrument of control was (and is) the pager. This device was issued to every member of the Parliamentary Labour Party. As with the mobile phone, it could be set to ring, or vibrate, or both. As with a mobile phone, substantial text messages were possible on the face of the pager and could be simultaneously relayed to all members of the Parliamentary Labour Party. In meetings or social gatherings around Westminster, apparently unrelated people could be seen suddenly and simultaneously clutching their vibrating trousers, thereby revealing themselves as members of the PLP. On many occasions the message simply related to an imminent Division in the Commons which was, of course, useful. On other occasions they were used by the Whips' Office to deliver Orwellian exhortations on some form of discipline.

'TERRORISM BILL. Colleagues should NOT give interviews to the media without consulting the Chief Whip.'

'Colleagues should be aware of a BBC Survey on Foot and Mouth. It is AGAINST PLP POLICY to respond.'

In my early months in Parliament I took delight in revealing some of the more extreme messages to Tony Bevins (*Independent*) and Michael White (*Guardian*) and, accordingly, some of these were reproduced, generally in diary form. This was, of course, a gross breach of discipline but it led, reasonably quickly, to a subtle softening of tone. The strictures gave way to urgent advice: 'Colleagues are reminded that it is contrary to

Party Policy to answer questionnaires on breast-feeding.' These helpful admonitions continue to the present day and are, no doubt, harmless enough.

In 1997, the office of the Parliamentary Labour Party was confronted by an unusual but, for the Whips, enormously serious problem. There were far too many Labour MPs. Following the 1997 election, there were 410 Members of Parliament bound to the Labour Whip. In the Lobby, crowd control became necessary. During the course of the early Divisions, it frequently took nearly half an hour for the entire Parliamentary Labour Party to file through the Division Gates. Serious overcrowding took place and, if Health and Safety regulations applied to the Palace of Westminster (they do not), they would have been breached on a daily basis. This particular problem was obviated by creating new lanes of egress in the voting lobbies, but the main political problem remained unsolved. The majority of Whips were Scots, and many were of a religious disposition. None know better than the Presbyterian Scot that (in the words of John Knox) the devil makes work for idle hands. What to do with 410 MPs? Given the fact that the Government, even at its most swollen, can accommodate barely 100 ministers, even down to the lowliest rank, there were still a huge number of potentially idle and, therefore, miscreant Members. The first solution was to provide every minister with a Parliamentary Private Secretary. Traditionally, PPSs were available only to Cabinet ministers. Now every junior minister had his own personal PPS. It was once said of the Guinness family that even their servants had servants, and thus it was with us. However, this cured but half of the problem. Even allowing for 100 PPSs (or bag carriers in the Westminster vernacular) over half the Parliamentary Labour Party remained theoretically unbidden and unattached to the Government in any way. They were simply backbenchers and, therefore, open to all forms of mischief.

One solution which figured briefly in the early years of the

Labour administration was to create a raft of 'champions'. These were neither fish nor fowl. Given the alarming title of Champions of Government Policy, backbenchers could become a champion of wind farms, nuclear power, women's rights, Housing Benefit, salt mining, dental care or anything else which conveyed a sense of self-importance. Otherwise the role had no status, purpose, power or influence. Unsurprisingly, it was swiftly scrapped.

Finally, a further solution was employed which is a delight to recount and to remember. In September 1997, all backbench Labour MPs received a document from the Labour Party Central Office. This resembled a form of contractual agreement and, indeed, required a signature. It began with the words 'PLEASE TREAT THIS AS A TOOLBOX'. The document then suggested that I (as a Member of the Labour Party) might avail myself of regular 'constituency weeks' away from Westminster, during the course of which I could (with a little diligence) visit every single home in my constituency. It was, in short, the final gesture of contempt towards the historic role of the parliamentary backbencher. The very idea of visiting, uninvited and without warning, every home in Medway was so offensively bizarre that it moved me to print; the *Guardian* was good enough to publish the following:

> I have a contract. I got it last month. It was drafted in Labour Party Headquarters at Millbank Tower in order to regulate my activities as an MP between now and the next election. With a fine sense of metaphor, the contract refers to itself as a 'Toolbox'.
>
> The point of this contract (which I was asked to sign at the top and bottom) was to ensure that I did certain things to my constituents in Medway. The most impressive was to visit 26,000 of them personally by the next election. I was suddenly gripped by a sense of enthusiasm. What a wonderful prospect for them and me! I read on, but quickly discerned an apparent flaw in this otherwise luminous and

poetic document. It contained no instructional help in what I should do to the 26,000 citizens of Rochester and Chatham and the Hoo Peninsula. Then suddenly I had it. There was a code. It explained why this contract, this elegant piece of prose, was also called a 'toolbox'. It was not a metaphor for the contract; it was a metaphor for me. Armed with a toolbox or, more accurately, as a toolbox, I was to go to 26,000 of my constituents and offer them some small but useful service. Exactly what service would probably depend upon their requirements and needs. Mentally I rehearsed my role:

'Good morning. I am Robert Marshall-Andrews QC, your Labour Member of Parliament but I am also a toolbox. No, please do not shut the door. Here is my Millbank identity card testifying that I am wholly qualified for this operation.'

'Of course you were in bed. This is only natural at 4.30 a.m. But please appreciate that I have another 25,642 constituents to visit. Most services, however small, take at least five minutes to complete to a high standard. No doubt you will appreciate that I need to start early. In fact, I hardly start at all. It is a matter of continuous process. Yes, it is hard from time to time.'

'What is this? Oh, this is my toolbox. I appreciate it looks more like a small handcart, but I must be prepared to carry out a vast range of services. The trailer behind the handcart? This is a reference library. Indeed it was the reference library before it closed.'

'Are you still there? I am sorry the head strap fell over my eyes. Yes, it is an interesting device. They are manufactured in Tibet to assist in the pulling of the handcart. They are available, at a small discount, to members of the Parliamentary Labour Party. Now I wonder if it is possible to offer you some small service?'

'Oh come, surely there is something? I cannot but notice that the hinge on the front gate was loose and the paint … I see. Well perhaps you have a pet that requires de-worming?'

'I see. Well, possibly dry rot or areas of infestation. Carpet mites can be especially hard to detect for the untrained eye. Compost? I happen to have a bag of high-nitrate horse-dung in the toolbox, well-rotted, brilliant for azaleas. Hedge clipping? Re-grouting? Knife sharpening? House clearance? Oh, come, come, what about all that nasty scale round the bath?'

'Oh very well, but this is very disappointing, really, I shall have to make a report. Perhaps you would sign … What? Pension? Your pension? No, I'm afraid that's a matter for Parliament, you know, those johnnies up in Westminster.'

'No, no, I'm afraid you have got that quite wrong, but don't worry, it's a really common error. It's what we call the old politics. Just think for a moment: if I were up there mucking about in Parliament I couldn't be down here looking at your U-bend now could I? And besides, it would be terribly irritating for the Government.'

Notwithstanding the farcical nature of the 'Toolbox' experiment, a number of my more innocent and younger colleagues availed themselves of the 'constituency week' and dutifully set about annoying vast numbers of their constituents.

One new MP, having taken no fewer than two constituency weeks, arrived back in the House to be informed that, as a reward, she was to be a champion of the Party policies on infant obesity. At that point she became a dissident.

All of this tomfoolery concealed a number of sinister political dimensions which I discovered and analysed slowly in the course of the next thirteen years. First, of course, it elevated the status of the Whips and the Party machine to that of an employer. As I came to repeat on many occasions (to the annoyance of my friends), a Member of Parliament is employed by no one, and least of all by the Party machine. Winston Churchill once observed that he had three priorities as a politician. The first was his country, the second was Parliament and the third was his Party. This noble principle has been steadily eroded by the growing power of the Party machine and the Whips. The well-known lobby group 'TheyWorkForYou.com' is a self-apparent misnomer. Members of Parliament do not work for their constituents. Of infinitely greater importance is that they do not work for the Whips. However, the concept of employment with all its controls became ever more pervasive with the arrival of the young professional politician on the parliamentary benches. In my particular intake in 1997, no fewer than 30 per cent of new Labour members had no or very little work experience outside politics or politically related (e.g. trade union) employment.

Inevitably they treated the Senior Whips as employers and the Whips responded accordingly. Shortly after the 1997 election, the Whips' Office produced duplicated forms which required completion by MPs to request any absence from Parliament for whatever reason. Boxes at the foot of the form indicated APPROVED or NOT APPROVED. I steadfastly refused to use them. If I needed to be absent from Parliament I provided the Chief Whip with a polite letter as a matter of courtesy. This misbehaviour was reported to my constituency Labour Party in a letter bearing a strong resemblance to a parental warning from the head teacher. It was read out to the monthly meeting, to the joy of my local members.

The second and related effect of this utterly discredited system lies in the erosion of the status and stature of MPs. It results in what probation officers or social workers would term 'a crisis of self-esteem'. This should not be confused with personal aggrandisement or *amour propre*. Members of Parliament may enjoy public approbation but this is simply an attribute of their office, and their office is everything. Thus, when Members of Parliament surrender their self-esteem to the power of the Whips or the Party machine, what they surrender is the office with which they have been entrusted. The mentality of the toady or the lackey is something perceived by the people and exploited by the press. But it is also a betrayal of trust. As in wider society, this Lilliputian state of mind begets the pettiness of action that is the handmaiden of delinquency. This, more than any other factor, was the hallmark of the expenses scandal which engulfed the final years of New Labour's administration.

The third and inevitable consequence of this abuse of power and discipline is the reluctance of men and women of stature and qualification to enter Parliament. No one who has succeeded in the great endeavours of a modern society, be they professional, financial, artistic or social, will easily subordinate themselves to such a system. Very few Gullivers will enter this Lilliputian world and subject themselves to its Lilliputian control. This, in turn, leads to a further distortion of the political system, namely the elevation of ministers through the House of Lords. Increasingly, the great and good are spared the petty corruption of the Whips and are elevated, effortlessly, to unaccountable power.

What effect does the whipping system actually have on the lives of MPs? The answer is both direct and complex. First, the approbation of the Senior Whips is a prerequisite of ministerial office and this was and is the major sanction. If, however, a back-bencher is one of the small and dwindling group who neither seek nor desire such office, the sanction doesn't work. Thereafter, serious and unbecoming conduct may result in referral to the National Executive Committee of the Party with a view to expulsion. This, too, is a limited sanction. The Party machines are aware of the growing public disaffection with tribally controlled politics. Placing dissident MPs publicly in the pillory is a sure route to even greater public aversion. I can recall only two occasions in which this ultimate sanction was employed. The first was sustainable (George Galloway) and the second, wholly and disgracefully undeserved (Ian Gibson). Both, however, effectively cost Labour the seats which were contested as a result of these expulsions. Thereafter, a myriad of minor petty punishments and sanctions may be employed. The most important of these is to be effectively disbarred from membership of Select Committees.

Parliamentary accommodation at Westminster also lies in the gift of the Whips. As a result of dissident behaviour, my accommodation steadily shrank. My final room measured, approximately, 8' × 10' and my researcher shared a room with six others mostly employed by Ed Balls, and occupied a space measuring a princely 5' × 5'. Had I continued in Parliament I would no doubt have found myself in some form of modern oubliette, with my research staff suspended below it.

There is also some threatening behaviour and bullying. During the voting procedure itself, infantile forms of intimidation are employed. Whips are stationed in the centre of the narrow entrances into the voting lobbies, attempting to emulate the nightclub and pub bouncers now prevalent in every constituency high street. To the seasoned rebel it is pretty tame, but to the initiate it conveys its own menace. Two of the best and most independent of Labour's intake of 2005, Katy Clark and Linda Riordan, were escorted into the dissident lobby by a small elderly phalanx of myself, Alan Simpson and Ian Gibson which might, in itself, have proved ineffective had it not been for the presence of Diane Abbott at the spearhead of the charge.

The most iniquitous effect of this rotten system is to perpetuate and ossify in Parliament social attitudes and lines of conflict which have entirely disappeared in the constituencies that we represent. In the class wars of the twentieth century, parliamentary discipline was necessary and inevitable. After the apparent demise of the Liberal Party, Parliament dutifully reflected the great social dialectics of the age. The stark fundamentals of wages, welfare and education drew their own lines in the parliamentary sand as clearly as those that separate the adversarial sides of the debating chamber. These great struggles created and dictated their own disciplines. The issues of liberty, equality and welfare were etched and superimposed on a class battle faithfully reflected in the pantheon of Parliament. The Britain that was dominated by these issues, by overwhelming common consent, no longer exists. The working class as a cultural and political entity is as relevant to political reality as the remnants of a landed aristocracy. The great issues of the age – climate change, civil liberties, religious intolerance and the movement of impover-ished populations – transcend the politics of class and demand the politics of conscience. The continued existence of a whip-ping system dragging its knuckles across the parliamentary floors awakens, rightly, nothing but public derision and contempt. This existed long before the expenses scandal and will exist long after it is forgotten.

In truth, the power of the Whip began to disintegrate over the last nine years of Labour's administration. From 2001, growing elements of the Parliamentary Labour Party began, collectively or individually, to challenge the Whips and the Party machine. In part this related to the policies and the legislation which a failing Government attempted to impose on an increasingly intractable Parliamentary Party. Foundation hospitals and top-up fees pro-vided substantial grounds for dissent, but the recurring theme was legislation aimed systematically at the curtailment and withdrawal of liberty. The Iraq War provoked the two largest rebellions against the Whip by MPs of any party for over 150 years. At a growing rate, the Government between 2001 and 2005 recorded a higher rate of rebellion among its backbenchers than any post-war Parliament. Against this background, the first session of the 2005 Parliament was remarkable for the behav-iour of Government backbench MPs. Indeed, what happened in the first session of the 2005 Government was unique in modern British political history. As Philip Cowley records in his excel-lent pamphlet 'Dissent amongst the Parliamentary Labour Party 2005 to 2006': 'The Government was defeated on four occasions (a record matched by no other post-war Government). The Gov-ernment won another vote with a majority of just one (being saved by a handful of inattentive opposition MPs) and managed to pass the Education and Inspections Bill only as a result of Opposition support.'

From 2005, in the face of this upsurge in parliamentary democracy, the Whips' Office had begun to fall apart. For the Government, desperate times required desperate measures; and Hilary Armstrong was appointed as Chief Whip. Armstrong's reputation needs no burnish from these pages. It is sufficient to record that her last act as a Member of Parliament at the end of the Labour administration in 2010, was to put down a procedural amendment designed to kill the parliamentary reforms of Select Committees achieved after ten years of dedicated cross-party campaigning, brilliantly led by Mark Fisher.

In short, she represents, with effortless poise, the politics of control. She can also be delightfully inefficient. This latter characteristic she demonstrated magnificently during the final vote that defeated the Government on the Racial and Religious Hatred Bill on 31 January 2006. This nasty piece of legislation, which would have criminalised racial and religious satire, was finally defeated by one vote. This glorious achievement was rendered all the more memorable by the fact that Armstrong, as Chief Whip, had told the Prime Minister to go home. Blair, famously, virtually never came to the House of Commons. The fact that he did come and was sent home in order for his Government to lose a vote is a rare political treasure. Armstrong's reaction to this personal humiliation was another revelation. Examples had to be made. As a matter of urgency, a scapegoat was needed to be found and publicly hanged. There were a number of obvious candidates, of which I was the favourite. This was, of course, duly leaked, and national newspapers helpfully obliged.

'REBEL RINGLEADER FACES LABOUR PLOT TO OUST HIM FROM SEAT'

ran a typical headline from the *Independent* alongside a picture of me under Big Ben, looking unhappily like Alan B'stard. I braced myself for imminent defenestration. For a moment, things became frenetic. Emails and letters arrived, if not in a flood at least in a respectable sluice. My good friends Alan Simpson, Ian Gibson and John McDonnell announced that if I was to go, they would go too (which, in my view, substantially increased my chances of expulsion). Rather more Labour members, let it be admitted, could not conceal their delight. In the event it came to nothing. Not even an ASBO. My attendance was requested in the Chief Whip's Office for what transpired to be a half-hearted caution, which I used as an opportunity to tell the Chief Whip that further attacks on civil liberties or freedom of speech would, inevitably, lose us the next election. She disagreed. Memorably, she said to me: 'Bob, people in my constituency do not give a toss about civil liberties.'

There are two alarming things about that statement. First, it may be true; and second, she obviously believed it was.

Finally, having re-read this chapter, I am concerned that parliamentary dissent may appear to be enjoyable. It is not. Most frequently, parliamentary rebellions are lost, and the satisfaction of beating your own party is a heavily qualified emotion. Often, though, it does help to reflect on the wise words of Oscar Wilde: 'To anyone who knows anything about history, disobedience is man's original virtue.'

good thing, and that bringing a wealth of experience or even a modicum of success to the parliamentary arena, can do nothing but contribute to the greater good of the legislature and, thereby, to Government and the people. The majority would, of course, be entirely right, although not for that single reason. Experience is enormously important in Parliament. Strangely, recent Parliaments have been unusually bereft of senior lawyers, and the well-known misconception that Parliament is comprised largely of lawyers is exactly that. However, a wide range of expertise is undoubtedly useful. One of the best backbench Members of Parliament during my time was undoubtedly Dr Ian Gibson, the Member of Parliament for Norwich North between 1997 and 2009. He was, and is, one of our foremost oncologists, who has done as much for the cure of cancer as any in his profession and who was awarded the Macmillan Gold Medal. His advice and his contributions to debates such as the genome debate were outstanding, and his private advice given to Members of Parliament faced with problems within their constituency was invaluable. There are other and obvious examples. The House, in my time, had a number of ex-officers and soldiers who were able to contribute to the debates on warfare which had unhappy frequency during the last Parliament. There is no shortage of educationalists and, there again, the House has been blessed by their presence. That is only part of the story. Where a new MP has never had any other occupation or profession and job other than that of, say, a parliamentary researcher then, naturally, the parliamentary career is the only career upon which he or she can rely, not only for an income but also for their success. This, *ipso facto*, makes them more likely to seek patronage and become a slave to the Whip. This is entirely understandable. Without the patronage of the Prime Minister they have no career; and this is, after all, the only career they possess. The overwhelming view, therefore, is entirely correct. To have Parliamentarians who have previous experience, preferably successful in other spheres of life, is good on two different grounds – experience and independence.

The first question is less easy to answer. Should parliamentarians have other occupations while they sit in Parliament? Should they have another 'job'? That, in itself, is something of a misnomer which is perpetuated in and outside of Parliament for various different reasons. Possibly encouraged by 'TheyWorkForYou.com' a number of my constituents asserted that I was their employee and thus it was my duty to do what they required. This is, of course, constitutional and practical nonsense. No man can have 175,000 different masters, many of whom have wholly different views as to what he should be doing in order to earn his money. Equally, the concept of employment is misapplied. A Member of Parliament works *for* no one. On the contrary, he represents everyone; certainly within his constituency but also, on a wider level, everyone in the country that he perceives to be jeopardised or threatened by legislation to which he is being asked to place his name. You do not, therefore, work for anybody. The position is complicated by the Party system. With a few exceptions, it is virtually impossible to obtain a parliamentary seat without being part of a political machine. In some ways, this power is waning as tribal voting becomes less relevant to a modern classless age. However, for those who seek parliamentary office, membership of and endorsement by a political party remains, generally, an imperative, and the process whereby that endorsement takes place achieves an ever greater importance. It is, therefore, very easy to perceive the parliamentary machine to be some form of employer. Indeed, when I first arrived in Parliament, my cohort included a large number of very young members with little work experience either within the House or outside it. Many approached the Whips in order to ask them 'What should they do?' By this, they meant when should they attend Parliament and what should they do when they were there. They found it difficult to understand that there are simply no rules as to the 'employment' of a Member of Parliament. No sanctions exist in the absence of gross misbehaviour, in which case the disciplinary mechanisms of the House (and now outside the House) come into play. The number and frequency of surgeries which a Member of Parliament chooses to have are entirely within his or her gift. The number of debates attended, the number of speeches that he or she makes, the number of committees that he or she chooses to belong to (if invited to join) are all entirely within the gift and purview of the individual MP. The overwhelming sanction, of course, is to be voted out of office by disgruntled constituents who perceive you to have done nothing or very little. This power, weighty though it is, is counterbalanced by an increasingly presidential electoral system and the continued existence of political parties. The days are going when it could be confidently said that a constituency would elect a donkey if it would wear a red or blue rosette but they are not completely over.

The issue therefore remains: what should a Member of Parliament do? Is it desirable or allowable that individual Members of Parliament should have outside work or interests while they remain members of the House? A hundred years ago that question would not have been difficult to answer. Not only was it allowable for Members of Parliament to have outside jobs or interests, it was generally expected that they should do so. MPs were unpaid, and relied either upon outside jobs or interests, or on some form of sponsorship in order to maintain themselves in Parliament. That stopped being the case in 1911, when Members of Parliament were voted a modest salary in order to carry out their parliamentary duties. Hot on the heels of the question of salary came expenses. At that point, the understandable misconception about 'employment' took hold, and it was but a short step for a number of people (again understandably) to reach the view that this stipend was money paid for a full-time 'job'. Quite what kind of job could only be a matter for the individual Member. Therein lay the problem.

It was a problem that I had to address when first I entered Parliament. Should I, for one reason or another, leave my practice as Queen's Counsel entirely, in order to carry out such parliamentary duties as I chose for myself as a parliamentarian? The rule which I set myself at the outset was that I should not continue to practise if I became a member of a Select Committee. For reasons which I have already explained, this did not come about. In those circumstances, I decided that I should maintain my practice at a lesser level provided that it did not interfere with my parliamentary obligations. Would this be possible? What would be the immediate repercussions? This I was soon to discover in graphic form.

In the days immediately after my election to Parliament, I was engaged in a trial for which I had previously been retained in Harrow Crown Court. I was defending a young man who had had the misfortune to steal a highly classified computer which contained state secrets of a not very important kind. He maintained that he had no idea that the computer (which he had admittedly stolen) fell into this category. In the end, that account was accepted by the jury and he was sentenced for stealing a computer rather than some form of terrorism or treason. This was a happy result for him. However, the case itself had a less happy result for me.

I had not at this stage cast a vote and had only recently received my first three line whip. This document arrived on the Friday before I attended the Harrow Crown Court. From it I learned that there would be Divisions starting at three o'clock on the Monday. This obviously conflicted with my court commitments and I, therefore, decided to telephone the Chief Pairing Whip to inform him that I would, on this occasion, regretfully be unable to attend but in future, when my life became more ordered, I had no reason to suppose that I would be absent from such votes. This conversation was never allowed to take place. After a number of telephone calls I finally spoke to the Chief

Pairing Whip, whose role is the enforcement of discipline in the Parliamentary Labour Party – a gentleman called Tommy McAvoy, whose constituency in Glasgow contained the ship-yards in which he had worked and had been a boiler-maker. This background, as I was soon to discover, has naturally affected his view of QCs from the south-east of England.

Having made contact by telephone with McAvoy, the following short conversation took place:

> **Me:** 'Hello, my name is Bob Marshall-Andrews; I'm the new Member of Parliament for Medway.'
> **TM:** 'Rr …'
> **Me:** 'I'm phoning up because I've received this whip which tells me I must be in Parliament at three o'clock.'
> **TM:** 'Rr …'
> **Me:** 'I am afraid that I am just not going to be able to make this.'

The noise which greeted this statement cannot be accurately described on paper. For a moment I thought he had bitten the telephone receiver. The meaning was clear and indicated disapproval.

I told him that I was very sorry but I had a previous engage-ment in court which it was impossible for me to break. Several other noises then followed, from which I ascertained that he expected me to report to him in order to discuss this state of affairs the minute that I arrived in Parliament.

Following the court case I did, indeed, arrive in Parliament for the first time and stood in the Chamber feeling the full weight of awe and responsibility which must have been felt by all new Members of Parliament since the plebiscite. The Division Bell rang to signal the second vote of the day and I made my way towards the Division Lobby. Finding myself within the lobby, I moved slowly among the milling hordes of my colleagues and finally passed through the Telling Desk where I gave my name to the clerk who recorded my First Ever Vote. I passed the Tellers who counted me out and stood again in the Chamber surrounded by new and experienced Members of Parliament. Mindful of the fact that I needed to speak to Tommy McAvoy, I asked an experienced-looking MP whether he had seen Mr McAvoy, as he was, of course, unknown to me.

'Yes,' said the Labour Member of Parliament, whom I subsequently came to know well. 'He's just gone into the Lobby.'

Unwisely, I entered the Lobby in order to try to find the Chief Pairing Whip and had done so when time was called and the doors were duly shut. Having discovered Tommy McAvoy, I announced myself and my constituency.

'Oh,' he said, 'It's *you*, is it?'

I said that yes, it was me and that I was very sorry that I had been unable to attend at the First Division which had taken place an hour previously.

I explained my problem, with which he seemed to have remarkably little sympathy. However, on my assurances that my court attendances would, in future, be kept to a minimum and would be unlikely to interfere with the seamless course of the vote, we parted on reasonable, if monosyllabic, terms.

All of this had taken a little while and we walked together through the Telling Desk where I dutifully gave my name, noticing, with the benefit of hindsight, a look of consternation on the clerk's face. I then passed through the Tellers and was duly counted through. I then returned to the Chamber, took up a seat which was to become my favourite position, and sat watching the proceedings which I had only previously imagined, or seen through a glass darkly. It soon became clear, even to me, that something had gone wrong. A small cluster of Opposition and Government Whips stood in the middle of the Chamber exchanging notes and numbers. As the Government was in possession of approximately 150 majority, the error, whatever it was, could not change the passing of the legislation and thus the vote was delivered to the Speaker and parliamentary proceedings continued. I was, however, aware of what had occurred and, even with my total lack of experience, I realized where the error lay. I, therefore, thought it honourable to inform the Whips of my own defalcation. Approaching Tommy McAvoy from behind, I waited politely until he had finished discussing the whipping problem with his colleague. I then intervened:

'Tommy,' I said.

'Oww,' he said. 'It's you again.'

'Yes,' I said. 'Tommy, I am very sorry.'

He said: 'What do you want?'

I said: 'Yes, Tommy, I'm very sorry, it's me.'

'What do you mean, it's you?'

'It's me. I'm afraid that I voted twice.'

It is not easy to describe the expression that came over Tommy McAvoy's face, but it must have been similar to that which any boiler-maker would have reserved for news that a particularly difficult boiler in a battleship had been installed upside down.

In a voice that had become a little strangled he said: 'You voted twice. What did you do that for?'

A rash moment then overcame me. It seemed to me that the opportunity was too good to miss.

'Well,' I said. 'You know that I missed the first vote, well I decided that I would vote twice on this one.'

McAvoy looked at me in a way which made it quite clear that he was attempting to make up his mind (with some struggle) as to whether I was very, very stupid or was attempting to pull his substantial leg. It took him a little while before he decided which one it was and adopting what was, for him, a kindly grimace, he said: 'No, laddie, look you cannae do it like that.'

In the years to come, the Whips' Office repeatedly denied me a place on a Select Committee. It was not for want of applications and I regret the rejections to this day. This did, however, enable me to continue a very modest practice at the Bar, confined mainly to the parliamentary recess. My constituents were aware of this, and in thirteen years none complained of neglect. It had one unlooked-for benefit. As described elsewhere (in the chapters Of Liberty and Terror) the Government produced a wave of criminal justice legislation that became steadily worse and more unworkable. With my limited experience in court I was able regularly to report back to Parliament on the catalogue of chaos and injustice which increased daily in our courts as a result of statutes we had passed.

CHAPTER 7

OF SPIN

In which we consider the origins of the black art, its effect on the electorate and the mischievous behaviour of your author in respect thereof – Reflect on the character and influence of Mr Peter Mandelson – Recount the particular and dark skills of Mr Alastair Campbell and their brilliant deployment in the Strange Saga of the Sale of Peerages (alleged).

The advent of New Labour famously brought a new verb into the political lexicon: *to spin*. The OED contains a somewhat kindly definition: 'to evolve, produce, contrive or devise in a manner suggestive of spinning (1555)'. Shakespeare knew something about spin. In Touchstone's famous monologue, second only to the lie direct is the lie circumstantial. It is, in truth, the more dangerous of the two. The lie direct, once discovered, invites discredit and remedy. The lie circumstantial relies on shades of meaning and shadows of partial fact resulting in nuance and innuendo. Disraeli's father, as novelist, refers to 'many secret agents [who] were spinning their dark intrigues'. In truth, spin means deceit or lying. It has, of course, existed in politics since Pericles but, in the hands of New Labour, it was turned into an art form. The worst and most dramatic pieces of spin were the dossiers which preceded the attack on Iraq, but countless other examples litter Labour's thirteen years and extend into virtually every crevice of policy and presentation. In the early years, spinning was, remarkably, enshrined in documents regularly issued to all members of the Parliamentary Labour Party. These luminous instructions generally bore the heading 'The Line to Take'; there followed several hundred words of patronising drivel and exhortations. Exclamation marks were liberally applied to emphasise the obvious and to promote enthusiasm:

'WHAT IS THE TORY ANSWER? TO CUT ALL THESE BENEFITS!!

THAT WILL PUT THE LIVES OF CHILDREN/ WOMEN/THE ELDERLY/ LIVESTOCK IN PERIL!!!'

These could, if necessary, be amplified. All members of the Parliamentary Labour Party (including ministers) were instructed to inform the Whips if they were invited to participate in any form of media presentation in order to receive a particularly well-spun or embroidered patchwork of meritorious political cant. On one occasion I obtained such a document before appearing on a televised public forum. One of my fellow panellists was a junior Home Office minister, destined, as it transpired, for higher office. In response to one question on, I believe, health policy and the effective privatisation of parts of the NHS, I was delighted to see that she read verbatim from the text with which we had both been supplied. Somewhat mischievously, I corrected one part of the answer where she had, inadvertently, deviated from the script, pointing out to the audience that I was quite happy to circulate the document and could certainly correct any other aspects of Government policy if the minister required a prompt. I provided a number of the more delightful examples to lobby journalists which was, no doubt, little short of a capital offence under the Party rules. As with many minor acts of insubordinate mischief, this may, at first, appear to have an infantile streak. However, it was intended to illuminate a much wider and more serious state of parliamentary and constitutional decline. The rigorous enforcement of political conformity is lamentable in itself and is discussed in other parts of this memoir. To do so in order to convey messages which are duplicitous or false is infinitely worse. It is also obvious to the public, not least by the wooden recitation of dire polemical prose. It feeds into the electorate a deadly contempt for political discourse and debate. It exhausts public goodwill and promotes understandable derision and disdain.

The supreme master of spin and other forms of media manipulation was, of course, Peter (now Lord) Mandelson. In view of his central, seminal importance and pervasive influence, whether holding office or not, throughout the whole of Labour's administration, it is tempting to draw parallels with Richelieu or Rasputin. In truth, he is an uncomfortable cross between Iago and Polonius: a man of undoubted charm, charisma and persuasiveness, concealing a mixture of vanity, venom and an extraordinary capacity for bungling error; a man who famously attracts extraordinary loyalty and bitter loathing; a man capable of particular detail and planning but apparently incapable of providing accurate personal information to building societies or forgetting to declare huge loans by way of mortgage. A mighty paradox indeed.

Having never met Peter Mandelson, I was surprised to learn, shortly after the 1997 result that, during the course of the election night itself, I was on his mind. Apparently, during the festivities at the Festival Hall, he had quietly made an exit and, in the privacy of his own room, drawn up a list of names. This bore the heading 'New Members to be Seen'. Even on a superficial analysis it was quite clear that this was not a list of those who might be considered worthy of affection or preferment. Quite the reverse. This was a list of those thought capable of trouble or subversion.

In some cases, extraordinary and unflattering footnotes had been made. Claire Curtis-Thomas, whose starred PhD marked her out as one of the cleverest of all Labour MPs, let alone the new intake, was described briefly as 'mentally unstable'. I occupied a gratifyingly high position although what I had done to deserve such preferment remains, to this day, unknown. Who leaked the list remains, of course, a mystery – although its provenance and its purpose have never been denied.

Ironically, shortly after its publication, the *Spectator* magazine was kind enough to present me with one of their annual awards. This particular award was entitled 'New Member to Watch'. (The fact that I have not received another award since, does, I am afraid, speak for itself.) During my short acceptance speech I made reference to the Mandelson list. I said that it was unfortunate that the *Sunday Times* should have published it in the way that they did. Newspapers, I said, were too often indifferent to the pain and suffering they caused. I said that I knew many new members on the backbenches of the Labour Party who had been driven close to tears when they realised that their names were not on it.

After the award I shared a bottle of champagne with Quentin Letts, one of Fleet Street's most feared and formidable commentators. He was good enough to congratulate me, and was kind about my reference to the Mandelson document.

'Who do you think,' I asked pensively, 'could have obtained that document and leaked it?'

Quentin looked at me with a sympathetic expression which might be reserved for the sighting of a pit pony that has blundered into the light.

'It wasn't removed', he said. 'Mandelson leaked it himself.'

'But why,' I asked, 'would he want to do that?'

I can remember Quentin rolling his eyeballs towards the ceiling before he said, 'Control, of course. He wants new backbenchers to know that they are being watched. I know you don't give a fig but there will be plenty who will. You wait and see. No one on the list will actually be "seen". That's not the point. The point is to induce fear and trepidation that you might be.'

My first direct confrontation with Peter Mandelson came as a result of my opposition to the Millennium Dome. Mandelson was, of course, the 'Dome Minister', a position which he had appropriated for himself. I yield to few people and even fewer politicians in my capacity for sybaritic enjoyment, and I like to think that I throw a pretty good party. I regarded the Millennium Dome project as the most deplorable and offensive waste of public money. Ephemeral by nature, plastic in construction and devoid of any coherent content, it seemed a suitable metaphor for New Labour and a dire reflection on the state of our nation and the times in which we live. (The disaster of the Dome and the consequences for New Labour are considered in detail in another chapter: Of Nemesis.)

I dutifully set in train what was to become a substantial rebellion on the Labour backbenches and this opposition was enthusiastically and increasingly adopted by the press. This eventually resulted in the only communication I have ever received from Peter Mandelson. Although we had never met, it was addressed to Bob and concluded, 'Yours, Peter.' It asked whether I would be good enough, at my convenience in the near future, to attend at his offices in order to discuss my opposition to this cherished project. I own up to being somewhat flattered, and I prepared for this encounter. Before replying, however, I spoke to an old and wise backbencher, a veteran of many political battles and a backbench scourge of the Thatcher Government. Rather proudly I showed him the letter.

'Don't touch it,' he said immediately. 'Don't even think about it.'

'What's wrong with going to talk to him?' I said, a little plaintively.

He, too, gave me the full pit pony look, before saying, 'Let me tell you exactly what will happen. You will have an absolutely charming conversation; all of your objections will be listened to and probably noted down. At some stage you will be asked a question similar to this: "Do you think that this project will bring any benefit to your constituents?" You will say, no. Indeed, as I understand it, most of the toxic waste from the site is being dumped in your constituency, and you will probably say no with some emphasis. Subsequently, Peter Mandelson will be asked a question (probably by the *Daily Mirror*) about your objection to the Dome and the rebellion that you have started. Peter Mandelson will say that he has spoken to you at length on the subject and your primary concern appears to be that there is no benefit to your constituents. Do you see what I mean?'

'But,' I said, 'that would not be entirely true.'

'Just so,' said my friend. 'But equally it would not be entirely *false*. This, my friend, is what is known as spin.'

In the event I politely declined the invitation and thus have no way of knowing whether that prediction would have been correct. It did, however, have the benefit of experience and wisdom and, indeed, would have been entirely consistent with the contemporary portrayal of other events, notably the Bernie Ecclestone donation to the Labour Party, unhappily coincidental with the lifting of the ban on tobacco advertising. This was spun as a complete coincidence which was, of course, believed by precisely nobody, particularly after Blair's protestation that 'I think I'm a pretty straight sort of guy'. It was subsequently reported to me that Peter Mandelson expressed the view, rather contrary to the placatory tone of his letter, that he was surprised that I inhabited the same planet as himself, let alone the same Party. That did, at least, provide us with a measure of mutuality.

If Peter Mandelson was the Chief Wizard of Spin, Alastair Campbell was, of course, the Sorcerer's Apprentice. His extraordinary influence over Blair and Downing Street remains one of the arresting phenomena of the ten years of that premiership. It was to combine the mysteries of spin with a ruthless instinct for self-survival.

Campbell's stock-in-trade, at which he was brilliant, was the concealment or the creation of news. In doing so, he recruited and retained a number of enthusiastic and breathless acolytes that included a young woman called Jo Moore. She was responsible for one of the more repellent manifestations of the black art. Within hours of the 9/11 atrocity in New York she expressed the view that this was 'a good day to bury bad news'. The leaking of this email led to an unedifying public spat between New Labour's junior administrators. It is noteworthy, however, that Jo Moore was not immediately dismissed but retained her job for a matter of weeks after publication of her email. This led to the widespread and entirely justified assumption that she knew in detail the location of the burial sites of many New Labour bodies.

By far the best example and most brilliant exposition of spin was related to the 'cash for peerages' scandal which erupted on to the political scene in March 2006. This magnificent brouhaha began with a most extraordinary statement by Jack Dromey, the Treasurer of the Labour Party, and related to approximately 12 million pounds' worth of 'loans' which had been made to the Labour Party prior to (and directly for) the election of 2005. These 'loans' had been made by twelve gentlemen who were all wealthy, the majority of whom enjoyed a close relationship with Lord Levy, the Prime Minister's tennis partner and general financial fixer for the New Labour machine. These loans made a massive difference to the Labour balance sheet and enabled the Party to fight a vigorous, well-funded General Election which, despite the disasters of Iraq and Afghanistan, was ultimately successful.

It was nearly a year later that Jack Dromey revealed to an astonished press and public that he, the Treasurer of the Labour Party, was wholly unaware of the loans or the massive indebtedness which the Party now, theoretically, carried. Loans to political parties (unlike donations) do not have to be revealed under election law and were not, therefore, reported to the Electoral Commission after the 2005 election. Failure to inform the Electoral Commission is one thing, but failure to inform the Treasurer of the Labour Party was, to put it mildly, quite another. At precisely this time, the political heat was suddenly and dramatically increased by the revelation that three of the 'lenders' had been recommended by the Prime Minister to enjoy Life Peerages. The reason given for this honour was, somewhat disingenuously, described as 'political services to the Labour Party'. Predictably, inquiries were demanded by just about everybody. Ian McCartney, then Chairman of the Labour Party, issued an immediate letter to all Labour MPs in which he acknowledged that some may 'have concerns', but pointed out that the largesse resulting from the loans had been employed in the election of most of them. In other words 'shut up'.

Concealing the loans from Jack Dromey had been a serious political mistake. Formerly Deputy General Secretary of the Transport and General Workers Union, long-term member of the National Executive Committee and married to Harriet Harman, Dromey was and is tough meat. He was also, for ten years, a board member of the National Council for Civil Liberties and knew a fit-up when he saw one. The Tories, no doubt applying the glasshouse principle, were remarkably quiet, but the Scottish Nationalists (who had no peerages to sell) led a widespread and vociferous demand for police action. This, in turn, led to a weighty and protracted investigation by Deputy Commissioner Yates (or 'Yates of the Yard' as he inevitably became known).

Compared to the death and destruction in Iraq, the whole affair was trivial, but it was, potentially, politically deadly. In particular, it exposed yet again the sweaty relationship between New Labour and new money; a relationship of which, ironically, Jack Dromey had been a particular and vociferous critic. What subsequently occurred was a master class in spin, orchestrated from

10 Downing Street by Alastair Campbell. Campbell had by this stage formally left No. 10, but his influence remained, as did the total dependency he had created. In his book *The New Machiavelli*, Jonathan Powell records that 'Alastair Campbell urged us to fight back and attack the police'. The form that this 'fight back' took was a steadily and bitterly fought confrontation with Scotland Yard. As such, it broke all the conventional political rules. The classic Government reaction to police inquiries is to provide effusive support and cooperation. The police are regularly praised for their continuing efforts, thereby creating an atmosphere of innocence and trust. Campbell would have none of it. As the investigation continued, official and unofficial briefing became increasingly aggressive and strident. The police, it was said or implied, were heavy-handed, insensitive and incompetent. The immediate spotlight shifted to the police themselves. It was suggested that the Yates team were, themselves, leaking and briefing to the press. This allegation was probably, of course, leaked and briefed from Downing Street and Yates complained bitterly that he was the target of the Downing Street spin machine.

It was all quite deliberately provocative. The Yates team gratifyingly responded to the provocation. In July 2006, Lord Levy was quite unnecessarily arrested in the early hours of the morning in the home in which he had resided for many years and from which he had no intention of decamping. It was correctly pointed out that a polite invitation to attend Victoria Street in order to be arrested would have been quite sufficient. Ruth Turner, head of public relations, was arrested without warning at 6 a.m. by four male policemen. The temperature steadily rose. All those who had provided 'loans' were meticulously investigated by the press. Everything centred on the 'sale' of honours and privileges rendered a criminal offence by the 1925 Honours (Prevention of Abuses) Act. At the end of 2006, the Prime Minister himself was interviewed. The briefing from No. 10 deliberately widened rather than narrowed the range of suspicions.

Allegations emerged of splits within the police hierarchy and a state of neurosis settled over New Scotland Yard. Lord Levy was arrested again, prompting further hyper-allegations of bias and overreaction. Finally, on 20 July 2007, the 'cash for peerages' investigation collapsed. The Crown Prosecution Service announced that no prosecutions would be brought and Lord Levy publicly opened several expensive bottles of champagne.

For No. 10 and Alastair Campbell it was a sensational success. What had been engineered had been the creation of a story. There was, in reality, never any real prospect of prosecution for the corrupt sale of honours. The evidence was fragmented and circumstantial, and those against whom it lay were possessed of immaculate character and could point to a culture, widely accepted over many years, whereby wealthy and influential men and women supported political causes and parties of which they approved and in which they believed. In these circumstances, it was the vociferous and vehement reaction of the Downing Street machine that ensured, above all, that the sale of peerages and police behaviour remained 'the story'. By persistently denying the crime of corruption, No. 10 had ensured that the investigation had concentrated increasingly on precisely that denial. It is an old ploy, well known to the professional criminal fraternity and immortalised in the story of Brer Rabbit and the briar patch. By this device, intentionally or otherwise, the serious and real investigation was completely finessed. The majority of the 'loans' were, of course, no such thing. What demanded scrutiny was the nature of the loans and the failure to include them on the Party accounts. The most cursory consideration of the Party's balance sheet would have caused most commercial lenders to consign the application to the basket of hopeless causes. To repay such massive sums with full commercial interest would have reduced the Labour Party to its financial knees if not bankruptcy. The loans can only have been incurred in the hope if not expectation that the generous lenders could be persuaded to become generous donors in due course. What merited the most searching investigation was not the sale of peerages but the sale of the Party. The accounts filed by the Labour Party in June 2005, and presented to the Labour Conference in October of that year, made no mention whatsoever of the massive liability undertaken by the Party in early 2005. The technical assertion that the accounts had a cut-off point at the end of 2004 is buried under the obligation known to any accountant that significant 'after acquired' debts must be placed in the accounts. This was the issue that demanded investigation. Despite attempts by numerous members of the public and a minority of politicians (including myself), such an investigation never took place. The whole affair has had, of course, unintended (and for the Labour Party near disastrous) consequences. The peerages affair discouraged any conversion of loans to donations which, effectively, has reduced the Labour Party to ruin. This, in turn, has accounted for the financially strapped and failed election campaign and, most important in political terms, renewed reliance on union support. Such are the wages of spin.

The most infamous documents in the brief history of spin are the dodgy dossiers which appeared in 2002 and which undoubtedly influenced the parliamentary votes that led us to disastrous war. These are separately considered in another chapter (see Chapter 20: Of Wars 4: Iraq). It is worth observing, however, that the culture of spin, the lie circumstantial, had by 2002 become so ingrained into the fibre of New Labour that these documents can be seen not only as an attempt to legitimise an inevitable conflict but as part of a culture of government which served again to compound a sense of political decay. As to Alastair Campbell himself, future historians will, no doubt, wonder how this engaging buccaneer from journalism's rough trade walked with statesmen and princes and contributed so much to the first casualty of war.

Racine once observed *'prier le faux pour connaître le vrai'* – preach that which is false in order to discover that which is true. It could make a fitting epitaph.

CHAPTER 8

OF WOMEN

In which we reflect on the desirability of women in politics and the contribution of childbirth thereto – Purchase a china mug to assist the cause – Pay tribute to our sisters whose courage defies patronage and bullying Whips and lament their rarity – Recount an unhappy visit to No. 10 and the unwise rendition of Paradise Lost *in the presence of Miss Cherie Booth with unhappy consequences redeemed only in part by observations on suicide by bombing.*

I had a mug that I purchased at the Labour Party Conference of 1987 which is now unhappily lost. But it was, for a time, a treasured object and I remember it well. It was decorated on both sides. On one side was a picture of a long-skirted suffragette. Her occupation was clear from the steadfast poise, the demeanour and the fact that she was carrying a large placard which bore the words 'Votes for Women'. On the reverse side was a picture of a thoroughly modern young lady wearing a t-shirt and jeans but otherwise in an almost identical pose. She was also carrying a banner on which was written the legend 'Seats for Women'. Above both ladies was an inscription on the porcelain reading 'Emily's list'.

I had noticed it on a stall which was piled high with the same mugs and assorted literature that included, I was pleased to see, Mary Chamberlain's first seminal work *Fen Women*. There was also the inevitable petition. Above the stall was a fixed banner which bore the words 'Emily's list' and below these 'Vote Seats for Women'. The stall was staffed by a young lady who could have been a model for the reverse of the mug. Bespectacled and stern, she exuded intelligence and commitment. I have always found such ladies very attractive; a feeling which has, generally speaking, been wholly unrequited. I approached the stall, introduced myself and asked what was the purpose of the list? It was, she said, a campaign to promote women as Members of Parliament, an institution in which they were grossly unrepresented. Excellent, I said, adding that I was in total agreement that any discrimination within the selection procedure for parliamentary seats should be condemned and forbidden. This sturdy response did not receive the approval I was hoping for. That, she said sternly, would be wholly inadequate. The aim was to discriminate positively in favour of women and, in particular, in the selection process. I replied that I could see that there was certainly an argument for an equal number of women on all short-lists. This again was obviously inadequate. *All-women shortlists were the only acceptable answer.*

'In how many seats?' I asked.

'All seats,' she replied, 'as they become available *at least.*'

I took the *at least* to mean that some form of cull should take place of existing Members in order that even more seats became available in the immediate future. I observed that such an arrangement would be of considerable advantage to women, always provided that sufficient could be found to be interested in such a process.

But what benefit, I enquired, did she foresee that this would have to Parliament and to the wider body politic?

The stallkeeper was clearly of the view that I was making

my way slowly up a learning curve. She carefully and patiently explained that women possessed many qualities that were invaluable in politics, particularly modern politics, qualities wholly lacking or deficient in most men. I asked for a list of these salient qualities. This was a question for which she was clearly prepared and she was able to provide a rehearsed list of qualities without pause: 'Independence, clarity of thought, rationality, emotional commitment, communication and the courage to take actions irrespective of personal sacrifice.'

The last attribute, she pointed out, derived itself as an essential part of childbirth and rearing. Did she, I enquired, believe women candidates should generally be mothers?

'Certainly not. It is not necessary to actually have experienced childbirth or rearing in order for this essential quality to be part of the female psyche. It's simply that the potential of childbirth and rearing ensures its presence.'

I said I thought this was a very impressive list. Short of punctuality and cleanliness, I could think of few other attributes which would be necessary for the modern politician. She obviously took the view that, in so far as I had required conversion, the process was now complete and she, therefore, invited me both to purchase a mug and to add my name to the petition which I noticed already bore a substantial number of signatures. I gladly purchased the mug, signed the petition unread and, thereby, I reflected later, in all probability subscribed to all the virtues and deficiencies she had outlined and the gender singularity they implied.

I kept the mug but, I confess, as I used it and observed both the legend and the figures thereon, I was possessed of an increasing unease and disappointment. To be sure, my time in Parliament saw many women of indomitable spirit who possessed, in spades, precisely the attributes and the qualities that had been radically revealed to me. My old colleague, Alice Mahon, might be advanced as an exemplar; a woman of iron principle and indefatigable energy whose parliamentary career was a model of eloquent, witty and constructive dissidence. Her successor in Halifax, Linda Riordan, was in her mould, as was Katy Clark, another of the 2005 in-take. Both lost no time in establishing their independence of mind and all other of Emily's traits by deciding to defy the Government Whips on their first vote on terrorism. There are others; Diane Abbott, Lynne Jones and Clare Short obviously deserve their place in Emily's pantheon, along with Barbara Follett, who made one of the finest speeches I have heard in the Commons expressing her dissent and her objection to the establishment of Control Orders in the British legal system.

However, it is equally necessary to say that the vast influx of young women that attended upon the 1997 election, and the steadily incremental increase in their numbers as of result of women-only shortlists (involving the concomitant rejection of men of character and ability), has not fulfilled Emily's hopes. It has conspicuously failed to improve either the general independence of ordinary Members of Parliament or their willingness to confront or, on occasions, defeat the power the Executive has continued to exercise over backbenchers. The interesting studies carried out by Professor Philip Cowley into dissents and dissidence among the Parliamentary Labour Party in 2005–2006 reveal uncomfortable facts for the proponents of Emily's list and the virtues on which it was undoubtedly founded. During this important period, the Government embarked on a programme of legislation aimed at serious restrictions of personal and civil liberty, and parliamentary battles and dissent were commonplace. (See chapters on Liberty and Terror.) On at least one occasion, 106 Labour MPs voted against their Whip. Of these only twenty were women and just four had been elected in 2005.

Analysis of the vote against the Iraq War (a significant bellwether of many of Emily's attributes), reveals an unhappy lack of support among women Labour backbenchers. In a long and hard-fought debate, four Labour women spoke against the war (Diane Abbott, Glenda Jackson, Alice Mahon and Lynne Jones). From 139 Labour MPs who voted against the war, just fifteen were women.

None of which is to say that there aren't formidable *femmes* in British politics and, in particular, Labour politics. But too often they are to be found outside the elected representatives of the Labour Party. Sue Nye, the fearsome gatekeeper to Gordon Brown, had little difficulty in flattening my implied criticism of Gordon during the course of an otherwise enjoyable supper thrown by Geoffrey Robinson. She was kind enough to at least partially reconstruct me during the course of the rest of the meal and we have since remained friendly, albeit distant.

The same cannot be said for the wife of the former Prime Minister, Cherie Blair, whose influence over British politics from the early 1990s (nicely suggested in Robert Harris's novel, *The Ghost*) should never be underestimated.

I was left in no doubt of this on my first invitation to 10 Downing Street. This occurred shortly after the election in 1997. The massive number of Labour invitees meant there were several parties and, for some reason, I found myself in the first alphabetical batch. An invitation was received from the Prime Minister and his wife. The card was personal to myself and carried with it an instruction that I should phone a given number 'for directions'. I took this to be a helpful offer to new Members representing, for instance, Aberystwyth, who had no previous knowledge of Whitehall or the whereabouts of Downing Street. I, therefore, declined the offer of directions and duly proceeded to the party. After a short while, I found myself in the company of Cherie Booth whom I had known briefly at the Bar. I thought that this small acquaintanceship might stand me in some good stead, which was my first error. Without a single pleasantry, she fixed me with a beady eye and enquired acidly:

'Where is your wife?'

I contemplated a witty reply, rejected it and answered cheerfully, 'Not invited.'

'Not invited?' hissed my hostess. 'Not invited? Didn't you get the directions?'

I confessed I had not applied for the directions. Cherie's lips set in something approaching a bloodline before she said, 'You will go to the bottom of the list.'

There was something in the way she said 'bottom' which left no doubt that no living thing, however pestilential or foul, would be likely to inhabit the space beneath that to which I had been consigned. (I have reflected, on occasions, that Gordon Brown might later have been squeezed into that area but, at this time, we were still in the honeymoon period of New Labour, however improbable.) I was somewhat at a loss to deal with this sudden and precipitous demotion and the words of Milton rose unstoppable to my lips:

'Him the Almighty Power
Hurled headlong flaming from the ethereal sky,
With hideous ruin and combustion down
To the bottomless perdition, there to dwell
In adamantine chains of penal fire.'

Cherie appeared to be about to reply and then uttered a sound that would have sent primitive man scuttling to his cave, turned on her heel and disappeared.

Predictably, this was to be my last social invitation to No. 10. It was five years before I was to have my only other political contact with Cherie Blair, which surprised us both. In June 2002, Cherie attended the Offices of Medical Aid for Palestine. During the course of the interviews surrounding this visit, she expressed the view that 'young Palestinians feel that they have got no hope but to blow themselves up'. Predictably, there was a tabloid outcry, suitably fuelled and manipulated by the power of the British/Israeli media machine. In view of my aversion to Blair's foreign policy and my affinity with the Palestinian cause, I was an obvious candidate for media debate and I found myself on the *Today* programme 'head to head' with Ann Widdecombe, who had condemned Cherie's comment.

Over my years in Parliament I developed a strong admiration for Ann Widdecombe bordering on political affection. When we both left Parliament in 2010, we exchanged warm letters of appreciation and good wishes for the future. On the issue of Cherie Blair's statement, we had a thoroughly robust and enjoyable public spat. Ann's condemnation of Cherie Blair was total and was based on her own strong religious convictions at the evil inherent in taking one's own life for the express purpose of taking others. I replied that, as a confirmed atheist, nonetheless I found many Christian teachings and aphorisms wholly admirable. Was it not Christ's exhortation to hate the sin but love the sinner? Was this not, I asked, precisely what Cherie Blair was saying? In the event we enjoyed an honourable draw. Somewhat unexpectedly I later received a telephone call from a lady in Cherie Blair's private office. She had been asked to tell me, she said, how much Cherie had appreciated my public support at this difficult time. It was good of her to acknowledge my efforts, albeit through the agency of staff. I did not think, however, that this would lead to a resumption of social invitations. And I was right.

CHAPTER 9

OF THE MEDIA

In which we reflect on the best and worst free press in the world and the tyranny of Mr Rupert Murdoch – Recount the perils of briefing the media in competition with the Whips – Lament the failure to obtain a public platform for opposition to the Iraq War as a result of the trial of Mr Burrell and the fornication of footmen – Pay tribute to the magnificent Any Questions *which allows me briefly and joyously to become Miss Jeanette Winterson – Explain the magic and menace of* Have I Got News for You *– Reveal a strange affection for most hacks and fail utterly to remember the devastating arguments of Mr Christopher Hitchens.*

In Britain it is a cliché. We have the best and we have the worst of it. The BBC remains a beacon, flashing weakly but a beacon nonetheless. The *Sun* newspaper, at the other end, remains a creeping stain. The effect of Murdoch is much debated, in and outside Parliament. For many he is the highest form of demonology. His crude vulgarity, it is said, casts a long influence over the gullible and the deprived. In my political experience, I have found this to be an exaggeration. As with many bullies, Murdoch's reputation relies precisely upon his own self-advancing and self-reinforcing press. This may be seen in the *Sun*'s treatment of parliamentary dissidents and, in particular, those who espouse almost any form of civil liberty. A direct example may be found in the *Sun*'s campaign against those in Parliament who stated their opposition to detention without trial in terrorist cases. The first (failed) attempt by the Government to impose long imprisonment without trial (ninety days) was vociferously supported by the Murdoch press and, in particular, by the *Sun*. Those MPs who were opposed to this wholly aberrant measure were pilloried, individually and collectively, by the paper itself. In particular, shortly before the vote we were individually named and shamed. Our photographs were set up in a rogues' gallery on page 5 and our telephone numbers were provided to *Sun* readers in order that they might engulf us with their vitriolic distaste for liberal friends of the towel-headed terrorist. There was some discussion in the Tea Room about the effect that this campaign was likely to have, both on ourselves and on the management of our offices. In the event I received more calls than most (three). Of those three calls, two were made in order to express support for the position that we were taking. One gentleman appeared to be incandescent with rage on a wholly different subject, namely immigration. When asked whether he supported ninety-days imprisonment, he expressed the view that 'it depended on who got it'.

The dialectic between the mass media and politics continues to absorb much of political culture and political life. The attempts by both to manipulate the other have become legion, commonplace and much despised. Spin has now become an essential part of the political lexicon and is convenient shorthand for deliberate and manipulative deceit. It has done much to corrode belief in the body politic. The media, however, is, in truth, the only weapon that is available to political dissidents. For reasons explored elsewhere in this book, the power of Parliament and parliamentarians within a parliamentary context has become vestigial. However, use of the media is as available to the backbenchers as it is for the Government itself, and nothing causes greater alarm in Government than the prospect of backbenchers utilising the media in order to express dissent. The attempts on the part of Whips and Government to dissuade (forbid even) backbenchers to fraternise or use the media in order to express dissent have a gloriously hypocritical and hollow ring when compared to the activities of Government itself. This became particularly apparent after the weekly meeting of the Labour Parliamentary Party in Parliament. The meetings are, by common consent, packed with Government supporters and toadies. Tremendous desk-thumping takes place at every opportunity during speeches given by members of the Government attacking the enemy without and within. It can be, to the uninitiated dissident, a fraught and traumatic experience. Outside, in the corridors, the parliamentary hacks are waiting to receive news on which they themselves can base their views on Party cohesion or dissent. The Government Whips and No. 10 advisers are the first out of the doors and thus the first to be surrounded by a small covey of journalists. These are precisely the people who minutes earlier had been exhorting members of the Parliamentary Labour Party not to speak to the waiting hacks. Further along the corridor the dissident few hold their own press conferences. This attracts huge quantities of bile. I can remember on one occasion, Barry Sheerman MP, a serious Government supporter, literally shrieking at me for daring to discuss the PLP meeting with waiting hacks while, just down the corridor, the Whips were doing precisely the same thing.

It is, however, a fickle business. Not infrequently, friends asked why I had been absent from the media for so long. 'Where have you been?' they enquire, after another crisis has passed without a comment from me. The answer, of course, is that the media pick their own ground and those who will inhabit it. This was brought home to me forcibly in the approach to the Iraq War.

At this time, in late 2002 and early 2003, I was desperate to get on any media of any kind in order to express my own opposition to the war and my deep foreboding as to its outcome. I also wanted to give public expression to the growing number of Members of Parliament, of all shades and all sides, who opposed the conflict and regarded the pronouncements and documents from No. 10 with total disbelief. I became increasingly frustrated. All my attempts to find a suitable media outlet were politely declined. Ironically, I was in frequent demand but not to deal with foreign policy. The reason was the high-profile trial at the Old Bailey of a man called Burrell. This gentleman, who has subsequently achieved notoriety as a minor celebrity, had been the chief butler to the late Princess Diana. Some time after her death, the police had raided Mr Burrell's home and had discovered, concealed in a garage, a substantial number of personal possessions and impedimenta which had been the property of the late princess. Mr Burrell was duly charged with theft, thus providing the media with a further opportunity to reflect upon the sublime and ethereal nature of Diana and the odious nature of anyone who could have so defiled her possessions and abused her office. For the popular press it was particularly gratifying, as the news could be dissected and divorced from any mention of Mr Dodi Fayed and the circumstances surrounding Diana's death. It was in this regard that I found myself in substantial, almost daily, demand from various aspects of the media. As a politician I was known to be a robust republican and I was also a QC with grounding in criminal work. In short, I was the perfect 'political' commentator on this continuing trial, an issue about which I cared precisely nothing. My interractions with the press and the media became somewhat repetitive. Typically, my wife would inform me that '5 Live are on the phone and want to talk to you'. Breathlessly, I would arrive at the telephone indicating that I would be delighted to discuss the recent pronouncements on Iraq or, alternatively, the veracity of the dodgy dossiers that were being produced. My offer would be politely declined, but my contribution would be eloquently and urgently sought to comment on the airwaves on the latest twist in the Burrell/ Diana saga. This became particularly intense as the Burrell trial concluded in the most dramatic way. Her Majesty the Queen, having watched the trial progress for over two weeks, suddenly remembered that she had, herself, given instructions that Mr Burrell should be provided with a number of Diana's possessions by way of keepsake and memorabilia as a demonstration of gratitude. This dramatic intervention was brought to the attention of the trial judge, my good friend, the redoubtable Anne Rafferty or, as the popular press had christened her, Mrs Justice Whiplash. Had Elizabeth Windsor been anything other than the Queen and Head of State, her evidence would have been severely tested in the witness box and her delay in providing this evidence would have attracted harsh and ringing admonition from Mrs Justice Whiplash. In the case of Her Majesty such a reaction was unthinkable. Mr Burrell was duly acquitted by direction of the Judge, and, no doubt, returned home to play with Princess Diana's personal effects in the privacy of his own garage. For me this was, of course, a blessed relief. My role as chief commentator on the Burrell trial was now over, and surely I would be summoned by the press and media for my trenchant views on the rapid escalation towards catastrophic conflict.

Unhappily, this was not to be. Almost coincident with the collapse of the Burrell trial, the press became seized of yet another royal scandal. The butlers and staff of Buckingham Palace, particularly those associated with the Prince of Wales, had apparently been engaging in florid sexual concourse with each other. Dark rumours began to surface of non-consensual behaviour of a homosexual nature. To all of this activity I was, of course, totally indifferent, and was preoccupied in Parliament with the massive build-up of armed forces preparing for the onslaught in Mesopotamia. I found myself, once again, in strong media demand. Newspaper journalists and broadcasting editors tend to operate on simple and prosaic lines faced with political commentary. As a result of Burrell, I had now become collectively designated as the leading expert on the behaviour of butlers, particularly of a royal variety. My efforts to assail the media on Iraq, therefore, again met with an insistence that I should apply my political commentary to the issue of fornicating (or alleged fornicating) footmen. It was during a morning interview on 5 Live that my reserve and patience finally cracked. Asked to comment on the butler scandal, I found myself observing 'non-consensual sodomy among royal valets is almost unknown in Baghdad. That is, however, no reason to believe that they possess weapons of mass destruction'.

'I am sorry,' said my bewildered interviewer, 'I didn't quite catch that.'

During my time in Parliament I was fortunate to be asked to appear on numerous panel programmes, both serious and satirical. Of the serious variety, by far the best is *Any Questions*. It is this ancient radio programme which gave birth to the now vastly inferior and vulgarised *Question Time* on BBC television. *Any Questions* is a pure joy. Panellists are either politicians, political journalists, writers, commentators or professionals with a strong political interest. Its most important and famous aspect is travelling to the people. It takes place in school halls and community centres selected from towns and villages throughout Britain that have volunteered to take part. The audience is drawn directly from that community. There is simply no better place to gauge the direction and weight of public opinion. The panels are, of course, politically balanced. The Labour Whips have, I understand, complained bitterly, but confidentially, about my inclusion on panels on the basis that the authentic (heavily tailored) views of the Labour Government are not only absent but are, on occasions, actively criticised by the 'Labour' panellist. That could account for my frequent invitations to appear. The programmes have been brilliantly chaired by Jonathan Dimbleby and the late and much lamented Nick Clarke.

Nick, one of the great commentators of his time, died from a terrible cancer which involved the total removal of one of his legs. For a short time he continued to chair the programme with this dreadful disability, which required the use of two full shoulder crutches. I was on the panel in his last programme, together with Polly Toynbee and the novelist, Kate Mosse. We were on the platform of a school hall and due to enter in procession (Nick first) from the wings. In a gross faux pas which, even now, causes me to shiver, I uttered the thespian's exhortation 'break a leg'. Realising immediately the crass nature of the remark, I turned to Nick and said, 'Oh my God, Nick. I am so sorry.' He laughed out loud and when we were assembled on the platform before the programme started, took great delight in telling the audience what I had said, whilst waving his crutches gleefully in the air.

The quality of *Any Questions* audiences was starkly demonstrated by my last appearance at Wokingham in a week that contained widely different pieces of news. The first was the tragic death of Baby P and the venomous press campaign which followed against the social workers of Haringey and, in particular, Sharon Shoesmith. The second was the raid on Damien Green's Commons' office which had, it transpired, been authorised from his home in Scotland by the Speaker, Michael Martin. The authorisation was given through the Serjeant-at-Arms, Jill Pay, one of the nicest and most distinguished holders of that office. Faced with a furious Commons, Martin had lost no opportunity publicly to blame the Serjeant-at-Arms for his own gaffe.

Both stories inevitably formed the subjects of questions from the audience. Asked whether the Speaker should resign, I replied with an unqualified affirmative. In doing so, I explained that Members of Parliament possessed personally no rights and privileges above an individual. However, the office they held did not belong to them but to the people that they represented. If that was violated, it was a violation of the people's rights and not of any individual MP. The response of the audience indicated quite clearly the view they had formed of the Speaker's conduct and could well have accounted for my failures to catch his eye in the House until his subsequent resignation.

The second question relating to Baby P was desperately difficult. The death was, of course, a tragedy, but the issue for me was the reaction of the popular media and, in particular, the *Sun* towards the social workers involved. I had decided before the programme that this issue could not legitimately be avoided, notwithstanding the fact that I anticipated from the audience an unpleasant period of hostility. I had drafted my answer carefully:

'Through this case let us give our thoughts to the social workers of Haringey, now much vilified. They are ill-paid public servants dedicated to their vocation. The choices that they are forced to make in these cases are desperate. It is not "what is best for the child" but what is least bad. They live with a daily diet of dysfunctional violence and deceit and they work in streets down which the editors of popular newspapers would not allow themselves to be driven, let alone to leave their cars. One of the most sickening spectacles of the week was a *Sun* reporter repeatedly demanding of my minister, Ed Balls, that he give credit to the *Sun* for their nasty campaign. I am very sorry that my minister did not have the courage to resist it.'

I delivered the answer verbatim and waited in some apprehension for the audience's reaction. When it came, it was in the form of overwhelming applause. I received a large number of letters. All of them, save one, supportive, some tearfully so. One social worker told me that she had been moved to stop the car she was driving to cheer at the radio. The *Sun* newspaper believes, fondly, that it speaks for the people. It would do well to listen to the audiences of *Any Questions* before it persists in that vainglorious claim.

It was through *Any Questions* that, briefly, I became Jeanette

Winterson. Jeanette has been a regular contributor to the programme. On this occasion we were together on a panel broadcasting from the Hay Festival in 2008. I had sat on panels with her before. Jeanette is a brilliant novelist and a fine panellist. She is also gay and has, in the past, provided invaluable views on tolerance and diversity. We always got on very well. The programme from Hay was a success, largely due to her effortless authority on the arts, politics in general and literature in particular. At the end of the programme, unfortunately, Jeanette had to leave because of a family bereavement. My friends, Jim and Ellie Naughtie were both in the audience and both were at Hay in order to enjoy the first day of the festival and to discuss their own books later in the week. At the party after the show I was asked by Jim where I was staying the night. I told him that the BBC had provided me with a car to take me to Pembrokeshire where I was staying for the rest of the weekend.

'You mustn't go,' said Jim. 'On the first day of the festival there is always a party at Revel Guest's mansion. It is a wonderful affair, you really must come. Jeanette Winterson was going to stay and I understand the BBC has booked her a rather good room. You can have that and make your own travel arrangements in the morning.'

I protested further that I was not invited to this great event.

'Nonsense,' said Jim. 'They would be delighted to see you.'

And so, it transpired, they were. The Guests' manor is a magnificent Victorian pile overlooking Hay and the surrounding countryside. Evelyn Waugh could not have written it. Fires roared in every grate and great dogs lay in front of them. Ancient, semi-legless tables were supported by piles of improving books and, in the interstices of the house, down darkened corridors plumbing clanked mournfully in the night. The main hall contained a vast dining table at which some thirty people, by the time we arrived, were well into their dinner and large quantities of fine wine. The literary great and good were assembled and I found a seat, generously vacated by Ed Victor, next to Rosie Boycott. The conversation was sparkling, the food excellent and the wine copious. By half past two in the morning I was in a state of ethereal happiness and about to fall asleep. Someone, to whom I owe a considerable debt of gratitude, summoned a taxi. Expostulating thanks, I was poured into the back and the driver was instructed to convey me to a destination which I did not catch which was, he was told, originally allocated to Jeanette Winterson. The journey was surprising and suspiciously long. Hay is surrounded by the most beautiful rolling countryside and the journey was an appropriately winding and somnambulant affair. The countryside was pitch black and on several occasions I fell asleep. During one period of consciousness I heard the driver receive a telephone call and confirm that he was on his way to 'Miss Winterson's house'. At approximately three o'clock in the morning, the journey ended and, grasping my briefcase (the only luggage I possessed), I stumbled from the taxi on to a thick gravel drive, above which towered a Queen Anne mansion, not dissimilar in dimensions from that which I had left. Descending the steps towards me was a blonde lady of quite indescribable beauty wearing a white dressing gown and followed by several dogs. Near dumbstruck, I uttered the first words which came into my head:

'Hello,' I said. 'I'm Jeanette Winterson.'

'Good,' said the lady. 'We have been expecting you. Come this way, please.'

I entered the house and ascended a magnificent spiral staircase led by a mêlée of blonde hair, white dressing gown and dogs. Passing several floors, I was shown into a room of startling grandeur. Vast windows were covered by thick French drapes. Ancient floorboards were liberally covered by magnificent Turkish rugs. Dark furniture radiated polish around the room and included an enormous four-poster bed.

'The bathroom is over there in the corner,' said my hostess. 'I'll see you in the morning.'

Rather disappointingly she disappeared with the dogs and I fell forward on to the bed and entered a deep and peaceful sleep. When I awoke I had not the remotest idea of time or place. As the night assembled itself in my mind, so did an increasing sense of alarm. Due to the magnificence of the hangings the room remained nearly black, but a chink of light revealed unmistakable day. I made my way to the bathroom and turned on the light, by which I discovered it was approximately 9.30. Bereft of both razor and toothbrush, I showered and gargled with the mouthwash that, fortunately, I always carry in my briefcase. I threw open the curtains and the whole of mid Wales lay before me, magnificent in the spring sunshine. I still had not the remotest idea where I was, which didn't seem to matter very much.

I assembled myself as best I could, packed my briefcase and gingerly descended the regal staircase. At its foot, I heard unmistakable family noises from a corridor which gave on to what, obviously, had previously been servants' quarters. At the end of this corridor I entered a vast kitchen, full of pine tables, breakfast smells, dogs and children. Standing over a kitchen range was last night's vision, now in jeans and a jumper, cooking bacon and talking to a tall and elegant man whom I took (rightly) to be her husband. Before I could apologise, I was warmly welcomed by the entire family and offered a seat at the breakfast table.

'Look,' I said. 'I think a number of apologies are in order. My name is …'

'Oh, we know who you are,' said Alice (as she transpired to be). 'You're Bob Marshall-Andrews. We've been in touch with the BBC.'

'Thank you,' I mumbled. 'But I really must apologise for keeping you up and also for my strange behaviour. I seem to remember telling you that I was Jeanette Winterson.'

This provoked some merriment from Alice and her husband, who had obviously discussed my arrival before.

'You did say you were Jeanette Winterson,' she said, sitting beside me at the table, 'and do you know it was really rather remarkable. I am a great fan of Jeanette Winterson and have read, I think, all of her novels – but I had never met her or seen photographs in the media. I do, however, know about her sexual preferences. I have never seen you before either and I am sorry to say that when you announced yourself to be Jeanette Winterson I did think that you actually *were* Jeanette Winterson.'

She then added hastily, while I laughed: 'But now we do know who you are, you are, of course, equally welcome.'

I finally left this piece of rural paradise at about twelve o'clock. The trains, she said, were quite impossible from the middle of Wales and a car had been found to drive me to Swansea. My driver was delightful and ancient and confessed to me that he had never left the area. Indeed, he had only on one occasion been as far as Swansea. At Swansea, I discovered that we had narrowly missed the train and I asked whether he would be prepared to drive me to Carmarthen. He agreed immediately adding, of course, that he had never been to Carmarthen. At Carmarthen, we again narrowly missed the train and I enquired whether he would drive me to Pembrokeshire. With the unnecessary observation that he had never been to Pembrokeshire, we set out and finally arrived at my ultimate destination, overlooking the Irish Sea, in time for a late lunch. When I asked my driver for the bill, he looked at me doubtfully. He had, he said, never undertaken a paid journey (or, indeed, any journey) of this length before. We then haggled. He asked me whether £20 would be all right. I answered sternly that it would not under any circumstances be sufficient and I would not pay him a penny less than £50. Notwithstanding his sheltered rural upbringing, he obviously had a stubborn streak, and he informed me that he would not accept a penny more than £30.

'£45,' I countered, 'and this is definitely my last offer.'

Finally we settled on £40, with £5 towards the petrol. He departed on the road to Hay. I just hope to this day that he is telling anyone who will listen that he 'had that Jeanette Winterson in the back of the car. She's got more money than sense.'

Next to *Any Questions*, I have enjoyed *Have I Got News For You*. I was first asked in 1998 and initially hesitated before acceptance. The programme had then (and has now) a grisly reputation for the treatment of its guests. My friend, Austin Mitchell, the wise and funny Member of Parliament for Great Grimsby, had been on the programme and before I accepted, I asked his advice.

'I am told,' I said, 'that it can be like being castrated in public.'

He thought for a moment before replying: 'No, no, no. It is much worse than that.'

I appeared first with my fellow guest Lloyd Grossman and we both met, unsurprisingly, in the lavatory before the programme began.

'Ah well,' he said, as we dried our hands, 'up the steps to the guillotine.'

Adopting the same theme, I said: 'Try to smile. It looks better in the basket.'

In the end I survived and subsequently, over the years, went four more rounds without noticeable public castration. It has, deservedly, become a magnificent national institution. It has been emulated but never remotely equalled. To answer the FAQs, it is not scripted. No one knows the answers and the questions are revealed half an hour before the programme starts. For the guests, filled with adrenaline and apprehension, it is coruscating and physically utterly exhausting. I had one immensely lucky break. In 2006, I appeared on the programme on Ian Hislop's side under the chairmanship of Jack Dee. It had just been revealed to the media that the Fees Administration in the House of Commons checked MPs' claims for items of furniture against the John Lewis list. As Members of Parliament, we had not the remotest idea that this yardstick was being used, but that had not the slightest effect on the story. Sitting immediately on Jack's right-hand side, I was able to see the shelves of the chairman's desk. Carefully placed on the second shelf I saw a copy of the John Lewis catalogue. Whilst Jack was reading the auto-cue, I gently removed it and place it below my own desk. I saw that a number of pages had been flagged and a quick check revealed furniture and items of particular extravagance and vulgarity. The programme had proceeded for about forty-five minutes out of its hour and a half when the John Lewis story arrived on the agenda. After a brief introduction, Jack reached below the desk to retrieve the tormenting article. As he groped to the back of the shelf, I pulled out the copy and asked whether he was looking for his John Lewis list. Ian Hislop and I then had considerable fun identifying items such as the velvet and tasselled chaise longue and asking Jack why he wanted to possess such an item and whether he wanted it for the bathroom.

After a while, he threw both hands in the air and said: 'Look, governor, it wasn't my fucking idea.'

It was fun but it was lucky and, even now, my blood runs slightly colder at the prospect of what might have been.

Westminster is, of course, the natural habitat for political hacks. Being a dissident Member of Parliament carries substantial disadvantages. You will never achieve high office (if you wish to); you will be disliked by approximately half of your colleagues on the backbenches and will be positively loathed by a small number and by the Whips. One of the reasons why you are thoroughly disliked is that you have a public voice. This, of course, is the main advantage. As you are prepared to speak so, gratifyingly, there are, apparently, people who are prepared to listen. Providing free-range analysis and opinions for the media and, thence, to a wider audience is, in fact, positively forbidden by the Party's parliamentary rules and this is one of the reasons why the public hold politicians in contempt. For me, providing a dissident voice was not only legitimate, it was essential. The dire state of Parliament and parliamentary procedure has greatly reduced the power of MPs to hold their own government to account within Westminster. No such inhibitions exist within the wider media. Sensible, even radical dissidence, expressed through the media is, in truth, far more powerful than dissent expressed in Parliament.

To have a public voice is gratifying, but it should not give rise to dangerous delusions. The first of these is that the voice and the small influence that it carries belong to you as an individual and not to your parliamentary status.

Shortly after leaving Parliament on 6 May 2010, I left my mobile phone in the office, which was in the process of being wound up. It was several days before I was able to retrieve it from Jill, my wonderful PA. Several hours later, I phoned her from London.

'What,' I said sternly, 'have you done to my mobile phone?'

'Nothing,' she said. 'Is there anything wrong with it?'

'Yes, there is,' I said. 'There are no messages on it and no one has phoned all day.'

'Yes,' she said brightly. 'It's been like that all week.'

The reason, of course, is blindingly obvious. The media and the public are interested in the existence of dissident voices within the Parliamentary Party of Government. In the views of ex-MPs they have absolutely no interest whatsoever.

I have become very fond of political hacks personally and as a class. One of them – the late, great Tony Bevins – was one of my best friends. Some, like Alan Watkins, were as wise politicians as any in Christendom. Many are gloriously funny. Some, like Mike White, affect a Jaquesian melancholy, but this barely conceals wit and humanity. Conference lunches with the likes of Simon Hoggart, Steve Bell and Martin Rowson are postcard memories of happy seaside bawdry. It was in the course of one of them that I was invited to comment on Tony Blair's 93 per cent popularity rating. Perhaps unwisely, I observed, '7 per cent; we can build on that'. This comment reappeared for thirteen years with increasing regularity, occasionally as a sign of prescience. (One of my New Labour colleagues once upbraided me, blaming that statement rather than Iraq for Blair's plummeting popularity.)

Only a very few hacks are venomous. Unusually, one excellent political editor recently wrote that something (I cannot remember exactly what) 'reminded us of how much we hate politicians'. I wonder who exactly is 'we'? I doubt whether many journalists have ever canvassed roads or walked the High Street of my constituency. If they did so with me, they would encounter no hatred. A bit of derision or banter here or there (there are twelve pubs in Rochester High Street) but generally they would find humour, kindness, goodwill and even a little sympathy of purpose. My surgeries were totally free from rant or rancour and occasionally there was even touching gratitude for the little we could do. When I announced my retirement, my postbag was movingly full of thanks and good wishes. There was one vitriolic rant (which was also anonymous and, inevitably, in green ink).

Private Eye, strangely, has never traded in personal spite, despite the jovial protestations of its great editors. Its lunches on the Formica tables of the Coach and Horses presided over by Richard Ingrams and Ian Hislop are the finest rough trade soirées society has to offer. They contain much completely forgotten wisdom. I remember an agreeable and ferocious row with Christopher Hitchens, which lasted all the afternoon. It ended in a long silence when we realised that we were quite alone, whereupon we simultaneously enquired of each other what we had been discussing.

OF LIBERTY AND TERROR 1:
THE HABIT OF CONTROL

In which we reflect on the extraordinary proclivity of New Labour to pass repressive laws and the reasons therefore – Recount the details of my first organised rebellion to preserve jury trial and the modest success thereof, and observe the near catastrophic consequences for Mr Jack Straw then Home Secretary.

In thirteen years, the New Labour Government passed more criminal justice legislation than became law in the whole of the nineteenth century. A formidable achievement. As to the number of new criminal offences that have been created, there is continuing debate. It is certainly more than 500. (The Liberal Democrats' claim of 3,200 displays an impressive amount of double accounting.) Yet more impressive is the number of new sentences and the rules, regulations, strictures and statutory exhortations that have been applied to the sentencing process. The result is a judicial nightmare. The prisons are massively over-crowded with prisoners who, by common consent, should not be serving anything like the sentences to which they have been sub-jected as a result of the statutory straitjacket that now confines judges. As a result of the same legislation, these same experienced judges (still by common consent the finest such cadre in the world) are now enjoined to recite meaningless mantras calculated to baffle defendants and inflame victims and their families. On the judicial seminars I still attend as Recorder and Deputy High Court Judge, I spend much time in urgent denial to my fellow judges that it is my fault. During the course of a debate on jury trials, I invited the junior minister holding the front bench to attend a judicial seminar in order to 'experience at first hand the raw anger of the judiciary at the meaningless sentences which they were increasingly forced to impose'. The only response I got from the front bench was from David Davis, then the Opposition Home Secretary, who asked if he could also attend to watch the spectacle.

How did we arrive at this dreadful state? How did a Party that prided itself upon its civil libertarian credentials descend into one of the most authoritarian regimes in British history, certainly since that of Lord Liverpool in the middle of the nineteenth century? The answer is an interesting reflection on Party politics. Amazingly, until the 1970s, law and order, crime and punishment, did not appear as a political issue in the election manifestos of any of the major parties. The reason for this (now startling) omission was simple. There was a political consensus that human wickedness was a matter for theology and not for politics. The conditions and circumstances which gave way to human criminality were something for the political arena. Education, housing, health and the general physical and mental wellbeing of the subject could, obviously, affect the propensity towards crime. This simple truth dates back to Lord Shaftesbury and beyond. However, crime and punishment itself was not perceived to be part of the political arena and neither side thought to blame the other for rising crime rates or, indeed, to attempt to achieve accolades for their fall. All this changed in the course of the 1970s.

The Labour Party had always been (indeed, prided itself on

being) the party of civil liberty. This stemmed from a history and tradition of trade union emancipation mixed with the softer liberal tendencies of the Bloomsbury intellectual and Shavian literature. In the 1970s, the Tories perceived this as a wonderful political opportunity. It was, they realised, a short step to allege that understanding and compassion for the sinner was, in fact, approbation for the sin. Thus, in the manifestos of the 1970s, the Tories launched their onslaught on law and order. Being 'soft on crime' was one of many albatrosses suspended around the emaciated neck of the Labour Party. It had a deadly political effect. It coincided with a number of other developments. The popular press embraced the whole concept of criminal behaviour as a political issue and, at the same time, sociology was becoming a science as opposed to an enjoyable pastime.

The result was particularly bad for Labour in working-class areas and, taken together with the sale of countless council houses, formed a Tory bridge into the working class. Those in charge of the New Labour Project knew this very well. It, therefore, became a part of the Project itself to ambush and then outflank the Tories on issues of law and order. The method employed was to blame lawlessness on liberty, thereby perpetuating an ancient totalitarian myth that the more liberty human beings enjoy, the more wicked they become. It is a particularly easy message to filter through the pages of the *Sun*. Thus New Labour embarked upon an extraordinary onslaught of authoritarian legislation, challenging some of the most revered and cherished institutions of British society, from jury trial to the rights of an individual to maintain silence in the face of accusation by the State. Fighting my own Government on this issue became the major *raison d'etre* of my political life.

The Government signalled its intentions at an early stage with a Bill to remove the right to elect trial by jury. Despite its ancient position as the cornerstone of British liberty, jury trial has long been anathema to the Home Office because it is difficult, if not impossible, effectively to control. Juries have both a political and judicial independence which cannot be regulated or administered and which has resulted, through the centuries, in 'perverse' verdicts to restrain the injustices of executive power. For this reason it was an obvious target for New Labour and, for thirteen years, assaults on the jury system became a recurring theme of Government.

The first attack came in the form of Mode of Trial Bill I. This short piece of legislation proposed that defendants in the vast majority of indictable cases should lose the right to elect trial by jury which would lie instead in the gift of individual magistrates. It was widely anticipated that magistrates would retain an increasing number of trials to themselves; that they would gradually assume a more judicial role and thus, within a short period, jury trial would be reduced to a limited number of the most serious and venal offences. Although barely ten clauses long, the importance of this Bill could not be overstated. Had it become law, it would have marked the end of eight centuries of trial by jury.

There was, however, a problem for the Government which arose from an extraordinary class deference and the wonderful concept of the *Respectable Defendant*. The Government apprehended, rightly, that a limited number of defendants in criminal cases possessed reputations so immaculate and pure that any conviction, however minor, would blight their entire lives. The respectable professional person who, in a moment of absent-mindedness, leaves WH Smith's with an unpaid copy of Martin Amis's new novel would, if convicted, lose far more than the sentence imposed. Their reputation and professional careers would very probably be ruined. This group of people required, so the Government perceived, a special form of protection. The Bill, therefore, required magistrates, in deciding whether jury trial was appropriate, expressly to consider the reputation of defendants and the likely damage a conviction would do to their way of life.

This Bill was the cause of my first rebellion and first attempt to organise a revolt on the Labour backbenches. One of the obvious grounds upon which the rebellion could be mounted (and which would ensure a wider bed of support) was the 'reputation clause'. It provided obvious grounds for criticism that the Government was creating a two-tier system of justice. There was a right for those who possessed a reputation, and none for those who did not. Thus, in losing your reputation by a criminal conviction, you also lost, in perpetuity, the likelihood that you would achieve jury trial for future offences. The obvious class basis of this distinction touched a chord with many of my Labour colleagues who might otherwise have been indifferent to the trial process. There were also a significant number, both inside and outside the campaign group, who believed that the principles of jury trial were deeply enshrined in the principles of the Labour movement and, thus, the rebellion grew.

In order to stoke these flames, I employed the much abused method of setting down an Early Day Motion. This anachronism is a process whereby Members of Parliament, individually or collectively, may put down a motion for early debate. In reality, this means that no debate will take place, but it is a method of engendering publicity and demonstrating to the Government that there is a substantial risk that their legislation may be opposed. The process of Early Day Motions has now fallen into serious disrepute by increased silliness on the part of backbench MPs using them for such purposes as congratulating their local football team on coming fifth in the Fourth Division. In those days, however, it was a potent weapon and, on my first Early Day Motion relating to jury trial, I managed to achieve close to a hundred signatures, something even a Government in possession of a 160-plus majority should have taken, at least, seriously. In the event they did not, and the Home Secretary, Jack Straw, ploughed ahead with this measure which would, though short in size, have had a huge and weighty effect on British civil liberties. I went to see Jack and asked him seriously to reconsider this legislation which he politely declined to do. It was a rejection which came close to costing him his political career.

In the event, the Bill moved towards its Second Reading. I put down a Reasoned Amendment which would, effectively, have killed the Bill in its tracks.

There was a spirited debate on the subject. The Tories (after the dark days of Michael Howard) rediscovered an attachment for civil libertarian principles and, during the course of this campaign, I made a number of allies across the floor of the House, who remained with me throughout the whole of my political career. David Davis and Dominic Grieve (then emerging as one of the best debaters in the House of Commons) were in the vanguard organising the Tory response. It was becoming an extraordinary parliamentary affair. The Labour Party, the traditional champion of rights and liberties, was fighting to destroy them in the face of Tory (and Liberal) opposition.

At the end of the debate, the House divided and the Labour majority was reduced to fifty-three. It was a significant moment. In parliamentary terms a majority of fifty-three is perfectly normal, but for a Government which had swept to power with a majority three times that size, it represented, effectively, a serious defeat. The Whips were furious. During the course of the vote itself, they were stationed as they were thereafter, on many occasions, at the foot of every gangway and doorway in order, by their very (largely Scottish) presence, to deter New Labour stragglers intent on entering the civil libertarian Tory and Liberal Lobby.

The effect of this vote was far-reaching, as I was subsequently to discover. The House of Lords, emboldened by the substantial fall in the Government's majority, debated the issue and, largely as a result of repeated and truthful assertions that the Bill represented not the view of the people but the will of the Whips, it was defeated. I spent much time in the Lords' Bar and in the corridors of the House of Lords talking to likely dissidents and re-forging a long and happy relationship with my fellow barrister, Baroness Helena Kennedy. Helena soon found herself, like me, in uncharted waters and, in so doing, encouraged her peers and colleagues by steadily rebelling against her own Government. As such, she has been a physical and political adornment to thirteen years of Parliament.

The Government was then faced with a dilemma. It either attempted to force the Act through by the use of its parliamentary leverage by the Parliament Act, or it retreated and redrafted the Bill. What the Home Office and the Home Secretary in fact decided was bizarre. They perceived, with some justification, that the Reputation Clause was one of the weaknesses in the Bill. They, therefore, performed an extraordinary volte-face. The Bill was reproduced with the Reputation Clause surgically removed. Indeed, it was not only removed but magistrates, having previously been directed to take reputation into account in the first Bill, were now specifically told that they *could not do so*. This opened up a merry riposte. Those of us who were totally opposed were now able confidently to ask what would happen to the elderly, absent-minded professional of immaculate reputation who walks out of WH Smith's with an unpaid-for copy of Martin Amis's novel. Were they to run the risk of the total loss of their lifestyle, their friends and their reputation, without the safeguard of jury trial which has been enjoyed by such professionals (and everyone else) for 800 years? The Government expressed some outrage at what they perceived to be a complete change of tack on the part of the opponents to the Bill. What Jack, unhappily, did not appear to understand, was that the volte-face lay with the Government.

In the following attempt to force the Bill into law, Jack was seriously to mislead the House and, had it not been for extraordinary events, the consequences for him could have been dire.

During the Second Reading debate, he announced that removing the right to elect trial by jury was supported by the police, the Magistrates' Association and 'The Lord Chief Justice'. This, he asserted (with some justification) gave the Act a certain grounding and gravitas. If the Lord Chief Justice was, indeed, in favour of such a measure, it was obviously something that would be persuasive to Members of the House of Commons, the vast majority of whom had no legal experience whatsoever. This assertion, however, gave me some pause for thought and after the Second Reading debate, I set about discovering if it were true. The Lord Chief Justice, at the time, was the late Tom Bingham, a liberal thinker of considerable reputation. I had met him once only briefly, but I determined to find out if, indeed, this draconian Bill enjoyed his support. I, therefore, wrote to the 'Chief' asking if I might have a personal interview, explained briefly the reason for my request and, in particular, my desire to ascertain his views on the Mode of Trial Bill. The Chief responded swiftly, and a meeting was arranged in his substantial rooms overlooking the Thames in the House of Lords. The conversation was friendly but short. I asked him if he could tell me whether he supported the Mode of Trial Bill in its present form. The question obviously made him a little uncomfortable and he replied, whilst gazing intently at the Thames, that he felt he was unable specifically to answer my question. This, in itself, sharpened the political antennae. I asked politely why he felt he was unable to give me an answer, to which he replied that he had 'had correspondence with the Home Secretary on the subject' and felt that courtesy, and his professional rules, forbade him from revealing the contents of that correspondence.

I may not be in the very forefront of political or legal perspicacity but immediately I began to sense that something was seriously wrong. In the event, Tom Bingham agreed that he would write to Jack in order to see whether the correspondence could be revealed to me and could be made public. I thanked him and immediately wrote my own letter to Jack, telling of my conversation with Tom Bingham, and assumed there would be no problem in my seeing the letters that had passed between him and the Lord Chief Justice. A deafening silence ensued.

After a couple of weeks, I wrote again, asking Jack if he had received a letter from the Lord Chief Justice and whether, as a result, he felt able to show me the correspondence. More silence.

Meanwhile, the Bill was making its way through its stages in the House of Commons, and within a short period of time went through Committee and was due to come back to the Commons to receive its final vote on a Tuesday.

It was obviously essential that I ascertained, before that date, the true standing of the Lord Chief Justice, so I wrote a stern letter to the Home Secretary indicating that I required a reply to my letters and that, regrettably, if I did not receive it, I would make his silence public and would, indeed, issue a press release to that effect. At this stage, I felt seriously out of my depth. I had been a Member of Parliament for barely twelve months, had already organised two rebellions against my own Government, and I was now in the process of 'shopping' the Home Secretary and his Department with a strong inference of cover-up if not deceit. For a Labour backbencher this was, even then, an unusual course of action.

In the event, I received a telephone call from Jack's private office and, in particular, from one of his junior officials, who lost no opportunity in informing me that it was 'all his fault'. My letters to the Home Secretary had 'gone astray' and the matter had not been placed upon his desk. However, now there was a measure of urgency, the Home Secretary would communicate with the Lord Chief Justice with a view to making their correspondence public.

Finally, on the Monday of the week of the debate, I received, by messenger, a copy of the correspondence between the Lord Chief Justice and the Home Secretary. It revealed, with absolute clarity, that far from enjoying the support of the Lord Chief Justice, the Bill had awakened his severe apprehensions.

A detailed letter to the Home Secretary set out Tom Bingham's grave concerns as to the effect which the Bill would have, not only for individuals who were charged, but on the wider criminal justice system. It was a careful, methodical and devastating critique of the legislation. This letter had been written to the Home Secretary less than a week before he had announced to the House of Commons that the Bill enjoyed the support of the Lord Chief Justice. In other words, in the clearest possible way, the House had been seriously misled in circumstances which would have profoundly influenced the parliamentary vote. Most of my Labour colleagues (then as now) will avoid any confrontation with the Government if they possibly can. The endorsement of a liberal Lord Chief Justice would have done much to lessen or, indeed, completely avoid a repetition of the Commons' vote on the first Bill that had so emboldened the House of Lords.

I contacted Tony Bevins, then political editor of the *Independent*.

'Fuck,' he said. 'This is monumental.'

One of the tabloid editors was also told the story and both assured me that it would appear as their front page lead. Had it done so, the effect would have been disastrous for the Bill and possibly for Jack. He would probably have survived, but to do so would have required all of his skill and resources as one of the great survivors of British politics.

It is a fact of politics, well tested, that grave and terrible events overshadow the mere reputations of men, and so it was on this occasion. On the day before publication of this 'monumental' political story, Concorde crashed, causing the deaths of many people and the end of the dream of supersonic civil aviation. Unsurprisingly, every newspaper contained nothing on their domestic pages other than the awfulness of the news and the analysis of its consequences. The story of the Home Secretary's misleading the House of Commons was reduced, even in the *Independent*, to a below-the-fold article on the sixth page.

Although I raised the matter again in a strong debate, the impact was, of course, noticeably diminished. The whole lamentable saga has been rehearsed on a number of occasions, not least by Peter Oborne in his influential work, *The Triumph of the Political Class*, but it is now no more than a footnote. The effect on the legislation, however, was indeed terminal. It limped through the Commons with a majority of fifty and made its way wearily to the Lords where, inevitably, it faced defeat. By this time Jack had, understandably, lost the energy or will for this political fight. The Bill gradually disappeared into the quicksand of parliamentary procedure, never to reappear.

It was, in its way, a monumental victory. The right to elect jury trial remains now as it has for centuries. The erosion of our civil liberties was, for the moment, halted, but the manner in which it occurred was, for me, an unforgettable lesson in parliamentary machination.

Despite this, we should not forget that Jack Straw was one of New Labour's better Home Secretaries, but he has a strange flaw. For a man of his immense political experience and stature, he has always been curiously deferential to his civil servants. On two occasions, he confided in me that changes he wished to make in legislation were simply impossible as a result of the intransigence of his own Department. This has always surprised me but, nonetheless, he remains at heart a liberal, and criticism of his civil libertarian record becomes ever more muted when considering his successors; in particular, David Blunkett.

CHAPTER 11

OF LIBERTY AND TERROR 2:
THE EROSION OF LIBERTY

In which we reflect briefly on the remarkable character and flaws of Mr David Blunkett and the authoritarian instincts of Mr Blair – Assess the powerful persons, institutions and circumstances assembled to encompass the erosion of liberties and the inadequacies of the parliamentary forces attempting to defend them – Recount a mild but deserved public rebuke by Mr Peter Hain and a sad and silly gibe relating muesli and the Guardian *newspaper.*

Despite the damage he did as Home Secretary, it is possible to feel a large reservoir of sympathy for David Blunkett. To have overcome a terrible disability from childhood and to have obtained the success and stature that he enjoyed is a remarkable, heroic achievement.

Perhaps because of this, he, more than any politician I know, reveals a complete identity between his politics and his personality. The latter drives the former to an extraordinary degree. At best, this results in massive industry and commitment. At worst, it reveals a large degree of venom. To this may be added an obvious and populist predilection towards punishment. The manifestation of the first quality traits can clearly be seen in the vast quantity of legislation that he personally undertook and drove through Parliament. However, some of his behaviour became bizarre and some, simply nasty. The assessment of his colleagues contained in his personal memoirs, his extraordinary joyous reaction to the suicide of Harold Shipman, and the persistent vituperation against 'airy fairy wet liberals and all that they stand for', underscored both personality and politics. His final embarrassing collapse crooning 'Pick Yourself Up' at a trade union pub party, carried uncomfortable echoes of Augustus Melmotte's self-destruction in Trollope's political masterpiece, *The Way We Live Now*.

Blunkett's appointment and his withering contempt for liberals and liberty should not be seen as an aberration. He faithfully and zealously represented the character of his Government and its architects. Blair and Brown are both, in different ways, natural authoritarians. In Brown, the rigid, often gloomy self-flagellation of the Manse can clearly be observed. Blair's piety, from which his repressive instincts flow, is both more nauseating and more dangerous. The desire to control, observed from the very first days of Blair's Government, is semi-Messianic and contains precisely the same flaws which, in time, encompassed the bombing of cities. Blunkett was Blair's longest serving and favourite Home Secretary in what amounted to a fundamentalist and self-vindicating relationship of righteous and punitive zeal.

The political motivations and the traits of personality become the more obvious when considering the incontrovertible fact that virtually none of the domestic criminal justice legislation passed in thirteen years was remotely necessary. I was able to consider precisely this point during the course of the opening debate of the 2007 Parliament. After summarising the vast growth in criminal justice legislation, I asked the Government a rhetorical question:

'Why has all this happened? Have our citizens become more

venal or wicked in this period? No, as the Government never tires of trumpeting, accurately, crime has fallen steadily and consistently in the course of the last ten years. We are, therefore, confronted by an extraordinary rule of mathematics for which knowledge of higher calculus is presumably necessary. It is that the fewer crimes that are committed, the more crimes it is necessary to create. We will eventually reach a point on the graph at which the crimes are so few and the new offences so many that every person arrested will be able to have their own personalised hall-marked crime that can bear their name in perpetuity.'

In creating a maelstrom of repressive legislation, the New Labour Government had a number of powerful allies and exploited or created popular mood and prejudice. These included the Home Office; the tabloid press; fear; and regional class bias against southern liberals and, even worse, liberal lawyers.

First, the Home Office. Much of the more pernicious legislation, including the repeated assaults on jury trial, had been gathering dust for years on the Home Office shelves. The character of the Home Office is one of the persistent wonders of Whitehall. Something extraordinary occurs within its walls. Perfectly decent and clever young men and women enter this vast part of the Civil Service, proud of their country's civil liberties and intent on a career dedicated to their nurture and propagation. Similarly, most ministers embarking on appointments at whatever rank within the Home Office, carry with them the liberal credentials that, even now, remain a hallmark of many national politicians. What happens to them within the walls of this ancient ministry is a subject for persistent conjecture. Certain it is that they change, and certain it is that, within weeks or months, they are formulating and proposing legislation which their earlier selves would have found inconceivable.

I discussed this phenomenon with one former Home Office

minister (a Tory) who, by then, had obviously undergone a form of rehabilitation. I asked him what he thought could be done about the Home Office finally to improve this culture. He mused for a little while, then expressed the view that it would be necessary to close the building entirely, to remove and destroy all the furniture and fittings, to hack the very plaster from the walls and remove all door and window frames. The resulting shell should be subjected to exorcism by each of the world's major religions and, thereafter, should remain empty for a period of ten years. I asked him about the Home Office staff and civil servants. Remove them all, he said, treat them humanely and properly and eventually give them employment in regional government offices. After the ten-year period, he said, the building should be totally refurbished, furnished with Scandinavian product and filled with new civil servants and staff whose DNA bore no connection, even remote, to those who had previously been employed. He did not appear to be joking.

New Labour's second major ally after the Home Office was the tabloid press and, in particular, the *Sun*. Its natural instincts, and, most important, those of its proprietor, chimed perfectly with both the personalities of New Labour and the political imperatives which they pursued. Like most press barons, Rupert Murdoch is a natural populist authoritarian. The stock-in-trade of the *Sun* is to vent its views on helpless and ill-paid targets such as social workers, who spend an increasing amount of time attempting to control the vulgarity and abuse daily exemplified and encouraged by that very newspaper. The cynical proprietors and purveyors of the *Sun* are fully aware, of course, that they create the very problems against which they mount their tabloid attacks. An essential corollary of this is the near hysterical support for almost any form of illiberal, punitive legislation, particularly if it is aimed at foreigners. Thus, New Labour not only had the political motive, personality and institutions necessary to embark on its 'justice' agenda, it was also guaranteed the enthusiastic support of the Home Office mandarins and the red-top media.

Next, the government employed the classic tactic for the removal of liberty; namely the installation of Fear.

Since 1997, fear has become an increasing and carefully nurtured aspect of British life. It is a savage irony that the national level of general trepidation and mutual distrust has, by a deliberate process, been increased in directly inverse proportion to the quantum of real risk. All of this has been assiduously and deliberately cultivated by Government. By the end of his period in office, Blair's transport around his own capital was unlike that of any previous Prime Minister. In order for him to progress the 250 yards from Downing Street to Westminster (a rare but necessary journey) one bullet-proofed limousine and four black-windowed armoured Range Rovers were pressed into service. On one occasion I wandered innocently on to the underground private road which runs the length of the Palace of Westminster. I was, fortunately, physically restrained by a police officer in black fatigues before I was reduced to pulp by the first Range Rover accelerating with wailing sirens through the Mother of Parliaments.

'Who's that then?' I said to the paramilitary officer, gently backing away from his sub-machine gun.

'Can't tell you,' he said, without a hint of irony.

None of this is original. The political nightmares created by George Orwell and Aldous Huxley were predicated entirely on the creation of meaningless fear in order to promote and popularise Government. Kafka's short story, 'The Burrow', concerns a small animal so terrified that he frantically digs himself deeper and deeper. There is no cause for his fear other than the certainty that only a terrible danger would have caused him to dig with such frenetic anxiety. The deeper the burrow, the more the fear is reinforced.

The prevailing fears employed by Government to bolster its

programme of legislation were, of course, terrorism and domestic crime and, in particular, widespread abusive anti-social behaviour. Both are real enough. Fundamentalist terrorism is an ugly threat and abusive behaviour and disrespect a curse of our age. Neither, however, required the avalanche of repressive and authoritarian legislation that has been passed in their name. (As to anti-social crime, it is a fine irony that while liberties are curtailed to deal with it, the principal cause is the 'freedom' implicit in the removal of restrictions on alcohol licensing. This has enabled commercial interests to pour profitable poison down the throats of the very young, thereby blighting and disfiguring cities and towns throughout Britain.)

Associated with the fear factor came a further Orwellian assertion that obsessive security is, in itself, some form of liberty. This extraordinary spin was regularly (as a matter of policy) embraced by many Government ministers, some of whom should have known much better. On one occasion, while defending the creation of a massive security screen across the Commons Chamber (see Chapter 16: Of Screens and Security), Peter Hain expressed the view 'that the greatest liberty of all was the freedom not to be blown up'. In giving that reply, he endorsed the confusion between civic safety and civil liberty which has been the rogue's argument, employed by dictators since the beginning of government.

I have long been a friend and admirer of Peter Hain and, many years previously, had been active in the same campaigns against apartheid. I was also one of his primary supporters in his campaign for the Deputy Leadership of the Labour Party. I was, however, disappointed that he appeared to be following this particular Government line. We were subsequently part of a large table at the South African Embassy at a dinner in honour of our old and mutual friend, Donald Woods, whose life was immortalised in Richard Attenborough's film, *Cry Freedom*. It was a table of distinguished South Africans, many of them former members or leaders of the ANC. Ill-advisedly, I gently upbraided Peter for his parliamentary answer and the confusion of a safe life and liberty. Peter smiled at me and said:

'I suppose you are right, Bob, but, then again, you have never had to live in a country where life and liberty were synonymous with each other.'

It was an elegant put-down in august company and, on reflection, I deserved it.

My other friendly confrontation with Peter on the issue of liberty occurred during the Mode of Trial Bill and the attempt to remove the right to jury trial. In 1976, Peter, then an anti-apartheid activist, had famously been framed by BOSS, the South African Secret Service. They had employed a 'double' of Peter to steal a quantity of money from the counter of a bureau-de-change in the immediate vicinity of the London flat where Peter was living with his parents. Arrest and identification followed. Peter elected trial by jury and was, famously, acquitted by a majority verdict. The fact that he had, indeed, been framed was to be revealed in the compelling book, *Inside BOSS*, by Gordon Winter, a former South African agent. (In the same book, he reveals that BOSS had also employed the Kray brothers to burgle Chequers, then the residence of Harold Wilson.)

During the course of the second debate on the Jury Bill, I pointed out that, had the Bill been law in 1976, Peter would have lost his right to jury trial and might well have been convicted in the magistrates' court whereby a fine political career would have been brought to a sad and savage end. Peter, nonetheless, voted in favour of the Bill, which led to our good-natured confrontation in the Lobby when I observed that he owed his very political existence to the jury system.

'Of course I was acquitted,' he said, 'but then I was innocent.'

The assertion that his innocence would have had the slightest effect when he, as an anti-apartheid student, came before a stipendiary magistrate in south-west London, betrayed, I thought, a touching and naïve faith in the English legal system at that level.

The final theme employed by the Government (and David Blunkett in particular) to buttress repeated statutory assaults on civil liberty, was a persistent attack on liberal lawyers and, in particular, liberals and lawyers from the southern counties. This was an aversion unhappily shared by a number of New Labour backbenchers from northern constituencies. On 19 November 2001, the House of Commons debated powers sought by the Government indefinitely to detain terrorist subjects without trial or judicial review. Blunkett had been speaking at the dispatch box for fully forty minutes, under sustained attack from all sides of the Commons, when he received the first indication of support. It came by way of a question from Kevin Hughes, MP for Doncaster North, who asked:

'Don't you find it bizarre, like I do, that the yogurt, muesli eating, *Guardian* reading fraternity are only too happy to want to protect the human rights of people who engage in terrorist acts but never once do they talk about the human rights of those affected by those terrorist acts?'

It was a question which the Home Secretary, David Blunkett, had little difficulty in answering. Indeed, he may well have written it himself in order to obtain some relief from the 'airy fairy' liberals by whom he was beset.

Lest there should be any doubt as to the prime target of this sally, Hughes gestured menacingly to the seat next to the gangway on the third tier which was, predictably, occupied by myself. It is just possible that it was intended to include Diane Abbott, who sat beside me, or even Chris Mullin, who was immediately in front. It was a sad but significant intervention by a sad man. Hughes, a former Yorkshire miner and NUM official, was to leave Parliament in 2005 and die of motor neurone disease shortly thereafter.

The sadness of Hughes' contribution lay partly in its clichéd banality, but also in the class and regional assumptions upon which it was based. It was to find a direct echo in the observations of the Chief Whip, already recorded at the beginning of this book: 'Where I come from no one gives a toss about civil liberties', and proceeds on the confident assumption that the working-class north above, say, Milton Keynes, combine a grainy, horny-handed contempt for civil liberties in addition to yogurt and hi-fibre cereal. The unspoken inference is that they (the southern intelligentsia) would benefit enormously from a few days down the pits followed by fell running and hare coursing, to cure their effete affection for habeas corpus. This would, I suppose, be irritating to a working-class Irishman like myself (let alone a black West Indian like Diane Abbott), if it were not such transparent rubbish. Dennis Skinner, for all his contempt for lawyers and southern ways, never faulted in the many rebellions on the issue of civil liberty and my growing postbag on the fundamental principles at stake contained no class or regional bias. Equally, bigotry and prejudice are well represented in the south-east and even in my own constituency, which became all too apparent in the 2001 election, months before the Terrorism debate. Simon Hoggart, a welcome visitor to my election campaign, lovingly recorded a confrontation with just such a constituent. It is one of Simon's finer pieces, which I treasure. It contains the following excerpt:

> Britain's most aggressive candidate stomped across the street in search of new voters to offend. According to the voter ID sheet, we are visiting someone the computer called a firm Tory. I asked Bob Marshall-Andrews why? Because I like to, he replied grimly and he does make a scary sight with his gimlet eyes, prop-forward's build and lawn strimmer haircut, the Labour candidate for Medway has been compared (by me admittedly) to a cross between Dennis the Menace and his dog, Gnasher.

The voter, a male pensioner, didn't stand a chance. As always Mr Marshall-Andrews starts gently to catch them off balance.

'Just come round to say hello,' he began, 'things going alright here?'

To any other politician this may seem like small talk but with this one it sounds as if it is going to be a demand for protection money.

'Not really,' said the man, 'your lot ain't done much for me. For a start they took away my mortgage relief.'

'But your mortgage is much lower now. How much is your mortgage? It has not been lower for twenty years.'

The chap didn't recall. 'They have done bugger all for me, now leave it out.'

Even though it was now clear that he was like Alf Garnett without the elfin charm, I wanted to shout out 'Sir, you are tangling with the wrong man' but he was unstoppable.

'I'm definitely not voting Labour. All these bloody asylum seekers coming in, taking all of our bits and bobs.'

'You don't want them to be sent home to be tortured, do you?' asked Mr Marshall-Andrews, by now rather unpleasant.

The man looked as though nothing would please him more, but he forced out the 'no' before saying:

'What about the rest of them, coming in by train, under the train, on top of the train?'

'What,' the candidate answered furiously, 'do you expect me to do? Do you want me to lie on the track, wait for the train and see an asylum seeker and pull him off?'

Mr Marshall-Andrew's majority is 5,326. At the present rate of attrition he should have it down to zero a few days before polling.

As the Government's legislative programme unfolded, I found myself leading, or in the vanguard of, rebellions against successive criminal justice and terrorist bills. The aversion to lawyers was employed against me overtly and in the informal briefing of the Whips. I became worried that I was impeding the efforts to obtain rebel votes on the Government benches simply because of my former profession. During the battle against Control Orders (Terrorism Act 2005), I was approached by a colleague who intended to vote against the Bill, notwithstanding pressure from his Whip, who had approached him with the words:

'We don't mind you voting for some wet liberal amendment, but we do mind you supporting a millionaire fat-cat lawyer like Marshall-Andrews who is in it for his own benefit.'

Indeed, for a New Labour MP to begin a speech in the Chamber with the words 'I am not a lawyer/doctor/professor' would ensure audible support from his or her friends and a philistine badge of honour. Whence this political culture came is interesting in itself. The working-class founders of the Labour movement, be they miners, production workers, seamen or labourers, had justification in their antipathy to the professional classes, who were bourgeois and were seen to enjoy status and privileges denied to working people. Generally, however, New Labour Members of Parliament hold no such working-class credentials and, by reason of mass education, the professions have long been open to a far wider class base. The prejudice, however, has if anything grown, due to the dramatically increasing number of Labour MPs who have had no other work or vocation beyond politics. For them, the execration of professionals becomes an essential element of the past which they feel it necessary to perpetuate in order to burnish their remaining credentials as custodians of the Left.

CHAPTER 12

OF LIBERTY AND TERROR 3:
THE FEAR OF TERRORISM

In which we reflect on Terrorism and the perils of Scouting for Boys – Perceive the fragile beginnings of a rebellion – Examine youthful protest and imprisonment without trial and begin to sense partial victory.

The threat or the fear of terrorism became the persistent alibi for the creation of several hundred new terrorism offences in the course of thirteen years of perpetual legislation. Any reasonable criminal lawyer would confirm that the vast majority of these offences were unnecessary. 'Terrorist offences', like murder, assault and deliberate damage to property, are offences against common law and statute which have formed part of the English legal system for 800 years. The sheer volume of offences concealed the sinister purpose of the accumulated legislation. This was not to create more offences, but to criminalise areas of life and activity to which these 'crimes' related.

The extent of dangers to come could be read into the very first section of the first Terrorist Act passed by the New Labour Government in the year 2000. That section enshrined the new interpretation and definition of 'terrorism' as including the 'use or threat of action made for the purpose of advancing a political, religious or ideological cause'. The 'action' included 'any action which creates a serious risk to the health and safety of the public or a section of the public or is designed seriously to interfere with or disrupt an electronic system'. Thus the threat of any serious damage or 'hacking' for an ideological purpose was at once endowed with terrorist status. The year, let it be remembered, was 2000.

This definition of terrorism was ominous. To prosecute those who commit criminal damage during the course of a demonstration represented an obvious and reasonable use of the criminal process. To prosecute such actions *as terrorism* offends against law, language and common sense.

Other aspects of this legislation bordered on farce. One of the terrorist offences created by the Bill, criminalised the possession of a vast range of educational literature which would include (I told a surprised Commons) Baden Powell's manual *Scouting for Boys*. Section 57 of the Act created an offence to possess *any article* giving rise to a suspicion that it was for a purpose connected to the preparation or instigation of an act of terrorism. Large parts of Baden Powell's famous work, the official bible of the largest male youth movement on earth, are dedicated to survival in hostile terrain. Techniques such as the creation of bivouac and camouflage would undoubtedly assist the potential terrorist or insurgent in many parts of the world to which the extra-territorial reach of the legislation was directed. Under the Act, it is for the suspected citizen to prove that possession of the offending item was *not* for a terrorist purpose. (I, myself, possess a copy of *Scouting for Boys*, partly as a nostalgic reminder of a brief and unhappy period as a wolf cub – one eye barely open – and partly because of the priceless chapter on the subject of *beastliness* (masturbation) which contains much useful advice on how young men should avoid the temptation of this odious pastime. This includes fierce periods of exercise followed by cold showers and, if all else fails, going to see your scout master who would ensure everything would 'come out alright'. Whether this purpose would constitute a reasonable cause for possession in the eyes of an officious member of the terrorist squad is an interesting speculation.)

At this stage in the Parliament, the Tories, under the leadership of William Hague, took the view that any terrorist legislation should be supported as a matter of political expediency (and even attempted to trump the Government by introducing powers of internment without trial), and thus these dire provisions finally passed into law in the face of only minor Labour rebellions and with Liberal Democrat support.

The legislation had an inevitable and expected result. In the years that followed, hundreds of dedicated and committed young people, protesting against the effects of globalisation and the environmental degradation of their planet, were duly corralled, 'kettled', searched, made subject to random forfeitures and finally arrested *as terrorists*. Perfectly innocent photographers, such as my friend and colleague, Austin Mitchell, were subjected to harassment, forfeiture and confiscation, and coachloads of perfectly innocent demonstrators were imprisoned for hours in their vehicles as potential terrorist subjects. The effect has been, simultaneously, to alienate hundreds and thousands of respectable young citizens and to debase the coinage of terrorist activity to the point of dangerous legal farce.

In the end, there was only a small rebellion; just sixteen backbench Labour MPs voted against the worst of the 2000 legislation. After barely three years of a Labour Government, otherwise independent and thoughtful members of the Parliamentary Party were disposed to extend the benefit of doubt. In the coming years, as the effects of the legislation became clear and the Government's demands for repressive statutes became more strident, this trust was to erode and then disappear, and voting patterns dramatically changed. Before that, however, further parliamentary battles lay in store and the first of these concerned the not insignificant issue of endless imprisonment without trial.

Following the election, the 2001 Anti-Terror, Crime and Security Act represented the first step towards Control Orders and Executive Detention. This monstrous piece of legislation provided the Home Secretary with the power to certify individuals as 'foreign terrorists' and, thereafter, to ensure their indefinite imprisonment without trial. It was driven through Parliament, Lords and Commons, in the space of one month. The Government's case, expounded by Blunkett, was simple. There were, it was said, a significant number of dangerous foreign terrorists present in Britain who could not be extradited to their country of origin as they would face torture and death. Assuming this to be unacceptable, it was, argued the Government, necessary to certify their status and hold them indefinitely without trial, all of which begged the most obvious question. If sufficient evidence existed confidently to assert that these were, indeed, dangerous terrorists, why should they not be charged? Repeated interventions in Parliament, by me and many others, elicited no satisfactory answer. One attempted reply by the then Solicitor General Mike O'Brien is worthy of recital:

> Mr O'Brien: 'As I understand it, my Rt Hon. Friend, the Home Secretary, is saying that we have good cause for believing that the people in question are involved in activities that might lead to terrorist offences or are supportive of such offences. That is a somewhat different prospect. Of course, if those involved had committed offences in this country, then we would be able to deal with them in our courts. That is the way we should deal with them but we are facing circumstances that are somewhat different.'

Attempts at translation may be sent to the author.

The Act contained an even worse proposal, which was to remove from the minister's decision to imprison any appeal by judicial review. In short, the Act provided an Executive power over the freedom of the individual, unknown in peacetime for 800 years, with no judicial oversight. At the end of a long speech, I observed that:

> 'This is the point at which I stick. I will never vote for a Bill as long as clause 29 is in it. It is a signpost to tyranny and I will not take a single step, no matter how few people are involved down that road.'

As the debate wore on, it became clear that the removal of judicial review had no vocal support within the Chamber and George Osborne made a rare contribution to civil liberties.

> 'It will drive a coach and horses through 800 years of legal history, stemming from habeas corpus, and we must be careful about excluding people from legal processes and about ruling out judicial review.'

At the time of writing these words, George Osborne has become the second most powerful man in Britain and one may fervently hope that his defence of civil liberty survives the joys of office.

The Government was not assisted by further Orwellian definitions of 'terrorist activity' to which I referred in the debate:

> 'In part, there are sinister overtones of the great Lewis Carroll. Hon Members would have noticed under clause 21 the definition of an international terrorist as someone who has been certified as a suspected international terrorist. The logic would have been well understood by Alice In Wonderland – "words are what I certify them to be".'

Backbench colleagues whom I had hardly known, and who had previously regarded me as a genial leper, made urgent *sotto voce* enquiries.

'Was it *really* the case that there was no appeal?'

'Did it really mean that there was no habeas corpus?'

Alarm and dissent began to spread.

Organisations such as Liberty, Justice and the legal professional associations had been caught by the speed with which the Bill had been introduced. Now they issued a stream of warnings and information that further increased the size of a likely revolt.

Friends on the Tory benches told me that the Opposition had still finally to decide on its vote, despite a natural reluctance to oppose anti-terrorist measures. For the first time I detected unease among the Whips and concessions began to be made. Judicial review, of a sort, was to be provided by SIAC, the Special Immigration Appeals Commission. This semi-judicial body had been created in 1997, in order, as the name implies, to hear immigration appeals. It was now to be pressed into service to provide 'judicial' oversight to executive imprisonment. In a further concession, the Government agreed that SIAC should have power to consider the Home Secretary's certificate and whether there were '*no reasonable grounds for making such a judgment*'.

It was, of course, no concession at all. What was billed as a concession was, in fact, a desperate attempt to exclude the judicial process in favour of a Government appointed tribunal. I printed another leaflet and, in the Chamber, was able to voice the concerns of many:

'Of course, if Hon Members had heard that SIAC, that Star Chamber of an organisation, with all its draconian powers over evidence, was to be used as an appeals procedure, not for deportation but for the indefinite incarceration of people without charge or trial, no one would have voted for it; or if they had they would have felt ashamed of themselves a great deal earlier than this. SIAC is not a body known to law. It is a Star Chamber and is manifestly inadequate as the only appeal court against the exercise of such powers.'

The Tory Whips, faced with being seen as soft on liberty or soft on terror, magnificently ordered abstention, and the Government majority was thus ensured. It came, however, at an unprecedented price. Seventy-seven Liberal Democrat and Labour rebels voted against the legislation. Approximately fifty Labour backbenchers either rebelled or abstained.

The press provided unusual support. *The Times* carried the headline 'Labour MPs Rebel Over Terror Bill', and a secondary article, 'Blunkett Barracked by Labour MPs'. In the *Guardian*, Michael White and Patrick Wintour offered salient support: 'MPs Savage Terror Bill. Both Houses keep up pressure as angry Blunkett gives ground.'

The Bill moved to the House of Lords where I became a regular visitor, explaining the intricacies of the Commons' vote and pointing out that the Bill would have been close to defeat had the Tories maintained a united opposition. The Lords threw it back, thereby commencing a game of legislative ping-pong with the most fundamental of our civil liberties. Eventually a constitutional and parliamentary crisis was averted by the extraordinary intervention of Lord Donaldson. An elderly Law Lord, whose previous notoriety had included chairmanship of the doomed National Industrial Relations Court, he suggested a simple solution. Create a new court. If SIAC was to behave as a court of law, it should become a court of law. Its constitution would be altered, High Court Judges would be introduced on a greater scale and it would become a 'Court of Record'.

The Tories and Tory Peers pronounced themselves satisfied and, thus, the Bill became law, courtesy of a constitutional bodge.

In one sense, the Labour rebellion had failed. Executive Detention Without Trial was now a part of British jurisprudence.

In parliamentary terms it was a small but significant success. For a growing number of Labour backbenchers the habit of disobedience had begun. In the next session of the 2001–2005 Parliament there were recorded more rebellions than in *any* first session of a Labour Government. It is, of course, dangerous and facile to measure the health of a Parliament by the extent of the dissidence within it, but it gives the lie to the lazy assumption that Parliament is comprised entirely of lickspittle toadies intent on self-preferment and the will of the Whips.

CHAPTER 13

OF LIBERTY AND TERROR 4: TRIALS, DOWNFALL AND LUCOZADE

In which we introduce a statutory monster – Go into battle for Trial by Jury – Applaud a Tory re conversation to Liberty – Recall the downfall of a Home Secretary – Witness the attempt of another to incarcerate British subjects without trial – Spend sleepless days in parliamentary struggle, including an unwise lunch with Mr Mark Fisher, and reflect on the beneficial effect of Lucozade on Peers of the Realm.

On 8 November 2002, the great doors of the Home Office opened and a monster was released from the vaults where it had been sewn together in 300 clauses and nineteen schedules. This Caliban legislation lumbered to the House of Commons and fell upon the body politic where, for a year, it would devour vast quantities of time, energy and patience. The Criminal Justice Act 2003, when finally passed, removed the right of silence from defendants, allowed the bad character of defendants to be placed before juries as proof of their guilt, introduced the concept of double jeopardy for those that had been acquitted, and allowed the admission of double hearsay whereby a defendant might be convicted and lose his liberty on the basis of what one person said another person had told someone else. It introduced a sentencing regime that has caused near despair throughout the criminal justice system, from the highest judge to the lowest advocate. It has forced judges to pass sentences that are unjust and incomprehensible to victims, defendants and the public. It has nearly doubled the size of the prison population, consigning to overcrowded and rank conditions young men and women who, by universal consent, should not be there and who will, inevitably, be brutalised by the process.

Where the provisions are not rank, they are often totally incomprehensible. In 2005, a judge passed a sentence on a defendant called Sweeney which was so bizarre and inadequate that he broke with long judicial tradition and carefully and publicly explained to a crowded courtroom the reasons for the preposterous sentence he was about to pass. In order to avoid repetition of this disaster, an amended section was hastily drafted, which was then replaced by a section which is, by common consent, totally impenetrable both as law and in sense and syntax.

This monstrous assault on the criminal justice system is the towering achievement of David Blunkett and the Home Office, driven forward by a Prime Minister whose concept of modernising the criminal justice system was to reduce it, like Sulla's victories, to unworkable ruin.

Dire though the effects of the Act undoubtedly are, they could have been infinitely worse. In the body of the Bill, the Government returned again to its remorseless attack on jury trial. Two provisions, in particular, would have grossly eroded this ancient liberty. The first was the loss of *the right to jury trial in serious and complex cases*. The second contained a disingenuous liberty, namely the option to choose trial by judge at the behest of the defendant alone. The dangers implicit in this so-called right were trenchantly observed by Vera Baird speaking at the Report Stage of the Bill:

'Will the Government be comfortable for long with the right for a defendant alone to opt for or against jury trial to be exercised arbitrarily with no recognition of the rights or wishes of the victim? The Home Secretary himself mentioned that point. But what about a black person in a racially aggravated case faced with a white defendant who exercises his option to be tried by a white judge and not by anyone from a black community. What about a female rape complainant who comes to court to find that a highly gendered situation, the male defendant has the right to exclude every other female from the case and the trial to be by male judge alone. The perception of these two problems is dangerous enough before one even considers the outcome. The new right will inevitably be abused by defendants. For example in Redcar, particular judges are known to be liberal and others are known to be particularly tough. If anyone asked me what I thought about the right to trial by judge, I would ask 'which Judge?' What will happen will be forum shopping of the worst imaginable sort.

For my part, I concentrated on the loss of the right to trial by jury in serious fraud cases. In doing so I reflected on the 'exquisite irony' of this particular attack on the jury system. In the same debate at the Report Stage I was able to say:

'During the consideration of Mode of Trial legislation, we were repeatedly told that our fears were groundless because the most serious offences would always be sacrosanct in terms of jury trial. Now, of course, we hear precisely the reverse. It is impossible not to draw the conclusion that the Government, having got its hands badly bitten twice on that occasion, are now applying themselves to the dog from the other end. The plain fact is that jury trial is anathema to the Home Office and, indeed, to this Government, and it is time that we recognised that fact.'

Motivators
1. Gill and Africa – the combination that brought me into politics and 2. Neil Kinnock who unwittingly persuaded me to go back.

3. 'Charged with defrauding the British Public of £600,000,000 under the influence of a shadowy figure, street name Mandy.' Playing the Judge summing up in *The Trial of the Dome* (aka Millenium) in 2000, part of the annual Parliamentary Palace of Varieties, the brain child of Myra Jessell, that raised £1 million in ten years for Macmillan nurses.

4. On the hustings, discussing national politics with a friendly constituent.

5. Turning the tables, interrogating Ian Hislop for Cancer Research: 'You are the most sued man in British history and yet you were head boy at Radley, a decent, though minor public school. Where did it all go so terribly wrong?'

Old Testament Prophets (aka the Usual Suspects)

6. Brian Sedgemore

7. Alan Simpson

8. Lynne Jones

9. Alice Mahon

10. Hilary Armstrong

11. David Blunkett

Control Orders: 10 & 11. Hilary Armstrong (Chief Whip) and David Blunkett the Home Secretary who initiated more Criminal Justice legislation than all his predecessors in the nineteenth century.

12. David Davies

13. Boris Johnson

Strange Tory Chums

14. Martin Rowson's wonderful cartoon commemorating my (erroneous) concession of defeat in the 2005 election (final majority 217). Lazarus (me) rises from the grave thrusting a V sign at the Messianic figure (Blair) who crosses his fingers to close the tomb. Rochester Castle is in the pastoral distance surrounded by sheep.

15. Calling for the resignation of the Speaker who allowed the police raid on Damien Green's office (then blamed the Sergeant at Arms). November 2008.

16. Debating the Terrorism Bill, 2005

17. Debating on Palestine. Following my journey to Gaza to record the death of 1400 civilians and the destruction of, buildings and farmland during the assault by Israeli forces in Operation Cast Lead.

17. **Beginning:** The new MP for Medway standing by the great river 5 a.m., 6 May 1997.

18. **End:** Farewell constituency lunch April 2010 with my agent Fred Bacon and Peter Hennessey. Peter made a fine valedictory speech about someone I didn't recognise

A year of continuous battle ensued as this vast piece of legislation lurched through its stages in Parliament. On the issue of jury trial, the band of Labour rebels steadily increased. The Government found itself facing a serious dilemma. Assertions that juries were incapable of trying complex cases carried the unavoidable implication that they were too stupid. As juries convict in the overwhelming majority of complex cases, this argument was swiftly abandoned. By the time the Bill ran out of its Commons' time, the Government's only argument had been reduced to the difficulties of obtaining 'representative' juries in long fraud cases. It was not a difficult argument to demolish.

'The universal view of those who practise is that these juries are, in fact, more representative than any others. They include, which is true, slightly more women than men which is no bad thing. They include, which is true, slightly more disabled people who are unable to work which is no bad thing. Those drawn from a pool of people who are not working at that time include the highly successful – no bad thing when one is dealing with serious fraud – and those that have the misfortune to be unemployed – again that is no bad thing. These supposedly unrepresentative people have no difficulty whatsoever in convicting in nearly 97 per cent of the cases they hear. This Government would not suggest for one moment that that was due to some feebleness of intellect.'

By this time, we possessed, on the backbenches and outside Parliament, an impressive Council of War. Both Vera and I produced a stream of written material, directed at Labour backbenchers, which supplemented that arriving on a daily basis from every liberal pressure group and the Law Society and Bar Council. Two other developments assisted our cause. The invasion of Iraq in March 2003 had awakened in many Labour backbenchers the (subsequently entirely justified) suspicion that their own Government had misled them by a steady process of deception. Faced with protestations from that very Government as to its future plans for jury trial, they reacted with a scepticism unimaginable five years before. At the same time, Oliver Letwin, Shadow Home Secretary, delivered the Tories on a three-line whip.

When the Division was called on jury trial, seventy Labour backbenchers voted against the government or abstained.

As with the Mode of Trial Bill, the signal to the House of Lords was crystal clear. The assault on jury trial did not enjoy the support of the people. It was the will of the Whips. Together with Vera, I resumed my regular pilgrimage to the Lords, providing details, figures and extracts from Hansard, revealing both the arguments and the lack of articulate support from the Government's benches. A substantial number of Labour peers joined the Opposition parties and the cross-benchers to defeat the jury clauses. It resulted, yet again, in a nerve-shredding game of political ping-pong with our most established liberties.

We split our resources as best we could. In the Commons, Vera, Brian Sedgemore, Alan Simpson, John McDonnell and I checked our numbers on an hourly basis. Unashamedly, I provided continuing intelligence to David Davis, who had succeeded Oliver Letwin. The House of Lords, assisted by the persuasive blandishments of Helena Kennedy, held firm. The clauses and amendments passed back and forth along the line of march, bound in red ribbon and carried solemnly by the Deputy Serjeant-at-Arms. Time, and the temper of the Home Secretary, began to expire. Finally, late at night, a deal was done. The 'right' to elect trial by judge alone disappeared completely from the Act. The serious fraud provisions remained but were unenforceable in the absence of further affirmative votes from both the Commons and the Lords. In other words, a new Act of Parliament would be required. It was a victory conceded with singular ill-grace. (The encounter with Blunkett and David Davis is recorded in Chapter 4.)

As the House adjourned and its members disappeared into the night, Vera Baird, Brian Sedgemore and I drank wearily together in the Pugin Room overlooking the Thames. We felt flattened by anti-climax. The fundamentals of jury trial remained unaltered, but vast tracts of the repressive legislation had been passed. We managed, I think, two bottles of the House of Commons' best before the late winter's journey home.

It was, sad to say, the last occasion in which Vera and I enjoyed such cordial terms. Subsequently our paths divided. She became Solicitor General in Gordon Brown's administration, and espoused the Government's cause during its attempt to extend detention without trial and to enforce secret inquests on deaths caused by the security services. Years later she lost her seat of Redcar in a massive swing against her. This occasioned some joy among civil rights campaigners and lawyers who had, by that time, seen her as a turncoat. It was a joy I did not share. Saving jury trial was a singular victory and the one of which, in thirteen years at Westminster, I remain most proud. Without Vera's voice we would probably have lost and that remains, as they say, big medicine.

The Government's capitulation on the issue of jury trial signalled a brief truce with its own backbenchers on the issue of civil liberty. It did not last long; twenty-eight days to be exact. On 17 December 2003, the Asylum and Immigration (Treatment of Claimants) Bill was placed before Parliament on Second Reading. It had two consequences that resulted in an unusually eclectic rebellion. The first was to render destitute the children of failed asylum seekers, a consequence which saw an unusual and unwilling band of rebels that included steadfast Blairites represented by Denis MacShane, Fiona MacTaggart and Barry Sheerman. The second consequence, unique in British legal history, was an attempt to remove judicial review from the decisions of the Immigration Appeal Tribunal. It reflected, of course, the now persistent desire of the New Labour Government to remove the

Executive from judicial scrutiny. The fact that they were prepared to risk a constitutional crisis on behalf of the Immigration Appeals Tribunal revealed an extraordinary degree of arrogance or historical illiteracy; possibly both. It turned, predictably, into a fine debate. As the Government was mounting a twin assault on infant welfare and civil liberty, the Chamber was remarkably full. I attempted to spell out the consequences of the judicial provisions:

> 'It is worth reflecting on precisely what that means. It means that the Tribunal, once established, can make any decision, however unreasonable, even if it is so unreasonable that no Tribunal could previously have arrived at it. The decision may be capricious but it will be immutable and without challenge. The Tribunal will be able to act entirely outside the powers that we in Parliament have given it and that, too, will be immutable and without challenge. That is the extent of the Bill which we are being asked to pass and it is entirely unique.
>
> It is interesting to reflect that no Tribunal in this country is free from judicial review. If a planning tribunal in deciding whether a conservatory may be put up makes a decision that for some reason is outside its powers, it is subject to judicial review. Here we are talking about a Tribunal that can decide whether a person is liable to torture or death, yet its decision will not be the subject of any review.'

The Tories abstained on Second Reading and the Labour rebellion, with Liberal Democrat support, reached seventy-eight votes. Inevitably the Government capitulated on both the issue of child support and on judicial review. However, faced with inevitable surrender, the Home Office could not resist one Parthian shot. The time for appeal was reduced to five days from ten. It was a miserable, snivelling change that smacked of petulance. That aside, this small battle for civil liberty had been won, hands down. I wrote a short note of appreciation to the Minister of State and received a generous reply. Truce reigned but, again, not for long.

Between 2000 and 2005, the loss of liberty occasioned by terrorist legislation excited little comment or interest outside Parliament. The reasons were relatively simple to understand. First, the more draconian provisions were perceived, rightly, to relate almost exclusively to foreigners. To that may be added the fact that these were foreigners who were suspected of terrorist activity or of planning terrorist offences. Their liberty or liberties did not excite the national mood and, indeed, in the view of the tabloid press, it was the very least that they deserved. Elsewhere in the free world, notably America, hundreds of terrorist suspects (all foreign) had, by 2005, already been imprisoned for years without trial, routinely beaten and tortured by being strapped to boards and nearly drowned.

The British Government set the tone. Its opposition to Guantanamo was at best lukewarm and at worst non-existent. A growing number of leaks and reports suggested that the Government was actively and passively complicit in the process of rendition, the export of suspects for the purposes of torture. As I write, the coalition government has announced a judicial inquiry into this practice, for which they deserve much praise.

In America, on 13 November 2001, by presidential dictat with no reference to Congress or the Supreme Court, George Bush ordained a system of arbitrary arrest, indefinite detention, secret trial and extreme punishment (including water boarding). This would have impressed the Inquisition. Arrest and imprisonment of terrorist suspects was to be entirely by order of the President, with no judicial process, no habeas corpus, no review. Detention could be indefinite. There was no provision for court bail. The identity of the prisoners and their location could be kept secret by decree. There was no automatic provision for legal representation and if conversations took place between lawyers and clients they could be wire-tapped without legal redress. A trial (if it existed) would be run by military tribunal without jury and in secret session. There was no right of attendance, no rules of evidence and no procedural checks.

I was invited to write a comment piece in the *Evening Standard* and did so.

This led to furious denunciation in the Murdoch press, where a gentleman, whose experience of water boarding was, presumably, vestigial, expressed the trenchant view 'that this is the justice that terrorists should get'.

The British Government, buoyed by the American example and the tabloid press and convinced of the populist value of more, rather than less, oppressive legislation announced further sweeping powers. The *Independent* of 22 November 2004 reported that 'David Blunkett, the Home Secretary, confirmed yesterday that ministers were planning a draft anti-terrorism bill which would include sweeping measures such as judge only trials, Control Orders for people suspected of terrorist acts and the use of wire-tap evidence in courts.'

Normally a cheerful campaigner, I was beginning to feel depressed. It was a mood caught and shared by many organisations and politicians, now weary with seven years of dogged (and largely unsuccessful) defence of civil liberties while the Government, founded by a party to which many of us had subscribed for most of our lives, set about their steady and cumulative erosion.

All this changed in 2005. In December 2004, the Law Lords had unanimously ruled that the holding of a terrorist suspect without trial at Belmarsh Prison was illegal. Immediately after this, the Chief Special Counsel (Ian Macdonald QC), appointed to represent the interests of the detainees, resigned. Shortly before this ruling, the judges within SIAC had exercised a rare spasm of independence and had released one of the detainees (after nearly three years in detention) in view of his clear mental illness. This decision had been described by David Blunkett (Home Secretary and Minister of the Crown) as 'bonkers', an observation which contributed to the growing public opinion that he was, himself, dangerously unstable. This, together with his champagne-popping joy at the suicide of Harold Shipman, his failure to declare expenses paid to his mistress, led to his inevitable resignation on 15 December 2004. So departed the most morbidly reactionary Home Secretary of modern times. Even for his most profound political critics (including me) there was sadness attached to the downfall of a man so driven and so disabled. Undeniably, however, there was a splendid irony in the fact his downfall was directly associated with the oppressive legislation which he had promoted with such zeal.

Blunkett was replaced by Charles Clarke. A big man in every physical and political sense who, unlike so many members of the New Labour Government, had never dabbled in Stalinist politics. He brought with him an impeccably robust pedigree. As with many clever and professional politicians, he knew a problem when he saw one and, on his arrival in office, he had one in spades.

The judgment of the Law Lords was interesting. Held as a victory for principle and civil liberty, it was, in reality, no such thing. It proceeded on the basis that a law designed only to criminalise 'foreign terrorists' was, *ipso facto*, discriminatory. The Government was, therefore, faced with a classic dilemma. It could scrap the existing (now useless) legislation providing for certification and detention without trial. Alternatively, it could avoid the issues of discrimination by extending detention without trial to everyone including, of course, British subjects.

Charles Clarke and I had known each other for many years, during which he referred to me (incomprehensibly) as 'young Bob'. In his previous period in the Home Office, he had worked closely and successfully with my wife on gun control and there existed between all of us an occasionally percussive friendship.

In the event, so far as civil liberties were concerned, the

Government could not resist the temptation to render the situation infinitely worse. Its solution lay in the creation of 'Control Orders'. These orders could be made by executive decree and could apply to all residents of the United Kingdom, whether foreign or British nationals. A vast array of orders and partial orders were available to the Home Secretary by executive decree. At one end of the scale lay 'secure detention', or imprisonment by any other name. If it were to apply to European citizens, it would require derogation from the European Convention on Human Rights and, *ipso facto*, would be in breach of the Human Rights Act.

This included the power of house arrest, restriction of movement, restriction of association, the search and retention of documents and physical tagging. To those who had cut their political teeth in the fight against South African apartheid, they bore an extraordinary and close relationship to the notorious Pass Laws which buttressed that system. This led to one of my more memorable experiences in the Commons when I listened to a speech made by Barbara Follett. Barbara was normally an impeccable Blairite (indeed, Blair was a social visitor to her house) but she had also lived in South Africa for over twenty years. So good was her speech and so profound was its immediate impact that I hope the reader will forgive being provided with a substantial excerpt:

Barbara Follett: 'I lived for many years in South Africa during the dark days of apartheid. During that time, Britain's legal system was held up as a beacon of light and hope as the prison bars of apartheid stayed closed around us. In 1961 the South African Government introduced the General Law Amendment Act which allowed people to be detained for twelve days without trial. By 1963 that had been extended to ninety days. By 1965 it was one hundred and eighty days. Two years later it became indefinite. At the same time, the apartheid regime was issuing Control Orders which restricted the right of some citizens to congregate at work and, in some cases, to leave the confines of their own homes. These orders had a devastating effect on the life of the subject and his or her family. I should know. My first husband was served with one of them in 1971. He lived under it for five years and it was only thanks to the generosity of the university at which he taught that he did not starve. He could not work, leave his home or travel to Cape Town to see his mother, and he barely saw his children.

'I know that this is Britain and not South Africa or Burma, but we must not underestimate the importance of what we are doing and the message that it sends to countries where we are talking about good governance. The example that we will send will stay with us for many years, removing the hope that we give as we could tonight may have a deleterious effect.

'My first husband was put under house arrest because the apartheid state believed he was a threat to its security. He probably was; he was campaigning to give black people the right to vote and join trade unions. Given the structure of the South African state, he was probably threatening it because it believed that only whites could vote and join trade unions. House arrest hampered him, but it did not stop him, which was probably why just before his five-year order was due to expire, he was shot dead in front of our two young daughters in their bedroom. I tried to comfort them in the days that followed by telling them that we were going to go to Britain, where people were not detained without trial or put under house arrest. When one tries to tell an eleven-year-old and a seven-year-old that not all parts of the world are as bad as others, one looks for example, and we in Britain were that example. I am glad that I am here today so that my now forty-year-old and thirty-six-year-old daughters can hear that we are still fighting to uphold that.'

I am a hardened politician ('a face lived in by squatters', as Simon Carr once described me). In my other life, I have defended and prosecuted the worst of human behaviour and I manage generally to avoid the lachrymose. It was difficult to do so listening to Barbara on that occasion, and I was not alone.

The other towering speech in defence of these fundamental liberties came from my old friend, Brian Sedgemore. It was the final speech he was to make in the House of Commons and the last speech he would ever make as a member of the Labour Party. It was a short speech and a brilliant indictment on the relationship between the mores of New Labour and the abnegation of Parliament:

> Brian Sedgemore: 'As this will almost certainly be my last speech in Parliament I will try hard not to upset anyone. However, our debate here tonight is a grim reminder of how the Prime Minister and the Home Secretary are betraying some of Labour's most cherished beliefs. Not content with tossing aside the ideas and ideals that inspire and inform ideology, they seem to be giving up on values, too. Liberty, without which democracy has no meaning, and the rule of law, without which state power cannot be contained, look to Parliament for their protection; but this Parliament, sad to say, is failing the nation badly. It is not just the Government but backbench members who are to blame. It seems that in situations such as this, politics becomes incompatible with conscience, principle, decency and self-respect. Regrettably, in such situations, the desire for power and position predominates.'

He continued:

> 'Have we all, individually and collectively, no shame? I suppose that once one has shown contempt for liberty by voting against it in the lobby, it becomes easier to do it a

second time and, after that, a third time. Thus even Members of Parliament who claim to believe in human rights, vote to destroy them.

'Many members have gone nap on the matter. They voted first to abolish trial by jury in less serious cases and secondly, to abolish trial by jury in more serious cases; thirdly, to approve an unlawful war, fourthly, to create a gulag in Belmarsh and, fifthly, to lock up innocent people in their homes. It is truly terrifying to imagine what those Members of Parliament will vote for next. I can describe all that only as New Labour's descent into hell, which is not a place I want to be.'

In a day of great speeches, my own was puny. I tried to draw attention not only to the content but to the form of the Bill:

'In part, the Bill is incomprehensible. I have seen and been reviewing statutes – many of them criminal statutes – for thirty-five years, and this Bill is one of the worst, despite its brevity. I spent over an hour attempting to understand clause 4 alone. That clause deals with the duration for which people can be detained under Control Orders and is, therefore, not unimportant; but I completely failed to understand it although I was reading my own language. If it had been translated into Arabic, Hindu, or Gujarati, the problem would have been even worse. We in this Chamber will, no doubt, argue about the effect this Bill will have on al-Qaeda but the effect is certain; they will not understand it.

I also drew attention to the undoubted fact that, following the demise of David Blunkett, thirteen people had been released from Belmarsh on the grounds that the new Home Secretary no longer found them to be dangerous. The conclusions were obvious:

'In the past three years, successive Home Secretaries – mainly one Home Secretary [David Blunkett] – have repeatedly told SIAC that these people are so dangerous that they cannot possibly be released from the miserable solitary confinement in which they have been interred. Now they are all to be let out because repentance is a wonderful and beautiful thing. Perhaps they have repented, but the idea that they have done so simultaneously would represent the greatest collective apostasy since St Paul's letter to the Corinthians. It is clear that SIAC has been misled for the past three years about these people in Belmarsh. It is felt the new Home Secretary is taking a different view, which demonstrates the arbitrary nature of the power which the Government are attempting to achieve.

'It cannot be repeated often enough that we will never decrease the sum total of human wickedness by decreasing the sum total of human liberty. If we act in that way, we run the extreme risk by increasing the sum total of human wickedness by denying these very liberties to those who deserve them. Looking back over the past seven years I am very sorry to reflect on the number of occasions when I have had boringly to repeat that phrase.'

The Conservative vote was, as always on terrorist issues, a potential problem. During the debate I had twice met David Davis, by then firmly established as the Shadow Home Secretary. There can be no doubt as to the heroic scale of his difficulties. The debate took place barely two months before a general election and the dissolution of Parliament. Many Tories were deeply troubled at the prospect of facing an electorate (and the tabloids) having failed to demonstrate a robust stand on terrorism.

David's own contribution was salient and conclusive:

'One of the primary aims of a terrorist is to provoke a reaction from the State which, in turn, will radicalise a part of the population and increase recruitment for the terrorist cause. There is a serious danger in that if the use of these Control Orders is seen to be unjust, even by a minority, that alone should be a telling argument of the power being exercised by the judiciary and not by the executive.

After three years in which none of these powers has been available against British citizens, and at a time when the Home Secretary himself says the security risk is the same as it was a year ago and the security services and police say they currently do not need the most draconian powers listed, why do we suddenly need this measure in fourteen days flat in the shadow of a general election. The Prime Minister has said that the security services do not need them. Did they tell him that in the past weeks? Did they tell him that they needed them instantly? I doubt it. To reiterate, the Home Secretary is taking powers to curb the freedom of British subjects by order, on suspicion based on limited and possibly doubtful evidence. He does this after his own department said the measure was draconian and unjustifiable less than a year ago, and he does it after no apparent change in the circumstances, in a rushed Bill with wholly inadequate scrutiny in either House of Parliament. That cannot be the way for a democracy that believes in the rule of law to proceed.'

In the end David delivered nearly all the Tories. It was not enough. On the main Division we lost, by the now familiar figure of seventy-six votes. Over thirty Labour backbenchers rebelled outright and fifty abstained. The Bill and I made our way to the Lords. The Lords voted against the Bill and tabled critical amendments, which included judicial oversight of the minister's decisions and, most importantly, a 'sunset clause' whereby the Bill was limited to a one-year duration before further legislation was required. What followed was one of the longest periods of deadlock in modern history, and the longest continuous sitting of the Lords for a century. Sitting in the Lords' Bar with Tim

Razzall, I sensed, for the first time in seven years, that we were beginning to win the issue of civil liberty. At that very moment I was informed that none other than Lord Irvine, Blair's mentor and first Lord Chancellor, had joined the rebels.

At Prime Minister's Questions on 8 March, I failed to catch the Speaker's eye but watched the Prime Minister when he claimed that changes in the burden of proof were necessary to restrict liberties. By Friday evening, both Houses were still in session after two long nights. Gaby Hinsliff of the *Observer* told me that elderly Peers had been seen drinking Lucozade Sport in the Lords' cafeteria. When I heard that news at lunchtime on Friday, I realised that victory was near; having made two full speeches, twisted innumerable arms in both Houses of Parliament and drafted reams of legal information, I thought, as the House was adjourned until 5 p.m., that I deserved a decent lunch. This I enjoyed enormously in the Garrick Club, together with Mark Fisher; it was nearly a mistake.

The Commons' debate continued at eight o'clock and centred on the sufficiency of judicial review negating the necessity for a sunset clause. Sitting next to me, Tam Dalyell was becoming increasingly frustrated after two sleepless nights.

'You must speak,' he whispered to me with aristocratic insistence.

'Bad idea,' I muttered in reply.

'No, you must speak. You must put an end to this nonsense.'

And so I did. In thirteen years in Parliament I made a golden, immutable rule that I would never speak in the Chamber unless stone-cold sober. This was the exception, and I approached Hansard the following day with a certain amount of trepidation. In the event, I was pleasantly surprised. I observed, halfway through my short contribution, that I had treated the Commons to a discourse on the history of judicial review and the ancient prerogative writs employed to curb executive and royal power. In truth, it wasn't bad. I might have got a rather better law degree had I taken my papers after a decent lunch. By the time I got to the end I was in a reasonably fluent state and I believe it was the last speech of the session.

'The Bill is seriously malformed. The Bill cannot be resuscitated and cured by definitions. What we need is a rebirth. What we need is a new Bill and we need it quickly. The period of a year which has been proposed in another place by a noble Lord of my Party [Lord Falconer] is worthy of support. One year is enough. We need to bring back in a year not this old malformed Bill, resurfaced and re-hatched, but a new Bill to deal with the problems of terrorism which are undoubtedly real.'

In short, the Government capitulated. It was entirely fitting that the biggest erosion of its massive majority occurred on the issue of civil liberty. In the final votes, no fewer than sixty Labour MPs voted against the Government on this central issue.

The change in the national press was dramatic:

EXTRAORDINARY SCENES AT WESTMINSTER
REVEAL A GOVERNMENT CLOSE TO DISARRAY AND
A BITTER STRUGGLE TO WIN THE NATION'S TRUST
Observer
CLARKE ATTACKED FROM ALL ANGLES OVER
CONTROL ORDERS.
MPs ANGRY. 60 REBEL MPs AGAINST
Guardian
MPs REVOLT AGAINST HOUSE ARREST LAW
Independent
SHAMELESS RAID TAKES ENORMOUS LIBERTY
The Times

BETTER SCRAP THE HUMAN RIGHTS ACT.
HOUSE ARREST OF BRITISH CITIZENS WITHOUT
TRIAL IS UNACCEPTABLE
Daily Telegraph

The Parliamentary Labour Party, in truth, would never be the same again.

Three months later, the 2005 election saw Labour haemorrhage more popular votes than at any time during its history. The hitherto massive and unassailable majority was reduced to barely sixty. Much of this was blamed on Iraq but, for the first time in my Parliamentary career, civil liberties became a doorstep issue. It emerged in different ways, but the common theme was a profound loss of trust. Thus the duplicity of Iraq and the authoritarian nature of Government came together in a deadly political brew. With this in mind, on my return to Westminster, I arrived with the fervent hope that the lesson had been learnt, that attacks on civil liberty would become a thing of the past and the nature of government by the Labour Party would resemble the political institution that I had revered and joined many years before. How wrong I was.

process of criminal justice and the (general) severity of sentencing. Their principal aversion is to liberties manifest in the process of arrest, trial and sentence, rather than the philosophical liberties of free speech and association. The Home Office has a strong populist instinct.

Permanent Secretaries of the Home Office tend to be averse to imprisonment without trial. This aversion would have been stimulated and enhanced by the political bloody nose administered by Parliament over Control Orders. Bearing this in mind, the serial assaults on liberty which occurred during the 2005 Parliament bore the unmistakable fingerprints of No. 10.

Clearly discernible in the pattern of restriction and control was religious zealotry. To anyone who finds this incredible or offensive, I would invite attention to salient parts of British life which would have come to pass by 2010 had Parliament not increasingly exercised the control it began to assert in the latter part of the previous Parliament. If the Government's proposed legislation had become law, British citizens would now (at the time of writing) be subject to *ninety days' detention without charge or trial on a vast number of 'terrorist' offences.* Among those offences would be approbation or the 'glorification' of terrorism *as perceived by somebody else and whatever the intention of the citizen.* That same citizen, by now, would have his or her identity secure on a secret and inaccessible database to which they supplied, *as a matter of compulsion,* the details of their accommodation, in addition to making themselves available at a pre-ordained location in order to have their personal biometric particulars (colour of eyes, size of head) measured and retained at that same time. That citizen would also, for good measure, be subject to prosecution and imprisonment if he or she did or said anything to bring the religion of another into disrepute, either by mockery, ridicule or otherwise. In short, Britain would be a different place.

The 2005–10 Parliament is widely perceived as having been one of the worst in recent parliamentary history. This perception stems from a fractious government at the point of political senility, a financial crisis followed by recession, and the scandal of parliamentary expenses. It is worth recording, however, that the gross assaults on liberty described above were substantially or totally defeated by that very Parliament due to unprecedented independence on the Government backbenches. This largely unsung and unreported fact is in stark contrast to the prevailing climate of derision that shrouded the final days of Labour's administration.

In 2005, these historic battles lay in the future, but we knew then that we faced an onslaught of repressive legislation different in scale and character from that of the preceding eight years. This bore the unmistakable imprimatur of Tony Blair. At the first Old Testaments Prophets' lunch we came to the conclusion that there was likely to be a parallel motivation. After the catastrophes of Iraq and Afghanistan and the extent of death, destruction and deprivation that they had caused, Blair was in a state of what seemed to be psychotic denial and was in need of public justification. The perceived extent of the terrorist threat provided just this. The greater the threat, the better the alibi. What better way to persuade a nation that the threat was immensely grave than to exhort the necessity of long periods of custody without trial for the maintenance of the public weal.

The Terrorism Bill of 2006 received its Second Reading in the Commons in October 2005. It provided, after arrest, for a period of detention in police custody for ninety days before charge, trial or release. Archbishop Tutu, himself, was to liken the power to that employed in apartheid South Africa and, indeed, it was a near facsimile. As to the necessity for this immediate descent into a police state, not a single justification was advanced, save for the fact that the Assistant Commissioner Hayman thought it would be a good idea. Unsurprisingly, on 9 November it was roundly defeated in the House of Commons in favour of an amendment substituting twenty-eight days, tabled by David Winnick MP.

Serious, hard-working and humourless, David has, over the years, generally adopted a seat very close to my own favoured position on one or other side of the gangway. I have, therefore, had a considerable period of time in which to observe him. He resembles a querulous French master in a boys' prep school and, during debates, has a habit of muttering insults barely *sotto voce* at Members of Parliament whom he disapproves of or dislikes, of which I was emphatically one. He once informed me that his dislike for me was based on my profession as a lawyer, for which he plainly had a profound aversion. He also possesses, as a political hallmark, a personal and pathological loathing of tyrannical and oppressive government, despite which he maintains, to this day, a strong affection for Tony Blair that reveals (in my view) a certain myopia. Whatever the differences between us, David is a staunch libertarian. He made a fine speech in favour of twenty-eight days and I was the first to congratulate him when he succeeded on the first Division.

Forty-eight hours before the ninety-day debate Charlie Clarke knew perfectly well that the Government would be defeated. I had been partly instrumental in organising the rebellion, and when I saw Charlie in the Pugin Room where we were both drinking at separate tables before supper, I stopped briefly, as I was leaving, and said:

'You are going to lose this, Charlie. You know that, don't you?'

The way in which he replied, 'We shall see, young Bob, we shall see', indicated that he was aware of impending parliamentary doom. I reflected, over supper, that his words might have another meaning, namely that he was about to retrench and accept a shorter period of either twenty-eight (or conceivably forty-two) days. He was eating in the same dining room, so I approached him again and asked whether, in fact, he was contemplating capitulation or compromise. He gave me exactly the same reply, which demonstrated to the experienced parliamentary ear that this is precisely what he intended. Indeed, as a result of subtle leaking from the Home Office, this fact was, by the evening before the debate, common currency. Unhappily, that evening Blair addressed the Parliamentary Labour Party and, unusually, in view of the importance of the vote the following day, I attended. Blair delivered a passionate defence of the ninety-day provision.

After nearly ten years in Government, it was perhaps inevitable that these meetings with the Parliamentary Labour Party should be attended almost entirely by the most sycophantic and biddable backbenchers, many of whom acted out of a forlorn hope of some form of preferment. This state of mind led to wild applause and desk-thumping at whatever Blair chose to say and however he said it. This was no exception, and his defence of a South African period of detention without trial received enthusiastic thumping from 150-odd members of the Parliamentary Labour Party. Blair left early, and Charlie Clarke stood up to make the next speech. He had barely started when he received an obviously urgent communication from a messenger. Having read it, he hastened his speech and disappeared. I saw him later looking a little crestfallen and asked (percipiently, as it transpired) if he had been 'got at' by the Prime Minister. He was, of course, non-committal, but certain it was that any hope or prospect of compromise thereafter disappeared. The following day he attempted, manfully, to promote a Division in which he had plainly no belief or confidence and it was duly lost. This little account says much, I would suggest, about the former Prime Minister. Blair did not bother to count the number of those who were enthusiastically thumping, nor did he bother to consult his own Whips or members of the Party. Simple adulation was sufficient for his self-belief in both the rectitude of his cause and his certainty of success. It is a characteristic which has caused many deaths and much destruction.

The ninety-day issue consumed much of the popular press,

of course, but infinitely more interesting was the debate, within the same Bill, of the 'glorification' provisions which created a serious 'terrorist' offence to *glorify* terrorism. This phrase, and the section itself, again bore the unmistakable hallmark of the Prime Minister. 'Glorification,' as I subsequently observed in the debate, 'may be a magnificent word in the music of Handel and the pen of Blake or Milton. It has absolutely no place in criminal jurisprudence. We do not do Beatitudes at the Old Bailey. We do criminal justice based on statutes.'

The section as recently drafted, however, was not simply floridly religious; it was positively and seriously dangerous. The danger lay in the absence of any element of intent. Thus, any statement which glorified terrorism *as perceived by the listener*, became a terrorist offence (and *ipso facto*, under the Bill, the subject of ninety-day imprisonment, detention without charge). The definition of domestic and international terrorism was so wide that any expression of opinion, during debates, academic studies, journalistic writing or otherwise, such as, say, 'the ANC in South Africa had fought a noble campaign against an oppressive apartheid regime', would have rendered the speaker immediately liable to a criminal offence (*for which he had no defence*). Similarly, Cherie Blair's public comment that young Palestinians could be hopelessly driven to be bombers would have amounted to a crime. I put this forcibly to Charlie, both before and during the debate. On both occasions he rejected the obvious construction of the Bill and simply stated 'it was not the Government's intention that it should cover such matters'. This was to become a recurring justification of New Labour ministers; namely, that the Government's intention would, by some mystic means, overcome the clear wording of a statute. Wearily I organised a further rebellion and, in doing so, had earnest conversations with both David Davis and Dominic Grieve, then the Shadow Attorney General. I had put down an amendment importing the element of intention into the offence. The Tories had put down a similar, though weaker, amendment suggesting that criminality would only arise if the statement was 'reckless'. This, in my view, was better but not good enough and we therefore agreed that their amendment (as the official Opposition amendment) should be taken first, but that they would indicate to the Clerk of the Commons their wish, if it were defeated, to be given the opportunity to vote on mine. In the event, after a fine and feisty debate, the Opposition amendment was called and was defeated by thirty-odd votes which, in itself, was a good result. Together with Dominic, I had previously persuaded the Clerk of the Commons (and, thereby, the Speaker) to call my amendment on the basis that it was distinct. When it was called I asked for another Division, which was duly held. I appointed my own Tellers but I was unable to speak to them before the vote was announced. What I did hear, however, was the junior minister, Angela Eagle, being informed of the numbers on the Division and quite audibly saying 'Oh, fuck.'

When the numbers were announced, it transpired that the Government had scraped home by *one vote*. To all intents and purposes, this was effectively a defeat. It was inevitable, given the closeness of the vote, that the House of Lords would block the Government's clause, if necessary on an indefinite basis. It was a not insubstantial victory and I still have the telling card on my mantelpiece. I was anxious, however, to repair any damage between myself and Charlie. I tracked him down in the Tea Room and offered my services to draft an appropriate compromise amendment which could be agreed between ourselves and the Government's minister in the Lords. Charlie had had a particularly bad twenty-four hours. The night before, he had been bullied by the Prime Minister into adopting an entirely indefensible position in the Commons. He had been badly humiliated on ninety days and now, to boot, he had effectively lost the glorification provisions to his own side.

'Look here, young Bob,' he said. 'Why don't you just fuck off?'

I took this with reasonable grace; it was, after all, an admonition to which I was becoming accustomed.

The story had one final twist. That evening I had promised to speak at the constituency dinner of my friend and colleague, Paul Flynn, the Member of Parliament for Newport West. The annual dinner commemorated the Newport uprising and the martyrs who were shot in that demonstration in the cause of trade union emancipation. We were staying with Paul in Newport, and Gill and I arrived in good time for a drink before we set out for the dinner. I was still quite flushed with the day's success, but disappointed that it was not a straightforward victory.

'Well, Paul,' I said, raising a glass of wine. 'That was damn close. We bloody nearly beat them.'

I perceived immediately that my good friend was somewhat uncomfortable.

'Paul,' I said. 'You were there, weren't you?'

'I was,' said Paul. 'But I voted the wrong way.'

It was not, of course, his fault. Paul is one of the very best, most independent and clever Members of Parliament, but his chronic suffering from arthritis is a daily public torture. In particular, he moves slowly and, on the crucial Division, had arrived late into the Lobby, immediately before the Division Bell and had been duly ushered into the 'wrong' Lobby by an officious Government Whip. Of course I forgave him immediately, but it is worth reflecting that had his vote been different, outright victory would have been obtained, a memory which I would have treasured even more, to this day.

In the event, the Government accepted, with poor grace, the Tory amendment. This, therefore, was now unstoppable and so, at least, some small progress was made on this mischievous piece of terrorist legislation – and Cherie Blair will not be charged with 'glorification', which is, I hope, an immense relief to her.

On Friday 3 February 2006, the *Independent* newspaper carried an article already referred to, under the headline: REBEL

RINGLEADER FACES LABOUR PLOT TO OUST HIM FROM SEAT.

The subject of the article was a reported 'crackdown' on Labour MPs in order to force through highly controversial measures on ID cards and anti-terror laws. Dire measures were promised, including the end of the use of 'slips to excuse themselves from Commons' votes' and the complete curtailment of foreign travel. However, that was apparently not enough in my case (not that I have enjoyed foreign travel as a Member of Parliament). The article continued: 'However, some Ministers have privately discussed taking tougher action against one of the veteran rebel ringleaders, Bob Marshall-Andrews, a QC and a leading campaigner against the war in Iraq. He was privately accused of colluding with Tory opponents of the Religious Hatred legislation. Some Ministers wanted him to be de-selected from his Medway constituency. "We don't mind him voting against the Government but colluding with the Tories is beyond the pale," one Labour insider said.'

On the same day as the article I met the deputy editor of the *Independent*, Colin Brown, walking through the cloister. Colin was one of the best of the lobby correspondents and a regular visitor at Old Testament Prophets' lunches.

'Where did this stuff come from?' I asked him as we headed towards the Strangers' Bar.

'The very top,' he said happily. '*Very top.*'

I said how pleased I was. One of the most depressing things in politics is to be plotted against by inferiors, and this cheered me up.

Jill, my PA, met me later in the day and told me that the headline had briefly surfaced on national radio.

The reason for this petulant nonsense was a quite spectacular own goal scored by Hilary Armstrong, the Chief Whip, during the final passage of the Racial and Religious Hatred Bill, legislation which clearly reflected the posturing piety of the Prime Minister.

The Act would create a new criminal offence of inducing religious hatred in another. So far, so good. Inducing hatred of anyone else, for whatever reason, is undesirable human behaviour and might easily be criminal if it is intended to cause violence or social unrest. The Bill, however, required no such criminal intention. The offence was committed if the inducement to hatred was reckless or careless. Thus the unintentional creation of racial hatred in some (unspecified) third party, however dysfunctional, bigoted or irrational that third party might be, became a serious criminal offence. This would include comedies or sketches debunking or vilifying religious orthodoxy or holding it up to ridicule. Not surprisingly, this attracted the excited attention of the celebrity circuit. Luvvies are not natural libertarians, but the prospect, as one of them put it to me succinctly, 'of being banged up for having a pop at the Prophet' caused an outbreak of angst in Notting Hill. And, of course, they had a perfectly good point. Since the Age of Reason we have always set our collective face against the protection of faith by statute. After a 200-year history of religious intolerance which led to nothing but bigotry and death, we came to understand perfectly that one cannot protect the faith without protecting the fundamentalist and the bigot who lie within it. And indeed, as I pointed out during the debate, legislation passed ostensibly to protect religion has precisely the reverse effect, as the people most protected are those who come closest to committing the offences we are attempting to place on the statute book. A loathing of bigotry and those that preach it would render me liable to prosecution under the very legislation passed to protect religious susceptibilities. We would not, as I observed, create a tolerant society but a legislative and cultural bearpit.

As a criminal lawyer, I was able to provide some small service by pointing out that 'recklessness' is the bastard part of intention and has caused more trouble in English criminal law than any other single concept.

In this particular rebellion, we were much fortified by the presence in our midst of comedians such as Rowan Atkinson, who made a speech at a parliamentary fringe meeting while the main debate took place in the Chamber. The House of Lords had done a good job in amending the worst parts of the Bill by reducing the criminal act to threatening words, and introducing the element of intention. The Old Testament Prophets had been busy organising a rebellion which was, I suppose, particularly apposite to our foundation. The religious aspects of the debate meant that we were joined by a number of strange bedfellows, including Ann Widdecombe.

On a whipped vote, the Government, on the first Division, suffered a humiliating defeat by ten votes. The second vote (the more important of the two) represented the glorious own goal by the Chief Whip. Having suffered a loss by ten votes and, not wishing the Prime Minister to be seen in another defeated lobby, she had advised Blair to stay in his room or return to Downing Street. In the event, the Government lost by just one vote. Had the Prime Minister voted, this dangerous and unpleasant piece of legislation would have made its way to the statute books.

My limited sympathy with the Chief Whip disappeared completely when the *Independent* reported the punitive measures to be taken against myself, puny though they undoubtedly were. It remains, however, a glorious irony that Blair's deliberate abstention saved one essential freedom of speech which he had sought, piously, to destroy.

Until its final deeply unlamented death at the hands of the Coalition, the project to inflict identity cards and compulsory identities on the British people represented one of the most dangerous and simultaneously the most farcical pieces of Blairite theology. The value claimed for the project, its size, effect or even its purpose, varied infinitely according to the minister who was burdened with its progress through a sceptical and, occasionally, alarmed Parliament. The Home Secretary, Charles Clarke (who manifestly loathed the whole thing), repeatedly stated that the identity project offered no benefit to the 'war against terrorism'. On this not unimportant subject, other ministers were ambivalent (or simply ignorant), whereas the Prime Minister expressed no doubt, when questioned, that it was an essential part of this noble endeavour. The extent or the use of this vast database which the Government intended to create was, likewise, the subject of conflicting and, on occasions, contradictory claims.

As time passed, the claims from No. 10 as to the benefits of this mass imposition began to bear an uncomfortable relationship to the escalation of weapons of mass destruction. By the time the Bill staggered through to its Third Reading on 18 October 2005, there was virtually no individual ailment or vice, and no collective crime or iniquity, that identity cards would not ameliorate or cure. Together with other members of the Old Testament Prophets and the usual suspects, I endeavoured to kill the entire Bill at its Second Reading on 28 June 2005. We tabled an Early Day Motion (EDM) calling on the House to decline even a Second Reading to the scheme. We did so on the grounds that:

'It will make no significant contribution to the reduction or eradication of terrorism, illegal immigration or illegal employment; contains no proper safeguard to limit or proscribe the information to be stored on identity cards or the national register or the agencies, organisations, national or international, to whom this information may be made available or will be given; fails to identify the biometric details to be stored or to acknowledge the effectiveness of the same or the margins of or the consequences of and the remedies for error; fails properly to limit or define the fees which may be levied by the Secretary of State; and provides for the costs of the scheme to be paid on the authority of the Secretary of State without providing to Parliament any proper estimates for the vast costs likely to be incurred.'

The EDM was drafted on the basis of the Government's early publications, but is one of those documents for which one may claim a measure of prescience. Put simply, the whole thing was a ghastly, unmitigated mess. It was also incredibly expensive. It also represented order, discipline, regulation and, above all, *control*.

As with many MPs, I encountered certain difficulties and reservations with my own, admirable, constituents. Not unreasonably, some asked why I was rebelling (again!) against a scheme that provided a harmless piece of plastic which could be employed in many useful ways such as access to benefits and health. Generally, these contentions swiftly evaporated when the Orwellian consequences and massive costs were carefully revealed. Nonetheless, one of the disturbing elements of this campaign was the slowness with which public hostility came to ignite.

The EDM itself had been the inspired handiwork of Lynne Jones, and formed the basis of uproarious debate. One of the more extraordinary claims that surfaced during its course was the effect that identity cards would have in preventing identity theft, a piece of casuistry similar to the claim that owning a car would, *ipso facto*, prevent it from being stolen. It was sustained by a remarkable Government document that contained the assertion that: 'A few items stolen from a rubbish bin, such as utility bills, can lead to huge financial losses as well as distress and inconvenience for victims in putting their record straight.'

It continued, without providing any form of source, by pointing out: 'On average, victims can spend sixty hours restoring their records.'

As I observed to the House, I found that difficult to believe. I know that British Telecom and British Gas can be tiresome when people try to put their records straight, and that one can spend a lot of time listening to music on hold, but I found the claim that one can spend two weeks of continuous time trying to put one's records straight as a result of documents being removed from one's dustbin, an unconvincing start to research.

The Government document went on to claim that the card system would prevent £250,000,000 in VAT fraud, a claim plainly bogus, as major VAT fraud is committed by companies.

At the end of the debate, the Government's majority was reduced to thirty-one. On a three-line whip this was, effectively, a defeat, and a guaranteed a rough passage through the House of Lords – which duly occurred.

The Third Reading debate at least provided the opportunity carefully to spell out the true implications of the legislation and, thereby, to provide a template which was available to incredulous constituents and the large number of non-constituents who wrote to me on this issue:

'Not since the Domesday Book in 1068 have we seen anything like it. That was a system of registration put into effect by the Normans – or the New Normans as I suspect they were known at the time. Not since then have the British people been required to attend, with their families, at a certain place, at a certain time in order to have their heads measured and the colour of their eyes taken. To be fair, under the present Bill, people will not have to declare the number of livestock that they possess or the number of items of clothing that they wear. However, we should not get too excited as under the terms of the secondary legislation people could be forced to give any other information that the Secretary of State prescribes.

'I can picture one of my constituents talking to me in my surgery saying "I have to go to Maidstone to have my head measured?" I will reply, "Yes, you have," and he will say, indicating his wife, "And she's got to have her head measured as well?" I will say, "Yes, indeed," then, pointing to his adolescent offspring, he will say, "And they have to have their heads measured as well?" and I will confirm that he is absolutely right. He will then say, "Why did you vote for this Bill?" I will then experience the glory of saying that I did not vote for it, and I voted against it on every conceivable opportunity. My constituent will want to know what will happen if they all refuse to have their heads measured and I will tell him that they will not be able to go to the public library (which will not upset him very much) but there will be other things he will be unable to do which may.'

There followed an interesting exchange between me and Martin Salter, the otherwise excellent Member of Parliament for Reading West. It went as follows:

Martin Salter: 'I always enjoy hearing my Learned Friend's oratory, but to develop his theme of explaining his glorious vote against the Bill to his constituents, did he make it clear to them at the election – I have seen some of his election publicity and it was very good – that although he was standing on the Labour Party manifesto, which included a pledge to introduce this Bill, he was personally opposed to it and would vote against it?'

Mr Marshall-Andrews: 'I am pleased to answer that question. The answer is yes, I did. Neither was it the only part of the Labour Manifesto that I told my constituents I was not standing on. I had pared it down quite thin by the end of the campaign.'

On Third Reading, the Government's majority, on a full three-line whip, was halved to a mere thirty-three. There followed a long and protracted battle with the House of Lords which delayed the worst aspect of the legislation until the departure of Tony Blair after which it effectively died, providing another small victory in the long rearguard action fought down the parliamentary Khyber Passes to preserve a wagon train of gradually diminishing liberties.

On 22 July 2005, Jean Charles de Menezes was pursued into Stockwell Underground Station by plain-clothes members of the Terrorist Squad. With barely any warning, he was shot; and when he lay helpless on the ground, he was repeatedly shot in the head. The resulting inquest, held before Sir Michael Wright, Assistant Deputy Coroner, revealed an appalling litany of error, failure and neurosis. Mr Menezes was a completely innocent man from Brazil and although his entirely decent and respectable family were robbed of their son, they were, at least, provided with the opportunity of watching an independent inquest held on oath into the public misfeasance which led to his death. The only criminal proceedings that resulted were an extraordinary indictment laid under health and safety legislation. There had been, however, a full inquest and, most important, an inquest before a jury.

In 2008, the New Labour Government attempted, in the Counter-Terrorism Bill, to provide for secret, non-jury inquests in cases that involved national security. A public outcry followed and the clause was hastily removed from the Act. It reappeared a year later in the last knockings of the Labour administration, in the Coroners and Justice Bill 2009. This was a rag-tag piece of legislation representing the floor sweepings of the Department for Constitutional Affairs. Legislation was introduced, for example, to prevent criminals benefiting from writing the memoirs of their crimes.

(Following the passage of the Bill, I received letters from two different sources, asking whether it would criminalise Blair's memoirs of the Iraq war. An interesting thought but, unhappily, one that was unlikely to attract the Director of Public Prosecutions.)

This was to be the Labour Government's final weary assault on the principle of jury trial and, it is worth recording, the only one in which they partially succeeded. This late last gasp also represented one of the rare failures of collaboration between the 'liberty rebels' in the House of Commons and the House of Lords. It occurred through error. In the Lords, the Liberal

Democrat peers (who had, over the preceding decade, an impeccable pedigree) failed to table the right amendment. When I learnt of this error, I presented myself before the Clerk to the Commons to see if there was any way in which we could, nonetheless, amend the legislation. I was told, unhappily, that there was none. On this occasion, however, we enjoyed the active support of Andrew Dismore, the Member of Parliament for Hendon, and Chairman of the Human Rights Committee. By a piece of masterly ingenuity, he managed to construct an amendment and to place it before the House for a vote. In the event, the Government succeeded by a majority of eight. In the process, it compromised on the degree of official overview by the Lord Chief Justice, which was a victory of a sort. It is an unhappy fact, however, that this last (albeit small) erosion of the jury principle was achieved by a tiny majority and thus relied entirely on the votes of Scottish Labour Members of Parliament whose constituents' liberties remained totally unaffected by legislation that related to them not at all.

It may well be argued that 700 years ago, the English denied many liberties to the Scots. In my thirteen years in Parliament, much legislation was passed which removed rights and liberties from the English and the Welsh. Much of this would never have become law without the votes of Scottish MPs whose own legal system remained totally unaltered.

It was difficult sometimes not to see it as a form of subliminal revenge.

CHAPTER 15

OF LIBERTY AND TERROR 6:
LIBERTY AND GORDON

In which heady optimism recounted at an ICAP lunch is vindicated, reported welcomed and firmly dashed – I discuss voting for forty-two days detention with a new Prime Minister confident that he is talking to someone else – And detention without trial is defeated again.

On 27 June 2007, Gordon Brown became Prime Minister. He succeeded the man with whom he had forged and founded the concept of New Labour and whom he now loathed beyond endurance. The feeling was entirely reciprocated, and it was inevitable that Blair would immediately signal his contempt for Parliament and democracy, take the Chiltern Hundreds and disappear to the profitable pantheons of a grateful Republican America. I had voted for Gordon to the amazement (and even hostility) of some of my best friends and colleagues on the dissident wing of the Labour benches. This distressed me. I had, with these selfsame foot soldiers, made common cause against repressive legislation and disastrous war. In these campaigns we had enjoyed some, albeit modest, successes and I was concerned and troubled by their disaffection. I was also troubled by denying a vote to John McDonnell. Nonetheless, I soldiered on. I believed in Gordon. For all his morose moods and occasional tantrums I believed him to be a good man, clever, literate and, unlike his predecessor, well grounded in the history and traditions of British socialism, one of which was a fundamental belief in our civil liberties as the defining characteristic of our nation.

In December 1997, the *Telegraph* had allowed me an article dedicated to the character of the Iron Chancellor. In it I sought to find an answer to his first, surprising, austerity measures.

'The answer,' I wrote, 'is toil and plunder. To Mr Brown New Labour means precisely what it says: new work. For this Chancellor it is not economics, it is ethics. Work purifies and liberates. They shall rise in the morning and they shall toil and to pay for this, we may plunder.'

Subsequently (in 1997) I met Gordon at a Christmas party thrown for those who remained dutifully in Westminster when our northern colleagues had departed. He had read the article and reminded me briefly of it.

'You got that right,' he said. 'Toil and plunder. Quite right.'

In short, I trusted his instincts.

On the week before Gordon's inevitable accession, I had lunch with Michael Spencer, the Chairman of ICAP (the inter-dealer money broker) and Treasurer of the Conservative Party. There is not a better lunch to be had in the City or better company in which to eat it. On this occasion, I found myself sitting next to the sublime Maggie Pagano, chief economics editor of the *Independent on Sunday*. She was looking to write an article on Gordon Brown which was not limited to the future state of the economy.

'In what way,' she asked, 'will he be most different from Tony Blair?'

Without hesitation I answered in two words: 'Civil liberties.'

This excited some interest around the table and I spent an enjoyable hour drinking Michael's fine claret and defending my surprising view of a liberal and reforming Prime Minister. That Sunday, Maggie duly carried the surprising news, quoting sources 'close to Gordon Brown'. She forecast a sea change in the nature of government. The erosion of civil liberties, she reported, was now a thing of the past. Brown would mark the clear distinction between his political philosophies and those of his predecessor.

The following week, in his first major Commons' appearance, Gordon, rather surprisingly, delivered just that. He intended, he said, to strengthen the role of Parliament, and to improve its powers of scrutiny, to be contained in a new constitutional accord. My own expressions of support were met, unsurprisingly, with ironic cheers, but I remained happy and vindicated in my vote. I resolved to capture the prevailing momentum and made contact with Wilf Stevenson, Chairman of the John Smith Institute, widely (and correctly) regarded as Gordon's personal think-tank. We had met Wilf and his wife Anne many years ago through our mutual friend, the architect Jan Kaplicky. After that meeting we had become friends and enjoyed a political affinity. Wilf was now firmly ensconced in No. 10 and this appeared to me to be the opportunity to create a new agenda for civil liberty and, with it, to alter the gloomy and repressive perception of New Labour and its Prime Minister. I drew up an impressive agenda for reform which included a drastic limitation to the issue and use of identity cards, the scrapping of electronic monitoring, a parliamentary inquiry into the abuse of terrorist legislation, the repeal of Control Orders and a judicial review to carry out 'slum clearance' of the incomprehensible provisions of numerous criminal justice statutes.

I met Wilf in the tiny canteen in the basement of No. 10. To my surprise he indicated his view that my proposals were far too modest. Was it not the case, he asked, that most terrorist legislation simply replicated existing crimes and could be scrapped altogether? I agreed energetically. We parted on a hopeful note. He took my proposals and agreed, kindly, to improve the grammar and syntax and to place them directly on the Prime Minister's desk. Finally, he agreed with my political analysis. Gordon's political reputation was gloomy, dour and authoritarian. An energetic civil liberties agenda not only symbolically reversed the nature of the Blair Government, but provided the clear antidote to his personal image.

I received a telephone call from Maggie Pagano, who was grateful for my intelligence on the new Prime Minister which had provided her with something of a scoop. I told her, rather grandly, that more was to come and, for a moment, enjoyed something which felt suspiciously close to influence. I was, of course, totally wrong. Nothing happened. Wilf, I have no doubt, genuinely shared my disappointment. Some months later, over dinner, he told me that the proposals had reached Gordon on a bad day and had returned to his office with the unmistakable ink markings of rejection.

But worse was to come. The Queen's Speech in November 2007 contained an unequivocal intention to reinstate the extension of police custody without charge or trial. The decision (which must have been that of the Prime Minister in person) was not simply wrong, it was totally incomprehensible. The ninety-day compromise had resulted in a maximum custody period of twenty-eight days. It transpired, on enquiry, that even this custody limit had not been used *once* in the two years following its passage into law.

The untenable nature of the Government's case was revealed, starkly, by the fact that no actual period of custody had, by the time of the debate on the Queen's Speech, been decided as definitive. It was, said Jack Straw (by now Lord Chancellor), a matter of consultation.

This meant that the Cabinet were totally divided on the issue. Thus, the liberty of the subject, the most priceless asset of the democracy, was reduced to the status of a lottery. Wearily I began to organise my final rebellion and applied myself to the Queen's

Speech debate. I was, by now, receiving substantial extra-parliamentary mail which I made some attempt to represent:

'The scepticism extends to the unavoidable fact that a period of 56 days, substantially less than before, is necessary for the police and the agencies to do their job. If that is the case why were we whipped two years ago to vote for 90 days? The threat has not receded since, so if 90 days were necessary then why aren't they necessary now? The conclusion to be drawn from that is that these figures are not based on scientific analysis by the police or other agencies but represented the greatest number of days that can be got past Westminster. 90 days will not work. The conclusion is a draw down process to see how close one can get before the weaker brethren in Parliament will give way. It is a bad way to do business, particularly on this issue.'

These questions were posed by many in the debate and remained unanswered by the new Home Secretary, Jacqui Smith, a decent woman several hundred metres out of her depth.

In the course of collecting names for yet another rebellion, it became clear to me that something quite profound had happened within the Parliamentary Labour Party. The dissident minority, historically numbering twenty to thirty votes, was growing, and the Whips were losing control. It became equally apparent that this change had a number of causes. The first, undoubtedly, was a growing aversion to the persistent and grinding assault on fundamental principles of liberty. The second was an aversion to Gordon Brown, and the third was the subliminal but tangible belief that a tired Government had run its course. My own figures told me that the Government faced certain defeat. The Whips' figures told a similar story. Official lists began to circulate and, inevitably, were leaked. Articles appeared in the national newspapers carrying surprisingly accurate lists of the disaffected. The Government, marked by internal disarray, began to panic. Two weeks before the vote an extraordinary compromise was offered. The entire basis of the Bill, it was now said, rested upon the possibility of an as yet unknown terrorist plot. If, it was argued, such a plot was suddenly uncovered involving the seizure of massive quantities of encrypted material, additional custody limits would be necessary for that plot in isolation. It was proposed (apparently seriously) that the powers should be exercised only where there was a significant risk of serious danger to life or property and Parliament would be specially recalled in order to consider the gravity of *that* plot. The idea of suddenly endowing MPs with the powers of policemen created an absurdity that needed no serious explanation even to the mass media, the majority of which had, by now, turned firmly against the legislation.

The figures of dissidents remained unchanged and desperation ensued. It was perceived by Downing Street that defeat on this issue would fatally undermine the credibility of the Prime Minister and his authority within Parliament, an analysis that was probably right. With three days to go, Gordon Brown embarked on an extraordinary round of telephone calls, individually seeking the support of potentially dissident members. In doing so, a number of strange blandishments were applied. Ian Gibson had long been an ardent campaigner against the blockade of Cuba. When the Prime Minister called him, he indicated that the Government might well offer a more vigorous support for this campaign. The inevitable leaking of these conversations led to a growing sense of incredulity within Parliament and outside. That Government policy could be tailored or traded for individual votes marked an extraordinary lurch towards pork-barrel politics.

My own call from the Prime Minister was even more bizarre. No one in No. 10 had told the Prime Minister that he was not only talking to a likely dissident but one of their organisers. He had obviously been provided with a useful crib sheet on matters likely to prove decisive or influential in my particular case. He had no doubt been informed (correctly) of my aversion to Blair and to his parliamentary faction. Gordon expressed the view that the present potential rebellion was being organised by sub-terranean Blairites such as Charles Clarke and Alan Milburn. Whether through astonishment or tact, I forbore from telling the Prime Minister that I was organising the rebellion and that, as far as I was aware, neither Charles Clarke nor Alan Milburn had organised a successful rebellion in their lives. Finally, he indicated that it might be possible to do something positive in the sphere of community housing. The only explanation for this extraordinary blandishment is that he had been provided with another MP's political priorities. Apart from a general inter-est in decent accommodation for my constituents, I had never been a housing expert, nor did its building or provision form part of my political priorities. I said, somewhat weakly, that I thought any improvement in social housing would be a jolly good thing. Gordon's unseen reaction indicated some forlorn hope that he had created a convert and I, I confess, had not the heart to disabuse him. Manifestly, however, it was no way to run a government.

With two days to go before inevitable defeat, I sought out Jack Straw and offered a means of escape. As a lawyer, he knew full well that the concept of returning an individual *ad hominem* case to Parliament on an issue of custody time limits was a con-stitutional outrage that would never survive public opinion, still less the House of Lords. I suggested that the Government should withdraw the current legislation with good grace, but publish a draft Bill, together with a programme and guillotine motion, which would enable that legislation to pass through both Houses of Parliament within the course of one day. Nothing could prevent the Government from taking such a measure and the effect would be theoretically the same. For a moment I saw a flicker of interest pass across the face of the Lord Chancellor before it relapsed into the cast of weary and inevitable defeat.

In the end, the result was worse than defeat could have been. The Government won by nine votes, which was accounted for entirely by the support of Northern Irish members. Their interest in the legislation was precisely nil, aside from the barely concealed promise of a substantial investment of millions of British pounds in Irish projects. This gerrymandering caused universal aversion and derision. The Bill faced inevitable defeat in the House of Lords, even without the remarkable maiden speech of Eliza Manningham-Buller, the former head of MI5 (and thus with a career spent dealing with national security), who said, in a devastating and short peroration, that she saw no reason for the legislation at all.

The Bill collapsed. The Government did not attempt to force it through the Commons again but, in any event, it would have been doomed to failure. At that stage, far too late, Jacqui Smith, the Home Secretary, adopted the provisional bill approach I had suggested to Jack. It was received with ironic jeers. By that stage, jeers were what it deserved.

The defeat of this nasty piece of legislation marked the end of the New Labour Government's persistent assault on centuries of civil liberties. For me, it represented the conclusion of a protracted and weary parliamentary battle. Generally the Government had succeeded through its use of its massive majorities. Occasionally it had not done so. The greatest significance for me was the fact that jury trial remained virtually unchanged and intact. This ancient right can now only be lost in the event of the most serious attempts to suborn or tamper with a sitting jury. In six years that power has been invoked on only one occasion and, for now, the floodgates remain firmly shut.

The battle, of course, was not only fought in Parliament and, indeed, we formed only one flank of a growing and powerful opposition to the erosion of liberty. In the press, it united great journalists of otherwise different views. Peter Oborne, Henry Porter and Simon Jenkins maintained consistent, devastating attacks from their unique points of vantage. Legal professional organisations provided highly researched material. Roy Amlot, Chairman of the Bar, attended every important debate during his office. At Liberty, Shami Chakrabarti became little short of a national icon leading dedicated teams with remorseless vigour.

As I write, the present Attorney General, Dominic Grieve, with whom I collaborated on many parliamentary campaigns, is preparing a Great Repeal Bill which I fondly hope will shred the worst, most incomprehensible and dangerous legislation that was forced through in the course of the past thirteen years. I wish him well, and the fact that I will not be there to see it passed is one of my few regrets in leaving the green benches.

CHAPTER 16

OF SCREENS AND SECURITY

In which we deplore the (failed) attempt to hit Mr Tony Blair with a projectile thrown from the public gallery – Lament the erection of a vast protective screen to separate Members of Parliament from their constituents – Reflect on the use of security to create a national neurosis – Recall the nasty attack on Mr Walter Wolfgang (82) by a New Labour thug and congratulate Mr David Cameron on his decision to walk to the Palace of Westminster.

On 19 May 2004, a visitor to the public gallery of the House of Commons threw a bag of powder at Tony Blair during Prime Minister's Questions. It was a fair shot which struck the seat directly beside the Prime Minister and a tiny proportion of the bag's contents settled on the Prime Minister's suit. The powder was entirely harmless and purple – a colour not, apparently, intended to convey any particular political message. The culprit, a member of the Fathers4Justice campaign group, was, of course, apprehended by the excellent House of Commons' staff, whose antique uniform of tights and knee-breeches belies the fact that all of them have a distinguished military background involving expertise in unarmed combat.

(I was once body-tackled by one of them, with whom I had become friendly, whilst I was running in a desperate attempt to reach the Voting Lobby before the doors were closed. As I picked myself up, somewhat shaken, I asked why he had treated me in this violent and unparliamentary way.

'You were running for the wrong Lobby, sir,' he said, giving me a reassuring pat. 'I knew you'd be voting for the Government on this one.')

The incident of the purple powder was widely reported but otherwise caused no more than a ripple in Westminster life. In the Tea Room there was some discussion as to the remarkable lack of violence shown towards politicians in general, and Prime Ministers in particular, over the history of British democracy. Wellington, we recollected, one of the most unpopular of all British Prime Ministers, had been pelted with vegetables when driving in his carriage outside Hyde Park. Otherwise only one British Prime Minister had been assassinated, the unfortunate Spencer Perceval, who was shot whilst leaving the debating chamber on 11 May 1812. The official history carries a charming ring of a gentler age. Someone cried out, 'Who is the villain who has done this?' To which the gunman immediately replied, 'I am that unhappy man.' His unhappiness was later compounded when he was convicted by a jury at the Old Bailey and was duly hanged.

During our discussions in the Tea Room, we also reflected on the fact that the murderer's name was Bellingham. Ironically, one of his direct descendants is a present Member of the House of Commons. Bellingham is a kind, delightful man and a thoughtful debater who has clearly avoided any genetic disadvantages that may have resulted from his ancestry.

A second irony was the fact that, several weeks before the powder incident, the Government, doubtless at the express wish of No. 10, had grossly disfigured the debating chamber of the Commons in order to avoid just such an event. We had returned from the Easter recess to discover that a massive glass screen, supported by metal pillars and stanchions, had been erected in front of the public gallery.

An elementary relay system had been installed which meant that foreign visitors and British constituents were able to hear their representatives speaking unintelligibly, as through a collective gas mask. The Prime Minister, who, in the preceding two years, had unleashed shock and awe on the people of Iraq, involving the use of the most destructive conventional explosives and white phosphorus, had plainly taken a strong view as to his own safety. No consultation had taken place with Members of Parliament or any other representatives of the British people to whom the Palace of Westminster ultimately belongs through the offices of the Crown. (In the subsequent debates, the Leader of the House, Peter Hain, attempted manfully to take the responsibility for the giant screen upon his own shoulders. The decision, he asserted, had been his and his alone in the interests of the safety of Members of Parliament, and was nothing to do with No. 10. This assertion, sad to relate, was, and is, believed by precisely nobody, an incredulity supported by a conspicuous silence from 10 Downing Street when the future of the screen was ultimately debated in Parliament (of which the Prime Minister was, after all, a member).

Together with Brian Sedgemore, I immediately tabled an Early Day Motion condemning the screen as an affront to democracy, an insult to our constituents and a gross waste of money (£1.3 million) to boot. Within days, the motion attracted nearly one hundred signatures and, in the face of this parliamentary rebellion, a debate on the retention of the screen (or its replacement) became inevitable. Predictably the screen also had its supporters, particularly within the pristine ranks of New Labour. From these I received a number of (remarkably similar) letters, accusing me of gross irresponsibility towards the Prime Minister and my parliamentary colleagues. One particular former junior minister became so agitated that she stopped me in the Library corridor and suggested that, without the screen, many members would simply refuse to go into the debating chamber. I enquired, perhaps disingenuously, whether this fear of the public gallery had accounted for her own near absence from parliamentary debates over the preceding three years. I was pleased to watch the struggle cross her face before she allowed herself to seize the opportunity and mutter that it had been a 'contributory factor' in her lack of attendance.

The debate finally took place on 22 April 2004. It was opened by the Leader of the House, Peter Hain, who stressed the need for security in order to guard against that tiny abhorrent part of society who might throw projectiles from the balcony.

I made my contribution from my favourite seat in the third row immediately behind the Government dispatch box. (It is undeniably the best dissident seat in the House. Unlike ministers, backbenchers are deprived of desks or lecterns or the dispatch box, and debate standing with the front of the body exposed. There is only one advantage over the dispatch box, namely height. From the third row you can tower over ministers from behind, which provides a satisfactory and atavistic atmosphere of threat.)

I referred to my position in the debate:

'There is a canard abroad. I have heard it whispered that those of us who bitterly oppose this thing, do so because we wish in some way those on the front bench to be put at greater risk. Nothing could be further from the truth, Mr Speaker. Indeed I can reveal to you that one of the reasons that I habitually attempt to take this particular seat during Prime Minster's Questions is so that I can, if necessary, suddenly interpose my own body between the Prime Minister and the Public or, indeed, the Press Gallery.'

In the remainder of my speech I attempted (as I have done on many occasions since) to illustrate the corrosive power of security over liberty:

'It will be a victory for the grimiest of organisations appended in the Terrorism Act 2000, including al-Qaeda, who will have the enormous satisfaction of knowing that simply through their existence and the threats that they can impose, they will have turned the Mother of Parliaments into a Lilliputian Assembly that they would perceive as cowering behind a wall of glass.'

Together with others, I attempted to encapsulate the elementary loss to parliamentary democracy:

'This building does not belong to Members of Parliament. It is a Royal Palace but it is also, in the best sense, the People's Palace. They come here not because of sufferance or invitation but as a right. They have a right to be here, not as voyeurs or listeners but to participate in the process. Of course, they cannot speak whilst they are here but their very presence alters the web and weft of what we do. When this House laughs, as it does, fortunately, on occasion, that laughter is echoed by the people who sit here and are with us. When the place is sad or solemn, that sadness and solemnity is felt not just down here but throughout the Chamber. Any interference with that is a gross distortion and intervention with the body politic and they will know it. There could not be a stronger metaphor for the alienation of people from politics than what we are proposing to put up. Of course there is risk, but we are here to take risks. We are not here to soak up the many privileges associated with being a Member. We are to bear and share the risks that our people bear and share. What rights have we over, for instance, those who preside over public order and public matters? What about the thousands of judges? Or the counsel that appear before them? What about the thousands of jurors who go into the jury box every day. Those juries are at risk, but are we going to put glass screens up in the public gallery in all our courts, thereby changing the very nature and the way in which we operate? We must accept the risk. It is unarguable that our action will increase the risk to people behind the screen. They are as much at risk as us, and if we isolate ourselves by an absolute equation we will increase the risk to them. We take risks when we hold our surgeries. I have no more intention of holding my surgeries behind glass than I have sitting in a Chamber behind glass because my constituents have the right to see me, not through a glass darkly that may improve the situation in some respects, but face to face both in these circumstances and here. If we vote for a permanent screen we will be contributing not to a national security but to a national neurosis. There will be no end to it.'

And so we came to vote. Theoretically, as this was a matter that related only to Parliament, it was a free vote. In fact, on the Labour side, the vote was heavily whipped. Labour Members had told me that their Whips had indicated the extreme displeasure that would be felt in Downing Street towards those who resisted the screen and thereby placed its occupant at risk. In the event, despite this pressure and inducements, the Division was lost by a mere seven votes. Overwhelmingly, it divided along Party lines. Barely twelve Conservative Members voted for the screen. The vast majority joined the Labour 'rebels' to oppose it. The vote was far more important than the sum of its parts. Thereafter, the nature of Parliament was changed beyond recognition. As I foretold, the public have become listeners and voyeurs and not participants in the reflections of their representatives. The process is, of course, deliberately symbiotic. The more the security, the greater the neurosis, and the greater the neurosis, the more willing the acceptance of totally unsubstantiated threat. The greater the sense of threat, the easier it becomes to pass and popularise legislation and measures which erode and corrode liberties that have existed for hundreds of years.

There is no better example of this neurosis than the treatment that was meted out to Walter Wolfgang at the Labour Conference of 2005. Walter and his family were wartime Jewish refugees. He joined the Labour Party at an early age and had been an active and dedicated member. As a delegate to conference in 1976 I remember him speaking from the platform on his twin passions of disarmament and import controls.

Twenty-nine years later, in 2005, this same activist, still dedicated, still loyal, physically frail at eighty-two and as much a threat to public safety as a Mozart symphony, again attended his Party's Conference. During the Foreign Secretary's speech, he suggested, vocally, that Jack Straw was being less than honest about Iraq. It was a view widely shared by hundreds in the Conference and millions outside. For this offence, Walter Wolfgang was seized by a massive, anonymous steward, physically manhandled from his own Conference and detained by police as a suspected terrorist. A nearby delegate attempted to intervene and was, himself, assaulted by another example of New Labour's finest. Hours later, Blair delivered the type of apology wholly typical of the man.

'I am sorry,' he said, 'but you must remember that I wasn't there.'

The event was not isolated. On the same day, my friend Austin Mitchell, the venerable, clever and amiable Member for Great Grimsby, had his camera snatched and the contents sanitised in order to eradicate photos of a Conference queue.

Blair's own behaviour came to reflect this prevailing neurosis. To attend Prime Minister's Questions, Blair employed three armoured vehicles and two outriders to negotiate the journey of 250 yards between Downing Street and Parliament. David Miliband, then Foreign Secretary and once a candidate for the Labour leadership, found this form of conveyance impressive.

Indeed, he suggested that the presidential armoured cortège, with its sirens and outriders, was Blair's essential hallmark and one which would entitle him to the Presidency of Europe.

In order to attend *his* first Prime Minister's Questions, David Cameron, the new Prime Minister and Leader of the Coalition, walked to the Commons. The outriders and armoured vehicles have been banished and, I suspect, the electoral benefit will be incalculable. Old Etonian and Bullingdon Club member he may be, but he walks the people's street at the people's pace. If, as an early part of this process, he moves the House of Commons to dismantle the screen that separates its deliberations from its public, he will do even more to re-establish the essential nature of British democracy.

CHAPTER 17

OF WARS 1:
THE JUST WAR

In which we discuss the Augustinian Theory of Siege and Shock and Awe with the Bishop of Oxford in Barbara Castle's sublime garden.

It was during an agreeably inebriated summer's lunch in Barbara Castle's garden that the Bishop of Oxford, Richard Harries, expounded on the Augustinian theory of siege. The context was an animated discussion about nuclear deterrence, a theory which enjoyed the bishop's support as a means to ensure peace. The guests included John and Penelope Mortimer, and the Bishop of Oxford thus found himself in a small but highly articulate minority. It was in order to buttress his argument for the humanitarian value of deterrence that he relied upon the works of St Augustine. The Augustinian theory of siege is a relatively simple concept, copied, in part, in the works of Machiavelli. It went as follows. When an invading army surrounded a city, the besieged leaders were presented with an ultimatum. Immediate surrender would have limited and generally benign consequences. The civic leaders and population would remain unharmed. They would be expected to feed and billet the invading army and provide suitable hospitality for the generals or commanders. Any misbehaviour by the invading soldiers would be strictly punished, and commercial, social and cultural life would continue undisturbed. After a brief period of rest and recuperation the invading army would move on, leaving a token presence of soldiers and administrators. There was, of course, a downside, in that the city became an unarmed vassal state. Taxes would be levied and paid to the invading power, methods of governance and administration which conflicted with the invaders' political mores would be abolished, as would individual liberties which were inappropriate to the satrap status to which the city was now consigned. The alternative was a 'no surrender' policy. If this was adopted, the siege would continue until such time that the city was successfully stormed or the inhabitants were reduced to surrender by starvation or disease. At this point, slaughter and rapine would immediately ensue. The male population would be put to the sword. The women and children, after inevitable abuse, would be taken into slavery, and the city itself would be reduced to rubble until, like Carthage, 'not one stone stood upon another'. In other words, shock and awe.

In discussion, the Bishop strongly advocated the theory of deterrence. He pointed out that it had been successfully employed by Alexander the Great (pre-Augustine) and Cromwell (post-Augustine). During Cromwell's notorious invasion of Ireland, the majority of cities surrendered when faced with the Augustinian ultimatum. The exception was Drogheda, the sacking of which remains a topical Celtic curse. The bishop deplored both war and violence, but argued that the threat of massive annihilation has always been a method whereby lives could be saved, albeit at the cost of liberty. The soundness of this analysis (which may well have been partly a formidable forensic exercise) was robustly challenged during the course of a delightful summer's afternoon in 1995 in the serenity of rural Berkshire. Much later, after sitting in Parliament through four wars, enthusiastically prosecuted by Tony Blair, I realised that the Augustinian theory was discernible in all the various ultimata that were delivered in Kosovo, Afghanistan and Iraq; namely total capitulation to demands or airborne devastation on a massive technological scale, involving all the modern military vernacular of cluster bombs, lazy dogs, bunker busters and uranium shells. Notwithstanding their overt religious piety, it is unlikely that either Blair or George Bush had considered the Augustinian theory, but its application in a modern context was pretty near faultless. The conflicts over twelve years established a predominant pattern. Identify a suitable (and suitably sized) rogue state, issue demands which cannot, in reality, be complied with; then unleash Armageddon from 28,000 feet.

At the end of the twentieth century this ancient theory of warfare became superimposed on the growing, urgent and important debate on the nature of national sovereignty and the right of other nations to intervene on humanitarian grounds. It was a debate to which I had made some contribution before my arrival in Parliament. I had corresponded on a number of occasions with the United Nations Commission on Sovereignty and Intervention – The Responsibility to Protect, set up specifically to consider this essential aspect of globalisation and the aspirations of common humanity at an international level. The old ground rules embodied in the United Nation's Charter and the Geneva Conventions were simple and stark. The sovereignty of states was sacrosanct. De facto government authority was the only benchmark. The international community was enjoined by its own rules to recognise governments that held effective control in countries, notwithstanding their odious nature and the brutal repression of their own people. Opposition to such governments and their ultimate removal was a matter for the people of that sovereign state. Intervention to relieve populations from subjugation, torture, abuse and civil strife was simply not a legal option, no matter how great the sufferings of its people.

By the millennium, after a century of ideological strife and vast totalitarian power associated with genocide and many forms of apartheid, the iron laws of sovereignty were the obvious subject of international review. This found its ultimate expression in the UN Commission – the august international body of eminent jurists and thinkers. These included, for the United Kingdom, Michael Ignatieff, with whom, ironically, I came into public conflict in Channel 4's seminal *NATO on Trial* during the Kosovo War.

The issues raised by this debate are profound. I have long believed that a structure for international intervention was possible and essential in a post-totalitarian world, acknowledging human rights to liberty and a criminal responsibility for those that abuse them. The statement is easy, the process anything but. It represents, literally, mankind's greatest challenge in the establishment of universal rights.

The iron doctrine of state sovereignty was not designed to stimulate oppression and abuse. It was designed to avert chaos and, above all, to stigmatise the intervention by the powerful into the territory of the weak on the pretext of humanitarian protection (exemplified by Hitler's invasion of the Sudetenland). The principle was underpinned in one of the rare Commons' debates on the Kosovo War, when I suffered an elegant rebuke by Alan Clark at his patrician and learned best.

In the course of the debate I had asserted my own belief in a New World Order:

> Robert Marshall-Andrews: 'We have reached, or should have reached, a time when we need to live in a new legal international framework which means we will no longer have to stand idly by wringing our hands and listening to the screams from our neighbour's house, unable to intervene because of the rules of sovereignty. My own position on the (Kosovo) war is this: unilateral action taken by NATO is more likely than anything else to defer the growth of such a

world order and will, in all probability, put back its inception for decades.'

Later, Alan Clark put the counter argument with academic precision:

'I invite my right honourable friends to consider when we think of NATO, one aspect of what is happening. The Prime Minister has said that the war is being fought for a "new internationalism". Javier Solana has said that its purpose is to establish a precedent for the "new strategic concept" of NATO, that it should be able to intervene in the international affairs of a sovereign state for humanitarian reasons. By definition, NATO never had that role when it was set up as a defensive alliance protecting the sovereign territory of its members.

'I repeat my caution to my honourable Friends on this matter. What is so insidious about that argument and that doctrine is that it replaces the old system of national legal systems creating free markets and national liberties. It is envisaged that there should be a new world order of universal human rights, with the inherent problem that a bogus notion of human rights can never provide a basis for the rule of either law or morality. Universal human rights are detached from any rootedness in either time or place; their application inevitably flails around capriciously, according to the latest whim or outrage or the latest fad or victimhood.

'Human rights are, by definition, antithetical to the concept of national sovereignty. The concept that there can be universal human rights implies that there can be a single global system of civil law, with NATO playing the role of world government or world government policemen.'

In the context of Blair's wars, involving as they did massive loss of life and incalculable damage to international stability and toleration, this moral and political debate cannot be overstated and should never be distorted. For Blair, emerging arguments for humanitarian intervention provided an essential justification for personal evangelism and vaunting belligerence.

Everything else was a tragedy of circumstance and opportunity. The ethnic cauldron of the Balkans, the resurgence of primitive and fundamentalist Islam, 9/11, George Bush and the Neo-Conservatives, and the grotesque person of Saddam Hussein, proved but the essential stages for this destructive vanity. To this dismal list may be added the natural duplicity of the New Labour administration, spin, and the abject failure of Parliament to control presidential hubris obsessed with military power. Blair's personal traits had many manifestations. One of them, among the worst, was the recitation at the beginning of Parliamentary Questions of the names of servicemen and women killed in the previous week. Distaste for this self-serving spectacle was particularly marked among those in the Commons who had themselves served in the Armed Forces. Tam Dalyell described it to me as 'sickening'. As both soldiers and parliamentarians, they knew full well that this hushed ceremony served but one cause, namely that of the Prime Minister.

A growing proportion of Parliament had opposed Blair's wars, but in the ten years of their duration the Commons was, with one exception, repeatedly denied a vote. The effect of reading the names of the dead was to create a semi-religious atmosphere in which all, perforce, were joined. The recitations also reduced the thirty minutes for PMQs and created a false climate of solidarity and approval entirely inconsistent with the critical analysis to follow. The families of the dead were given, effectively, no choice. After one particularly long recital, Tam told me that he had calculated that Churchill would have taken two days of Parliamentary Answers to read the fallen on D-Day alone. And what of the wounded? Modern battlefield medicine now ensures survival, albeit chronically and severely disabled, where historically wounds were fatal. Why are they not given parliamentary time?

The answer is, of course, entirely theatrical. For a politician like Blair, death in one of his conflicts was a glorious sacrifice. The wounded are an uncomfortable reminder of continuing pain. The dispatch box is no place for the disabled, the disfigured and the destitute.

Against this background, Blair led Britain into five conflicts of which three were 'major wars' employing large parts of British military capacity. In their cause and consequences, hundreds of soldiers were sacrificed, thousands of civilians died and hundreds of thousands were rendered homeless, helpless and destitute.

In 1997, before a single war, Blair's popularity rating throughout the country was 93 per cent. In 2009, an opinion poll found that 40 per cent of his own people thought he should be tried as a war criminal. In part this political descent was contrived by himself, in part by a small unelected, unaccountable band of acolytes (Jonathan Powell, Alastair Campbell and Sally Morgan, *et al.*) and in part by a dire alchemy with the Neo-Conservatives of America.

Blair's wars were universally a disaster. I will not try to emulate the seminal analysis in John Kampfner's *Blair's Wars,* which deserves the accolades it has received. I want to reflect on the parliamentary drama that preceded and accompanied these conflicts. At times it was difficult not to see Parliament as the chorus in Greek tragedy. We had voices, an audience and the power of commentary, but, like the wailing chorus, we were unable to stop the unfolding catastrophes in our own Parliament. Shakespearian metaphor became a recurrent theme. I always saw Blair's essential tragic flaws as those of Coriolanus (vanity and contempt) but I happily defer to a magnificent peroration by Sir Peter Tapsell which ended with his description of Britain's Prime Minister as 'more steeped in blood than any Scotsman since Macbeth'.

History may see Blair's wars as separate conflicts, meeting and merging unforeseen challenges in a changing world. It is how he would wish them to be seen. In his evidence to the Chilcot Inquiry he maintained in a carefully rehearsed reply that 9/11 had 'changed the calculus [sic] of risk'. In reality it was no such thing; 9/11 provided simply the circumstance and opportunity. The bellicose bible of the American Neo-Conservatives, 'Project for a New American Century', with its inherent global evangelism, was written ten years before al-Qaeda became a threat, let alone a reality. The dragon's teeth of Afghanistan and Iraq had been sown in the Balkans two years before the destruction of the Twin Towers.

CHAPTER 18

OF WARS 2:
THE BALKANS

*In which we record the history and cause of the Kosovo War and its
disastrous consequences – Reflect on the impotence of Parliament –
Record the advent of spin in the recording of war and the ominous
beginnings of Messianic motives for conflict.*

Of all Blair's wars, the Kosovo War should be seen as the
most dangerous. Not because it caused death (1,200 civilian fatalities is meagre compared to later wars) but because it
gave birth to gross duplicity and an enduring self-myth of a
global Messiah.

In future wars, and particularly in the case of Iraq, the myth of
the Kosovan 'success' was repeatedly and deliberately employed.
In 2005, desperate by then to justify the debacle in Iraq, Blair
told a meeting at a Labour Party Conference that 'I do not regret
ridding the world of Milosevic and I do not regret ridding the
world of Saddam Hussein.' The use of the imperial first person
had, by then, become commonplace. Of far greater significance
was the massive distortion of historical fact. Even assuming it
to be Blair's direct responsibility (rather than the United States
or the other eighteen signatories to NATO), the Kosovo War

emphatically did not 'get rid of Milosevic'. On the contrary, it reinforced his regime, his power and his ghastly authority. For eighteen months after the conclusion of the Kosovo War, Milosevic gained enhanced power and enhanced popularity. In 2000, I went to Belgrade with Alice Mahon. Our purpose was to examine the effects of the war and, in particular, the position of refugees. Our hosts were ardent opponents of the Milosevic regime. Clever, brave and articulate young doctors, they left us in no doubt that the Kosovo War had not only destroyed substantial parts of their own country and killed many civilians, but had been responsible for gravely weakening the opposition to the dictator. In these circumstances, Blair's statement 'I got rid of Milosevic' can be seen as a fine example of the debate which has always surrounded Blair's personality. Is he lying or is he mad? It is a question repeatedly asked in connection with the Iraq War and one that is difficult to answer. I have always tended towards the latter view, but, as with Caligula and Coriolanus, there is no easy reply.

The events which led to the Kosovo War were both simple and complex. The complexities lie in the wider ethnic, religious and economic conflicts inherent in the Balkans. The British Foreign Office is given to statements of '*grande sagacité*' said to be the essential blocks of British foreign policy. Of these, the maxim 'Stay out of the Balkans' was one of the most imperative. The Byzantine political complexities of this region have been notorious for centuries, but certain aspects of the break-up of Yugoslavia were relatively easy to understand if impossible to reconcile or solve. The 'Bosnian' question fell into this category. Bosnia is divided, both ethnically and religiously, between Bosnian Muslims and the Christian Bosnian Serbs. As with many Balkan conflicts, this ancient division had been exacerbated by the Second World War, the Nazi occupation and the relentless persecution of the Serbs throughout Yugoslavia. With the break up of Yugoslavia, Bosnia assumed a form of autonomy.

The army, however, had been largely comprised of Serbs, and strong links existed between the army and Serbia itself. In the resulting civil war, the Bosnian Serbs therefore maintained a significant military advantage and notorious military commanders, notably Ratko Mladic and Radovan Karadzic. The result was the brutal siege of Sarajevo, and the incarceration and massacre of civilians of which the slaughter at Srebrenica was the largest and the worst. (One of my close friends within my constituency, a magnificent socialist and consultant surgeon called John Beavis, spent the siege in Sarajevo, operating on civilian casualties from a reinforced basement. Any remote sympathy with the perpetrators of this atrocity could not possibly survive his personal testimony.) Ultimately, peace was secured by exhaustion and the brokerage of a united international community. The legacy of the conflict, however, was profound, particularly within the American administration led, in this instance, by Madeleine Albright. This powerful and formidable woman was famous for her uncompromising views on foreign policy; it was she who quoted Jorge Luis Borges's description of the Falklands War as two old bald men fighting over a comb. Her views on the Bosnian conflict were equally forthright. She deplored the failure by the international community to intervene in order to protect the Muslim community. She was particularly scornful of British efforts; once, reputedly, referring to Pauline Neville-Jones as Pauline Neville-Chamberlain. Her views were strongly expressed to President Clinton, then undergoing his own domestic difficulties in the substantial shape of Monica Lewinsky and possible impeachment. The American administration was determined that nothing resembling Bosnia should happen again and that NATO should be prepared to exercise a global role, irrespective of the United Nations, or fade into gradual inconsequence.

The historic stage was, therefore, fatally set for the escalation of civil warfare in Kosovo and the Messianic arrival of Tony Blair into the arena where, to the alarm of the Foreign Office, he was shortly to announce his own 'doctrine of international community'.

The Bosnian conflict occurred and was resolved before I entered Parliament. Politically, however, I had always favoured intervention in that country. Given the destruction of Yugoslavia, the notion of 'sovereignty' seemed a matter of doubtful legal consequence. Whatever one's views on the emerging philosophy of sovereignty and intervention, Bosnia was a special case. Its citizens had no recognizable state to which they could look for protection or, indeed, by whom they could be persecuted. Intervention, I considered, was a matter of international responsibility.

Ironically, Kosovo was completely different. Geographically it is a tiny area, barely larger than Yorkshire. Historically it has always been a part of Serbia and, indeed, is referred to in Serbian mythology as the 'jewel in the Serbian crown'. It has two main ethnic communities representing the greater states upon which it borders. The larger part of the population is Albanian (predominantly Muslim) and the smaller part Serbian (predominantly Christian). There was, however, within Kosovo a long tradition of tolerance and peaceful coexistence. Pristina, the capital, was traditionally a multi-ethnic community. In most of the country, Christian and Muslim lived side by side, as they had for centuries. In 1998, ethnic strife and violence was largely confined to the north in the Drenica valley. The Serbian government was represented on the ground by special forces and policemen. The opposition was represented by the Liberation Army, the KLA. Apart from the Muslim religion, the KLA bore no resemblance whatsoever to the Muslim communities in Bosnia. The KLA had been designated by America as a terrorist organisation and controlled the massive trade in narcotics which provided one of Albania's main sources of income. It was a ruthless, well-organised force, perfectly capable of carrying out its own atrocities, which it did in the summer of 1998 by murdering forty

Serbian policemen, an exercise it was to repeat in January 1999. Retaliation by Serbian special forces was wholly disproportionate and in one attack on a village, forty-five civilians, all young men, were killed. The civilian atrocities, however terrible, were insignificant by the standards of the Bosnian conflict but were a sufficient catalyst for war. NATO, on behalf of the international community, prepared itself to intervene in a Balkan conflict which had, in reality, been resolved in Bosnia over a year before.

Fuelled by an extraordinary mixture of guilt and a new sense of international evangelism, NATO's massive armaments, led by the US Air Force, prepared to exact reparation. A peace conference was called at the French town of Rambouillet. NATO, led by Robin Cook, placed before Milosevic the terms by which he had to abide in order to prevent the imminent onslaught. The terms were, as Henry Kissinger observed, such that no national leader could possibly sign them. They provided for NATO troops to 'manoeuvre, billet, bivouac, train or carry out search or inspection anywhere in Serbia'. Milosevic refused, and on 24 March 1999, the aerial bombardment began. Parliament had been informed of this by the Prime Minister on 22 March. There was no consultation, no debate and, effectively, no warning. British Tornadoes joined American counterparts. On the first night of bombing, forty targets were identified. A limited number of targets were allocated to the RAF. In order to avoid any NATO casualties, the bombers were flying at 20,000 feet and missed every one.

Parliament was informed that the bombing campaign was anticipated to be short. Official estimates were said to be seventy-two hours, a punishment exercise in order to induce capitulation; the Augustinian theory of siege with the assistance of cruise missiles. Capitulation did not occur. Reports from Belgrade indicated that the Serbian population was rallying behind Milosevic. Without any reference to the British Parliament, the number of targets was expanded. Reservoirs, bridges, oil refineries, hospitals, state buildings and Serbian embassies within Belgrade, all became legitimate targets. In these early stages, it revealed one of the most extraordinary characteristics of modern warfare, namely pinpoint accuracy. On my subsequent visit to Belgrade, my guides pointed out blackened bombsites where buildings had been removed, like extracted teeth, from the urban landscapes. There were hundreds of them, meticulously and carefully destroyed in an airborne onslaught which lasted for eighty days; 36,000 sorties, flown by 720 aircraft.

The effect in Kosovo itself was devastating. On the borders of Macedonia, NATO had mobilised a substantial army, which did precisely nothing. The Serbian Army was assembled through-out Kosovo in order to meet the invading troops. Deprived of a military enemy, the soldiers were, nonetheless, able to watch the vapour trails of aircraft and missiles flying above their heads with the aim of destroying the infrastructure of their own country. Inevitably, they turned upon the Albanian population whom they blamed for the conflict, notwithstanding the apparent toler-ance of centuries. Within days, a trickle of refugees had become a massive and unstoppable flood. An estimated 850,000 civilians crossed the border with Macedonia and camped on the Mace-donian hillsides. The world's press now had the ethnic cleans-ing which they required. John Kampfner reports that one of Blair's closest colleagues told him 'our whole policy was saved by the refugees. Milosevic provided the evidence to prove the case for the bombing.' The strategy of painless, high-level bombing created its own disasters. On 14 April, American F-16s, flying at over 16,000 feet, bombed a refugee convoy. More than seventy Kosovan Albanians, whose village had already been burnt, were themselves burnt in the firestorm. In Parliament, the mood became increasingly hostile to the war. The demand for a debate, both from within and outside the Government, became relent-less. Ministers began to panic. I met two junior ministers in the Tea Room talking openly of resignation.

Meanwhile, information denied to Parliament was being propagated at an extraordinary level by NATO itself. This was done on the television by a gentleman called Jamie Shea, 'a NATO spokesman'. Several of my constituents drew the immediate distinction between this conflict and the Falklands War. During the Falklands campaign, information was issued through the BBC by a gentleman called Ian McDonald. He was a civil servant who must have been chosen for his utterly impassive, bespectacled face and his ability to deliver any news in a monotone which moved not a semi-quaver to accompany tragedy or victory, however black or glorious. At the end of the campaign he revealed himself to be a perfectly affable and genial person, who told his interviewer that he had deliberately taken the decision never to portray any emotion. What was important, he said, was the unvarnished truth, devoid of emotion.

None of these presentation problems applied to Mr Shea. An employee of NATO, his assessment of the war was inevitably partisan and became ever more optimistic. 'We were,' he said, 'degrading the Milosevic war machine.' 'Actual' figures appeared from NATO, including the destruction of a hundred Serbian tanks. Following the war, official American intelligence put the total number at fourteen.

On other occasions, broadcasts and announcements varied between farce and tragedy. On 7 May, an American cruise missile hit the Chinese Embassy in Belgrade, killing a number of Chinese non-combatants. NATO's immediate public response was to place the blame on Serbian double agents who had deliberately misdirected the intelligence used for cruise missiles. This ludicrous postulation was subsequently reversed when it was revealed that the Americans were using a seven-year-old map. Worse still was the assurance given during one of the NATO broadcasts that 'NATO would target military targets only' (12 April). To this was added the assurance that 'television and radio towers are only struck if they are integrated into military facilities' and that there was no policy to 'strike television or radio transmitters as such'. Twelve days later, quite deliberately and without warning, NATO bombed the main television station in Belgrade, killing a number of innocent civilians. Nor were the announcements restricted to factual analysis. Gradually they took on a more Orwellian ring. NATO was the representative of democracy and this war was, itself, a war for democratic principles.

And still, in Britain, there was no definitive parliamentary debate and no vote. In order to make up for the parliamentary deficit, Channel 4 staged a debate on the war entitled *NATO on Trial*. I appeared for the prosecution, together with Germaine Greer. Michael Ignatieff led for the defence. The television audience ultimately convicted NATO by a substantial majority. However, I retained the recording as a fond memory of a rare opportunity to cross-examine NATO's representative in the person of Mr Shea. For the purposes of this memoir I allow myself the indulgence of a short verbatim extract:

Jon Snow: I would like, please, for Bob Marshall-Andrews for the prosecution to cross-examine.
Bob Marshall-Andrews: Mr Shea, you work for NATO, do you not?
Jamie Shea: I do indeed.
BMA: You work for NATO, you are its spokesperson? You are accountable to NATO?
JS: Yes.
BMA: We have heard many times from Michael Ignatieff and others, that one of the problems with NATO is, and one of the reasons why this war is being conducted in the way that it is, is that you are answerable to nineteen democratic states. Do you agree with that?
JS: Yes, and I think that is a source of strength.
BMA: Yes, nineteen democratic states and, no doubt, you would say that this is a war for democracy. Yes?
JS: I think it is a war for human rights.

BMA: Yes. Would you mind explaining why the House of Commons in this country, with its members that represent people sitting in this hall, have been denied on four separate occasions the right to vote on this war?

JS: That is a question not for NATO; that is a question for constitutional procedures in the United Kingdom and I have no say over that. Let me, however, state that many NATO countries where constitutional arrangements are different, such as in Germany – the German Bundestag and other parliaments have, overwhelmingly, voted in favour of this action and continue to do so.

BMA: Can you answer my question? Why in Britain have we, I, been denied the right to vote on this war? Can you answer this question?

JS: This is not for me to say. I am a NATO representative.

BMA: Exactly. That is the answer I wanted. You are responsible to nobody except NATO, which is not responsible to anybody. Yes?

On 18 May 1999, the Commons was granted the right to a debate but not to a vote. In the event, the debate was outstanding but the absence of a vote, despicable. It did, however, have moments which I shall remember, including the last speech of Alan Clark, already referred to in the context of sovereignty. He concluded with a statement on patriotism which, as I told him afterwards, defined my own position with a clarity I would gladly repeat:

'If NATO continues to behave in its present reckless, indiscriminate and brutal manner – devoid, it seems, of any comprehensible, tactical plan – which is greatly separated from the original concepts under which the organisation was set up and from the deference that it originally owed, and should owe, to the Security Council of the United Nations and the resolutions thereof, the alliance will have been gravely damaged. The outcome of its activities will be uncertain and probably give rise to disappointment, disillusion and much human suffering. ...

'I know ... that the anxiety that is felt in this Chamber is an echo of the anxiety that is felt throughout the country as to what is being done in our name and in the name of our country.

'I wholly reject any suggestion that to say these things is unpatriotic in some way. Is it unpatriotic to remind the House of Commons that members of our armed forces enlist to defend British people and British interests – not to kill non-combatants? Is it unpatriotic to point out – as I have been reproached for doing in this Chamber – that, where non-combatants have been killed, it is not, and never has been, the fault or the responsibility of our armed forces? It is the responsibility of those with whom they are currently associated.

'Those distinctions – that relating to global conduct and the concept to NATO and that relating to the proper function and role of our armed forces and the debt that we all owe them, and which I gladly pay – are matters that, at all times during this hideous and hateful experience, the House of Commons must have at the forefront of its mind.'

In the end, after eighty days of siege and bombardment, the Serbian War was brought to an end by the intervention of the Russians, who brokered a treaty. By it, NATO withdrew from Kosovo and relinquished its claims to occupy either Kosovo or Serbia. A United Nations force was to be placed within Kosovo and a conference on Kosovo's future was to be inaugurated. The Serbian war machine (said to have been totally degraded) lost just fourteen tanks, nineteen APCs (armoured personnel carriers) and twenty artillery pieces. The damage to Serbian infrastructure – its roads, bridges and public buildings – was colossal. The Danube was blocked and polluted for years, and there was widespread loss of agricultural land. Milosevic was hailed as a hero by his own people. Kosovo itself was divided into armed and fortified regions which remain to this day. In military terms the war was a total failure; but it was worse than that. It had created an appetite. During the later days of the conflict, Blair had walked the hillsides of Macedonia, resplendent in a pink shirt, 'passing among' the refugees which his own war had created, and spoke movingly about the wretchedness that he saw – apparently indifferent to its true cause, namely the relentless bombing he had ordered.

It created an appetite and an alibi. It was to form the repeated justification for a moral crusade against Afghanistan and Iraq and the abstraction of terrorism. The refugees hailed him as a saviour, which was hardly surprising, as he was their immediate hope of redemption. They did not know that encouraging the Messianic self-regard was the worst thing they could have done for future world stability. The nature of the conflict (aerial bombardment from 20,000 feet) also added its own terrible stimulus. During the course of the bombardment, General Wesley Clark observed: 'Milosevic must have thought he was fighting God.' Little did he know.

CHAPTER 19

OF WARS 3:
THE GREAT GAME

In which we remember 9/11 and the inevitable march to the unwinnable war – Reflect on the majestic impotence of parliamentary debate – Recollect the joy of Mr Donald Rumsfeld as 1 million 'rations' are dropped by American bombers, and witness the false dawn of liberation.

I watched the destruction of the Twin Towers in my constituency office, where we had spent the morning occupied by the closure of a primary school in a deprived area of Chatham. I knew the school well. It had a fine head, was full of bright, well-behaved children, and was a pleasure to visit. Four thousand miles away, on the morning of 11 September 2001, the President of the United States was sitting in a primary school listening to reading from similar children in America. The news of the attack was whispered quietly into his ear during the breathless recital of childhood fiction. His reaction, or lack of it, has been roundly condemned and mocked, not least by Michael Moore, in his blockbuster polemic, *Fahrenheit 9/11*. I have always considered this mockery to be unfair. I yield to no one in my loathing and contempt for the former President of the United States and his ghastly administration. Together they presided over death and destruction on a massive scale, introduced systematic torture into the American system of law, and presided over the darkest period of American history. But the classroom criticism is unfair. Whatever its mental acuity, the brain is numbed by news of catastrophe. As I watched the Towers fall, I suffered the same anaesthetic. I found myself relentlessly and silently reciting the words of Doctor Faustus – 'And burned the topless towers of Ilium'. It was only later, when the American bombs rained on Afghanistan, that I realised its significance:

> 'Was this the face that launched a thousand ships
> And burned the topless towers of Ilium?'

The Commons was recalled. I had no intention of trying to speak and sat next to Mark Fisher in the public gallery. Blair was at his deceptive best. The speeches on all sides were exemplary. Calm, sombre, responsible (with the sole exception of Dennis Skinner who attempted to ignite the class war by enlisting the sacrifice of the New York firefighters and contrasting the pusillanimous behaviour of George Bush). This contribution was required neither by the firefighters nor by Dennis. I expect he regrets it.

Later, over tea, we were filled with a dark sense of foreboding. We all knew then that the atrocity of 9/11 had created a massive *casus belli* on a vast, indiscriminate scale. However innocent of its perpetration, no perceived enemy would escape its consequences. Provocation on this scale would have tested the wisest of American statesmen. The reaction to it required a Truman, a Roosevelt or even an Eisenhower.

Instead America had George W. Bush and the Neo-Conservatives, the authors of the 'Project for a New American Century' and the high priests of American military might.

Across the Atlantic, but 'shoulder to shoulder', was a British

Prime Minister, fresh from the hillsides of Macedonia, gripped by the fervour of moral righteousness and with the 'hand of history on his shoulder'. It could scarcely have been worse. My sense of gloom deepened when I listened to Blair's conference speech days later.

'The kaleidoscope,' he said, 'has been shaken. The pieces are in flux. Soon they will settle again. Before they do, let us re-order this world around us.'

Clichéd and meaningless the metaphor may be, but it reflected a form of government already causing alarm and despair – vaunting, vainglorious and quixotic. And then into the speech came Africa. This giant, complex and wonderful continent received two sentences: *'The state of Africa is a scar on the conscience of the world. But if the world has a community focused on it, we can heal it; but if we don't, it will become deeper and angrier.'*

At the time, I had spent years promoting conservation and outreach projects in East Africa with the aim of protecting the environment and improving education and health. This was the first time I can remember that Blair acknowledged the problem's existence. It formed a transparent antidote for a conference likely to be hostile to an open allegiance with George Bush. It was, of course, mere cant, but I can remember thinking firmly, on behalf of the Dark Continent, 'Please leave us alone.'

Blair's speech to the Labour Party Conference was, in effect, a declaration of war on Afghanistan; the first time a Labour Party Conference has been used for such a purpose. In front of a highly partisan audience he did it very well:

'This is a battle with only one outcome – our victory not theirs. Be in no doubt, Bin Laden and his people organised this atrocity. Taliban aid and abet him. He will not desist from further acts of terror. They will not stop helping him. Yes, we should try to understand the causes of terrorism, but let there be no moral ambiguity about this; nothing could ever justify the events of 11 September and it is to turn justice on its head to pretend that it could.'

In the cold light of 9/11, he added these prophetic words: 'The conflict will not be the end. We will not walk away as the outside world has done so many times before.'

In the ensuing two weeks, until 4 October, the Labour Government's Cabinet met only once. There was no formal or substantive discussion on the imminent act of war. Adopting the invertebrate pose for which they were to become notorious, the members of Blair's Cabinet ran through a domestic agenda, smiled at photographers as they arrived at Downing Street, and otherwise shut up. On 4 October, Parliament was recalled in an emergency session. War was, effectively, announced. There was no vote or debate. I attempted to speak and failed, as did a number of the more usual suspects. The basis for war had been set out in a dossier prepared on 20 September by Alastair Campbell with the assistance of John Scarlett, Head of the Secret Intelligence Service (SIS). The document itself was based on sound intelligence, factual and, in its assessment, accurate. It was remarkably effective, and formed a direct and unhappy precedent for the dodgy and duplicitous documents that were to precede the war in Iraq.

I took the initial and cautious view (as did many of my colleagues) that the legal and moral case for intervention in Afghanistan was sound. By then, there was no serious doubt that 9/11 was the work of Osama Bin Laden and al-Qaeda. Apprehension and arrest of those responsible for the atrocity was a legitimate exercise of extra-territorial power, and demands to the Taliban regime for Bin Laden's extradition, futile though they were, proved sufficient for international legality.

Just as Parliament was provided with no vote, it was also provided with no details. Different ministers announced different rules and objectives for war, indicating clearly total obscurity at

Cabinet level. The Prime Minister's central message had more clarity, which must now be appreciated with the priceless benefit of hindsight. The war was, emphatically, not about regime change. The Taliban, albeit loathsome, were not the primary target. Their crime was to harbour and succour the fugitive Bin Laden. Police arrest, not punishment, was the point of the exercise and, it was implied, the operation would be surgically swift and successful.

This total fiction was maintained for barely seven days. Within that time it became clear to us in Parliament and, more slowly, to the British people, that this brutal exercise was to be pursued on a Kosovan model. The similarities were stark. No American or British troops were to be risked in open combat, and ground fighting was to be carried out by the Northern Alliance.

This rough grouping of warlords bore a distinct resemblance to the Kosovan KLA. As with the KLA, their primary stock-in-trade was drugs, and they did a fine line in terror and oppression. One of their premier members, General Dostum, had his own brand of criminal justice and trial which involved attaching prisoners to tank tracks prior to their manoeuvring over rough ground. For this friendly alliance, the full weight of American airpower was to be deployed, assisted on a minor scale by their British counterparts in the RAF. As with Kosovo, bombing was to proceed at extreme high altitude, reducing the risk of military casualities to, effectively, zero. As I pointed out in the House of Commons by a simple (almost algebraic) equation, this transferred risk from combatants in the air to non-combatants on the ground, and within a matter of days, the inevitable collateral damage formed a familiar litany of excuse and regret. Protestations by the British Government that this campaign did not represent a punishment beating were quickly dispelled by the American administration itself. After three days of bombing, Donald Rumsfeld complained bitterly and publicly at the absence of targets. This deficit was apparently cured, which enabled him to tell a cheering business dinner in Chicago that American planes had now flown 1,800 sorties and dropped 'one million rations'. 'Rations' included any form of explosive, from bunker busters and lazy dogs at one end to cluster bombs at the other. Day after day, Afghanistan, one of the poorest and most backward countries on earth, was being systematically bombed into the Stone Age as punishment for an unspeakable crime committed and directed by Saudi Arabians on American soil. In the Commons, the Government bowed to demands for a debate. The first took place on 16 October 2001.

As a rare acknowledgement of the trouble which we had caused, the parliamentary opposition to the conflict was significantly represented on the Speaker's list. As with so many such debates, the Press Gallery was virtually empty and the media reacted with indifference. In the absence of a vote this is perhaps unsurprising.

I remember, in particular, the beginning of Hugh Robertson's speech. One of the more thoughtful and able Tories, he quietly established the authority of his previous career:

> 'I start by adding my support for the Government's handling of the crisis thus far. I want to speak not merely to do that but because I believe we have reached a turning point in the conflict. I ask to speak not because I have any great history of a moralist or the legal expertise of some Labour members but simply because when this country last went to war I went as a young soldier of 28 years old. I want to bring some of those experiences to bear on the debate.'

Long after that debate, Hugh and I discussed our differing views. On one thing we are both agreed. The economic and humanitarian construction of Afghanistan has proved unobtainable, and his wise admonition that 'it is far easier to start a conflict than to bring it to a successful conclusion' was, thereafter, totally and fatally ignored. Immediately after Hugh's speech, I was called to put the opposition case. It earned me the opprobrium of both the Government and many of my backbench colleagues and for that reason I quote it in part and, in doing so, enlist the support of hindsight:

Robert Marshall-Andrews (Medway): 'There are, one perceives, three leaders in the world who believe that the bombing of Afghanistan – including the bombing of the pitiful remains of its infrastructure and the death of hundreds, perhaps thousands of civilians – is in the interests of their cause and should be part of their strategy. Those three leaders are first, of course, the President of the United States; secondly, the Prime Minister of the United Kingdom and perhaps those in NATO who support him; and thirdly, Osama Bin Laden himself.

'No one should doubt that the psychotic international criminal knows full well – no doubt, it is part of his plan – that with every single bomb which drops on Afghan soil and with every single cluster bomb or bunker buster that is dropped on a defenceless enemy from 30,000 feet, we sow the dragon's teeth. As a classical mythology, from that soil will emerge not our warriors but warriors who will fight for Osama Bin Laden and al-Qaeda and whose numbers will multiply. Above all, they will be armed with the hatred of the United States which brought them into being. That fact is not lost on our fragile and uneasy allies and neighbours in Pakistan and Saudi Arabia, who know and have said that the words and actions of the so-called coalition and America have proved collectively to be the biggest recruiting tent for terrorism since 11 September that one could possibly dread.

'We began by announcing a war, first, on terrorism. That is an absurdity, as one cannot make war on an abstract noun, although the President of the United States attempts to make war on most forms of syntax. As one cannot make war on an abstract noun, we are told we are at war with Osama Bin Laden, which endows him with precisely the status that he seeks. From being a criminal, he has become a warrior, and he will move on to become a martyr.'

I was followed by George Galloway. George glories in his reputation as political rough trade. But in his day, he was one of the finest orators in the House and, for this speech, duly received the Spectator Award. Two parts, in particular, deserve to be engraved on any book of contemporary history:

'If this conflict stretches – as it seems it must – through a difficult winter with large numbers of casualties through hunger and other reasons, there is a real danger that Pakistan will be tipped into what I call a Talibanisation of its politics. I do not need to remind the House that a Talibanised Pakistan will be a nuclear-armed Pakistan.

'This will be my final point. This war is being waged on the wrong target. The attack on 11 September had nothing to do with the Afghan people. None of the terrorists who attacked America were Afghans. As my hon. Friend, Tam Dalyell, said, the attack was planned from European and North American bases. The Afghan people have been hijacked by the Afghan/Arab formations of extremists, paid for by Saudi Arabia during the war against the Najiibullah Government, armed with American weapons and, as I said, even trained in our own country. It is the Afghan/Arab terrorists who flew out of the swamp of grievance. It is not the Taliban who are shielding Bin Laden, it is the other way round. Bin Laden's forces are the only organised force in the whole country with money and the logical ability to run themselves as a quasi-state. So to pound mercilessly the civilian population of Afghanistan is morally grotesque. To expect to keep international opinion on our side with the equivalent of Mike Tyson in a ring with a five-year-old child, beating it mercilessly, round after round, is ridiculous beyond words. If we leave morals aside and talk openly only of efficacy, we see the real danger of what we are doing.'

There were less memorable speeches and interventions. A (then) Labour backbencher called Jim Murphy demanded to know why we were not strategically bombing the poppy fields which comprised the economy of the Taliban and Afghanistan. In doing so, he proved a collective ignorance of the size of Afghanistan, the size of the cultivation of the heroin poppy, the political and economic effects on an impoverished community, the elementary laws of supply and demand, and the environmental catastrophe caused by the incendiary bombing of agricultural land. Apart from those drawbacks, as they say, his contribution was fine. It will surprise no student of New Labour politics that he was destined to advance swiftly through Blair's Government into the Foreign Office itself and, thereafter, into the Cabinet.

Until the end of October, the war and the bombing continued remorselessly. It did so with no democratic mandate from the British people and no vote from their Parliament. On 1 November, we formed a small non-party group under the redoubtable leadership of Tam Dalyell, Father of the House, old Etonian, former Guardsman and tireless campaigner for truth in war. We decided upon a procedural device designed not to provide a definitive vote but to draw attention to the absence of such a process. The motion was defeated by 373 votes to thirteen. The thirteen 'rebels' formed a strange, eclectic and eccentric group and some of us were far from friends. Now, however, as the Afghan disaster reaches its final and bloody phase, I record this little list with a sad sense of nostalgia: Abbott, Corbyn, Dalyell, Galloway, Jones (Lynne), Lloyd, Marshall-Andrews, McDonnell, Price, Robertson (Angus), Simpson (Alan), Weir, Williams (Hywel) and Wood.

On 7 November 2001, under the protective cover of the greatest air force in the world, the Northern Alliance entered Kabul. Immediate victory was claimed for the coalition. The Taliban, it was said, had been routed and destroyed. Any political reticence about regime change was now expressly banished.

Triumphal reports were given to Parliament, and heavily barbed comment was showered on the heads of those who had opposed the march for democracy and freedom. This political venom was particularly notable among some of my women colleagues on or around the junior Government benches. The 'liberation' of the capital was accompanied by pictures of a group of women joyfully tearing off and discarding their black burkas. This joyous scene had, it subsequently appeared, been designed and set up by camera teams from *News International*. They were, no doubt, operating under express instructions to deliver the strongest possible message of female emancipation. 'Katy from Kabul' as one of my colleagues remarked.

The parliamentary effects of Afghanistan were swiftly subsumed into the greater catastrophe of Iraq. But for many of us, on both sides of the Commons, who opposed the war it was an uncomfortable time in Parliament.

As I write this memoir, a new Foreign Secretary has announced a timetable for withdrawal from Afghanistan, nine years after the 'fall' of Kabul and the deaths of over 300 British servicemen and women in the hostile terrain of Helmand. The wisdom of setting a timetable for ultimate failure must be a matter for question. I share a widespread and justified admiration for the British Armed Forces. It is not the blind adulation of the *Sun* or the dispatch box, and I do not seek to justify or mitigate the violent death of prisoners in British hands. On Afghanistan I feel no sense of vindication, let alone satisfaction. We were right that the war would prove a catastrophe and I regret that we were. It is possible that a massive investment of money and civilian effort could have transformed the face of Afghanistan. I doubt it but it was, in any event, never a possibility. The Project for the New American Century is not based on philanthropy or tolerance. Unhappily, in 2001, the dire consequences of its implementation by the government of George Bush and his British supporters were only just beginning.

CHAPTER 20

OF WARS 4:
IRAQ

In which we consider the nature of the Neo-Conservative admin-istration of George W. Bush – Record the Downing Street memo of July 2002 and the duplicity and deceit which led us remorse-lessly to war – Record the parliamentary battles which narrowly failed to avert catastrophe – Analyse the extraordinary conduct of the Attorney General and the pusillanimous behaviour of Cabinet and lament the continued deliberate failure to appoint any inquiry with the means or ability to investigate the greatest disaster of British foreign policy and the immeasurable suffering it has caused.

On 26 January 1998, eighteen American politicians wrote to President Clinton in these unequivocal terms:

'We are writing to you because we are convinced that current American policy towards Iraq is not succeeding and we may soon face a threat in the Middle East, more serious than we have known since the end of the Cold War. In your up-coming State of the Union address you have an opportu-nity to chart a clear and determined recourse for meeting this threat. We urge you to seize that opportunity and to enunciate a new strategy that will secure the interests of the US and our friends and allies around the world. That strategy should aim, above all, at the removal of Saddam Hussein's regime from power. We stand ready to offer our full support in this difficult and necessary endeavour.'

After dealing with the military threat of Saddam Hussein and the possibility of military weapons of mass destruction, the letter continues:

'We urge you to articulate this aim and turn your administration's attention to implementing a strategy of removing Saddam's regime from power. This will require a complement of diplomatic power and political and military efforts. Although we are fully aware of the dangers and difficulties in implementing this policy, we believe the dangers of failing to do so are far greater. We believe the US has the authority under existing UN resolutions to take the necessary steps, including military steps to protect our vital interests in the Gulf. In any case, American policy cannot continue to be crippled by a misguided insistence on unanimity in the UN Security Council.'

The authors of this document included Richard Pearl, Donald Rumsfeld and Paul Wolfowitz, a group of Republican politicians known generally in Washington as 'the Crazies'. They were also responsible for the 'Project for a New American Century', the most bellicose statement of military politics by any nation since the Second World War.

In 2000, George Bush Jnr became the 43rd President of the United States and set about forming a government. His political advisors and his most senior officers of State were drawn directly from the ranks of 'the Crazies' whose early actions, such as immediate withdrawal from the Kyoto Protocol on climate change, signalled their intention to proceed precisely in accordance with their established political credo.

The letter of 1998 should have been well known to the British Ministerial Committee on Intelligence by May 2002. I am confident of this for two reasons: firstly, the views expressed within the letter were obviously of profound importance when considering American policy towards Iraq and, secondly, because I sent an unacknowledged letter to the Secretary of the Committee in May 2002 enclosing the document. I say, *should have known*, because it has subsequently transpired that, in the whole of the build-up to the Iraq War, the Committee did not meet on a single occasion.

Years after the Crazies sent their portentous letter to President Clinton, a group of British men and women met to consider Iraq. The meeting was recorded in a memorandum which was headed 'secret and strictly personal'. It was drafted by Matthew Rycroft, Foreign Policy Aide to Downing Street. The minute, by way of memorandum, was sent to David Manning, then the Prime Minister's closest advisor. Copies were sent to those who had been present at this strictly secret meeting who included the Defence Secretary (Geoff Hoon), the Attorney General (Lord Goldsmith), Sir Richard Wilson (Cabinet Secretary), John Scarlett (Joint Intelligence Committee), Francis Richards (GCHQ), Sir Michael Boyce (Chief of Defence Staff), Jonathan Powell and Sally Morgan (the Prime Minister's personal appointees), Alastair Campbell (Press and Media Secretary) and the Prime Minister, Tony Blair. The meeting received a report from Sir Richard Dearlove. Dearlove, known as 'C', was the Head of British Security and he reported on the recent talks he had concluded in Washington. His report was as follows:

'There was a perceptible shift in attitude. Military action was now seen as inevitable. Bush wanted to remove Saddam Hussein through military action, justified by the resumption of terrorism and WMD, but the intelligence and facts were being fixed around the policy. The NSC [National Security

Council] had no patience with the UN route and no enthusiasm for publishing material on the Iraq regime's record. There was little discussion in Washington on the aftermath after military action.'

The date of this meeting was 23 July 2002. The veracity of the minute has never been questioned. It was published on 1 May 2005, by the *Sunday Times* to whom it had been leaked.

As I have subsequently said on numerous occasions in Parliament, when the issue of an Iraq Inquiry has been raised, not one single word of Sir Richard Dearlove's report was ever placed before Parliament or, through Parliament, to the British people. On the contrary, Parliament on numerous occasions was told precisely the reverse of what it contained. Indeed, the extent of the deceit involved may be measured against replies given by Blair in the House of Commons on 24 September 2002, barely eight weeks after the 'secret' meeting. During the course of his statement, he said:

'As for precipitate action, I do not believe the United States is interested, any more than ourselves.'

Later, an exchange took place between Blair and Tony Wright, the MP for Cannock Chase:

Tony Wright: 'If a strategic choice opens up between international action to keep Saddam in his box and unilateral American action to destroy that box, what choice should we make?'

The Prime Minister: 'We should make sure – I hope that is what we have been trying to do – that the United States and the international community are working to the same agenda and I believe that they are.'

When I read the *Sunday Times* on 1 May 2005, I immediately called up my Hansard to check my memory of the statement and questions of 24 September 2002, which was also the parliamentary 'launch' of the now notorious '45 minute' dossier. Armed with both, in the following week I spoke to Graham Allen, whose inspired organisation of the parliamentary anti-war group came agonisingly close to defeating the war on the floor of the House of Commons. We speculated on the potential effect of a truthful answer at that stage. Can you imagine, we asked ourselves, the reaction of the House of Commons and the country had the Prime Minister added the truthful statement, 'I must, however, inform the House that our best intelligence is that America believes that the war is inevitable and is fixing the intelligence around the facts'? Had he done so, Britain would not have gone to war in Iraq.

Instead, the illusion of a potentially peaceful solution was maintained to the very brink of conflict. On 10 March 2003, Jack Straw, in the course of a statement to the House, said:

'There is no reason whatever why, within a matter of days, Iraq cannot indicate clearly its desire fully and actively to co-operate. There is no reason at all. I profoundly hope that the Iraqi regime will, even at this late stage, seize the chance to disarm peacefully. The only other peaceful alternative would be for Saddam Hussein to heed the calls of a number of Arab leaders and go into exile.'

On 25 February 2003, the Prime Minister had repeated the piety of 24 September:

'I hope most people do believe that even now he could disarm. I detest his regime. Most people do – but, even now, he could save it by complying with the UN's demand. Even now we are prepared to go the extra step to achieve disarmament peacefully.'

In the war debate itself, on 18 March 2003, hours before shock and awe was unleashed on the Iraqi capital, the Prime Minister intoned the same litany:

> 'If Saddam meets these tests we will extend the work programme of the inspectors. If he does not meet these tests, we take action.'

Throughout 2002 and 2003, I had bitterly opposed the war, both inside and outside Parliament. By then, I had reached the stage where I instinctively disbelieved every word or any assertion relating to war made by the Prime Minister. I had also been invited by Channel 4 to prosecute in the *War on Terrorism on Trial* which was broadcast on 8 September 2002. One of my principal witnesses was Sir Michael Quinlan, one of the most distinguished and respected Permanent Secretaries at the Ministry of Defence and co-author with Charles Guthrie of the definitive *Just War*. His opposition to the concept of the war was calm, lucid and devastating. I still have the formal witness statement he provided and which I used for the basis of his evidence. One conclusion has proved almost unbearably prescient:

> 'The doctrine of just war rests on centuries of reasoned reflection and underlies much of the modern law of war. Attacking Iraq would be deeply questionable against several of its tests such as just cause, proportionality and right authority. If further strengthening containment be thought necessary, there are ways to achieve that; the international community could declare that Iraqi use of biological or chemical weapons would be treated unequivocally as a crime against humanity.'

Probably as a result of his evidence, the studio audience voted overwhelmingly to condemn the prosecution of the 'war on terror' in the context of Iraq. At the reception after the programme, I asked Sir Michael to consider the existence of Weapons of Mass Destruction. After a moment's reflection he said:

> 'I have no doubt that he has had some nasty stuff. Whether he still has it I consider to be extremely doubtful. It is quite inconceivable that he retains the means to deliver it.'

I met this brilliant and scholarly man on a number of occasions before his tragic death in February 2009. When I reminded him once of our conversation, he smiled disarmingly and said: 'Ah yes, but I was wrong, wasn't I? He didn't have anything at all.'

Ironically, soon after our conversation, I experienced my only moment of serious and alarming doubt. This occurred during the Prime Minister's statement of 24 September, to which I have already referred. Although the intelligence report (the first dossier) was published on that day, there had been no time for Members of Parliament to consider or digest its content. During the course of his statement, the Prime Minister uttered his now notorious analysis. Speaking of the report, he said:

> 'It concludes that Iraq has chemical and biological weapons, that Saddam has continued to produce them, that he has existing and active military plans for the use of chemical and biological weapons which can be activated within 45 minutes, including against his own Shia population, and that he is actively trying to acquire nuclear weapons capability.'

Sitting barely 10 feet away from the Prime Minister, I experienced a sense of shock. Was there really intelligence that Saddam had 'existing and active military plans for the use of chemical and biological weapons'? Equally was there intelligence that they could be 'activated within *45 minutes*'?

Ultimately, publication to the Butler Committee of the actual intelligence revealed Blair's statement to the Commons as being misleading to the point of deception.

The words 'existing' and 'active' do not appear in the intelligence analysis. Instead, we find the phrase 'intelligence indicates that as part of Iraq's military planning, Saddam is willing to use chemical and biological weapons'. Intelligence was, of course, unnecessary for this purpose as Saddam had already done so. As to *future active planning*, there was silence. In addition, the intelligence assessment indicates that 'Saddam attaches great importance to the possession of chemical and biological weapons which he regards as the *basis for Iraqi regional power*. He believes that respect for Iraq lies in the possession of these weapons and the missiles capable of delivering them.'

Even the most simple strategic mind (such as my own) can immediately appreciate the distinction between 'existing and active military plans for the use' and the possession of weapons to achieve status.

Nonetheless, sitting in the House of Commons and hearing these chilling words, I experienced a real spasm of self-doubt. Were my constituents really in danger of massive death and destruction at a 45 minutes' notice? How could I responsibly oppose the war in those circumstances? When I finally considered the dossier, my feelings of doubt vanished and were replaced not only by scepticism and disbelief, but by a real sense of anger that the susceptibilities of the public should be manipulated with such arrogance and contempt. When delivered at the dispatch box, it was, as with so many of Blair's pronouncements, horribly credible, and the press reacted accordingly.

In the excellent Tricycle Theatre production on the trial of Tony Blair, entitled *Called to Account*, I was asked the question by both the prosecuting and defence 'counsel' whether I considered the Prime Minister was being dishonest or lying? The answer that I gave is one that I have maintained on many occasions since:

'I would find that a very difficult question to answer. Shake-speare talks about the "seven orders of the lie" and duplicity comes in many forms. We have all, in our professional life, had experience of clients who are plainly lying but have managed to persuade themselves they are not lying. Query: are they lying? It is a philosophical point. I simply don't know what the Prime Minister persuaded himself to do. Assuming that he was not delusional, then, yes, we were deliberately misled.'

In September 2002, my immediate reaction was less philo-sophical. On leaving the Chamber I stopped in the Members' Lobby with Alan Simpson.

'Well,' I said, 'this is either a massive lie we are being told or else we are totally wrong.'

Alan thought about it and said, 'I think I know which it is.'

In repeated statements to the House of Commons until the fateful vote on 18 March 2003, the Prime Minister maintained that regime change was not the objective of either the American or the British Government. He had good reason to do so. At the meeting of 23 July 2002, the Attorney General, Lord Goldsmith, had warned that any war for the purpose of regime change would be illegal.

The conclusion is quite inescapable. Between July 2002 and March 2003, Parliament was grossly and repeatedly misled by ministers from whom it was entitled to expect total veracity on an issue of national war.

Revelation of the 'Downing Street memo' came in 2005 after myriad reports from the Intelligence and Security Committee (September 2003), the Foreign Affairs Committee (July 2003) and the Butler Report (July 2004). In all the evidence given to those committees, not one minister revealed the stark fact that, according to the best British intelligence, our American allies, from July 2002, viewed war as inevitable in pursuit of regime change and that they were 'fixing the intelligence to fit'.

The three months from December 2002 to March 2003 saw the inexorable march to war. In the Commons, the mood was febrile. For the anti-war lobby (mainly but not all on the Labour and Liberal Democrat benches) the mood veered wildly from optimism to despair. In the early days there were a number of real causes for optimism. The first was the growing number of rebels on the Labour benches. This was manifest by both the number and the names of those signing up to parliamentary Early Day Motions insisting on United Nations' resolutions, demanding greater accountability and ultimately a parliamentary vote. Included among these activists could be identified a growing cadre not normally associated with the 'usual suspects'. Cynics observed that self-interest may well have been part of their motive. Public aversion to the war was evident both in our daily post and in the growing number of meetings and demonstrations, which had their culmination in the March demonstration which numbered over a million participants in London alone.

Self-serving or not, the anti-war Labour MPs began to assume a critical mass which could no longer be dismissed or ignored by the Whips. The second flash of optimism was created, ironically, by the publication of the 'dodgy' dossier of January 2003. This masterpiece was created by Alastair Campbell and displayed all the formidable talents he had previously honed as a tabloid journalist. Like the *Sun* newspaper, Campbell's original stable, it was not short on pretension. The strap line *Iraq: Its Infrastructure of Concealment, Deception and Intimidation* certainly indicated a refreshing lack of balance. Unfortunately for Alastair, substantial parts of the dossier were lifted straight from the work of a Californian PhD student called Ibrahim al-Marashi. (No one has ever ascertained whether this thesis contributed to the doctorate eventually gained by Dr al-Marashi in 2004.) Campbell certainly saw that it had a certain number of shortcomings in its semantics which were to be subtly altered in the dodgy dossier itself.

The term 'monitoring' employed by al-Marashi, for instance, inexplicably became 'spying' on the pages of Alastair Campbell's oeuvre. The plagiarism was swiftly spotted and revealed by Brian Whitaker and Michael White in the *Guardian* on 7 February 2003. Leaks from the Foreign Office, freely available throughout Westminster, indicated that Jack Straw was 'incandescent' with rage. The Security Services, now well embedded into the political machinery, also stated that the dossier had not been cleared with them. In short, it was, as one very senior Labour minister who had held most great offices of state observed to me, 'an absolute grade A fuck-up'. Outside Parliament it vastly improved the anti-war cause and inside Parliament the number of potential rebels increased still further. A nice irony was provided by Colin Powell in America, who managed to provide a brief eulogy for the dossier before it was totally discredited. Cautiously, we began to feel a real sense of hope that either the war could be prevented or Britain's participation could be avoided. In my case, this optimism was increased by the legal issues of which I was becoming aware. I was privately informed by a member of the Bar, that high-ranking civil servants and army officers were increasingly alarmed at the potential illegality of the war. Unlike America, Britain was a signatory to the International Criminal Court Statute, rendering its citizens liable for the pursuit of unlawful war. Matrix Chambers founded by, among others, Cherie Blair, published an opinion to the effect that the war was illegal and gained no legitimacy from the existing United Nations' resolutions. I agreed with this view and attempted to put it before Jack Straw during one of his Commons' statements when he touched upon the 'revival theory' then being canvassed as a legal justification. I think Jack foresaw the nature of the intervention and, unusually for him, declined to give way.

Things also appeared to improve when Colin Powell, in early February, gave a now famous presentation to the United Nations. For the pro-war lobby it was a distinctly embarrassing affair and could well have been transferred, completely unaltered, into any one of the weekly topical comedies or game shows. Part of it consisted of a PowerPoint demonstration of 'sites' identified by American intelligence. One or two contained pictures of a lorry which, on close inspection, appeared to have some form of logo on the side resembling the advertisement for Tesco's home delivery. Other pictures were of a ploughed field indicating, according to the Head of the State Department, recent excavations of weapons of mass destruction. After the presentation, several of my constituents wrote to me with the same enquiry, namely, why had this intelligence not been brought to the attention of Hans Blix and the hundreds of weapons inspectors firmly embedded on Iraqi soil so they could literally dig them up? My polite but informal enquiries of Foreign Office ministers elicited no satisfactory response.

The case for war lay in ruins, but there was one aspect of the continuing debate that caused me concern. The pro-war party, led by the *Sun* outside Parliament and the Prime Minister within it, had begun loudly (the *Sun*) or more subtly (the Prime Minister) to vilify the war's opponents as anti-American. This was accompanied by the inevitable Churchillian references and those who had 'always opposed war against evil'. I wanted to use a parliamentary debate to deal firmly with this argument. I was given the opportunity in a general debate on defence in the world on 22 January 2003. Unusually, I circulated the text before the speech to a number of those prominently opposing the war and, I am pleased to say, received their approbation. In the speech I tried to explain the American paradox which, I said, 'is something I have lived with all my life':

> 'There is no country on the globe that has a greater breadth of internal freedoms, there is no country in the world that is more reviled for the perception, very often the accurate perception, that it actively denies those freedoms to others and

the present example of that, transparently, is the Palestinian Arabs. No country in the world, in my lifetime, has done more for the cause of peace and I have in mind the Marshall Plan which has underpinned economically the peace that we have enjoyed in Europe, and no country, in my lifetime, has been a greater cause for war. There is no country at the moment more committed to the war on the abstract noun of terrorism and yet there is no country in the world in my lifetime which has given more aid, succour and encouragement to more terrorist groups, more military dictatorships and more rogue states. To simply take a list, in no particular order, one recollects the corrupt Diem regime in Vietnam, the military overthrow of the democratically elected government of Salvador Allende in Chile and the support of the Contra guerillas in Nicaragua. One also recollects, ironically, the unalloyed support of Saddam Hussein in his war against Iran. In those days, the United Nations' weapons inspectors need have gone no further than the customs of the United States or even, possibly, the customs at Dover. My family, I am proud to say, fulfilled a number of roles in their generation in the Second World War. They never let me forget, as a child, the debt that we owed to American men and women and to America. Those of us who oppose the war do not harbour festering anti-American feelings within us. Our opposition is to the nature of the American regime which is as bad as any I can remember within that paradox. It is ruled, governed and motivated by a ghastly mixture of fundamental Christian evangelism, ruthless Zionism and the oil economy. That mix, if it is allowed to rule us in our international affairs, will bring us nothing but disaster.'

It was a measure of the public interest in the war that the speech, made in Parliament at 3 o'clock in the afternoon, brought a substantial post. With three exceptions (to the phrase 'ruthless Zionism'), all were in favour. I felt yet another surge of optimism. The final cause for hope lay in the United Nations. As opposition to the war intensified, so did pronouncements in the Commons, both by Blair and Jack Straw, that massive efforts were being made by Britain and America to obtain a suitable resolution in the Security Council. At one such debate, Tam Dalyell expressed the view to me that the Government was providing itself with an exit strategy, secretly hoping that the failure of a new resolution would provide the political justification for withdrawal. I felt ever happier.

The first serious reversal came, ironically, from France. At the beginning of March, President Chirac was asked to sum up his view of the vote in the Security Council. His answer was as follows:

> 'My position is that, whatever the circumstances, France will vote no because she considers this evening that there are no grounds for waging war in order to achieve the goal we have set ourselves, that is to disarm Iraq.'

I listened to his statement on the news and felt, even then, a mild sense of disquiet which was fully justified. The following day, Chirac's statement was spun out of all recognition. As I had anticipated, the words 'whatever the circumstances' were elevated to headline status while the words 'this evening' were buried. In one sentence Chirac had unwittingly provided precisely what the war lobby required. Jack Straw called the Chirac statement 'extraordinary'. The spin was all too clear. If the French were going to veto a Security Council resolution *whatever the circumstances*, then there was no point in seeking to achieve a resolution at all. It also provided the Government and the Murdoch press a magnificent opportunity to mount a collateral attack on the French. Once again it was the 'cheese-eating surrender monkeys' obstructing the just war against evil. At one stroke, the temperature changed. Hating Saddam Hussein was a comparatively recent phenomenon. Hating the French was Shakespearean.

The Government called a vote on a procedural motion on Iraq. The motion fell short of the endorsement for war but was plainly the Government's dress rehearsal. A strict three-line whip was placed on all Labour members, which was bitterly resented given the nature of the vote. In the tea rooms and bars, feverish counting began by both the Whips and the anti-war campaign, frequently sitting at adjacent tables. One Whip told me, confidentially, that the Government anticipated a rebellion of ninety. Blair was in the Commons for the debate but left at an early stage. While I was standing in the Members' Lobby, I was approached by a sympathetic journalist who, on this occasion, leaked information *to me*.

'I think you might like to know,' he said, 'that Blair has gone back for a televised phone-in on the war.'

'Thank you,' I said.

Within the hour we had disseminated written and verbal messages. While the House of Commons was debating the principle of war and subject to a three-line whip, the Prime Minister had gone straight to 'the people'. The opposition vote accelerated. In the end, 120 Labour members rebelled.

After that, things got better. On 7 March, Hans Blix announced to the United Nations that he was receiving cooperation from Iraq. It was not perfect, but he had been able to visit all sites which he had designated. Memorably, he poured scorn on the assertions that there was no disarmament. He pointed to the destruction of seventy missiles, saying 'these are not toothpicks'.

Then Robin Cook resigned. During the course of his resignation speech, I sat immediately behind him. I was three feet away, but it was a monumental performance at whatever distance. This eminent Cabinet minister and former Foreign Secretary simply did not believe that Iraq possessed weapons of mass destruction in the established sense.

At the end of Robin's speech, the packed Commons reacted in a way that I saw only once in my thirteen years in Parliament

– prolonged applause. As I watched my clapping colleagues, I remember wondering how many would hold to the rebels' cause.

After his statement I spoke to him briefly in the Members' Lobby. I asked: 'Do they know something you don't?'

'Oh yes,' he said. 'But it's not about Iraq.'

In the end it was not enough. On 18 March, the House of Commons voted for war. By any standards it was a great debate. I was lucky to be able to speak. Many were not. The Deputy Speaker confided in me that it was my reward for attending every single Iraq hearing. I would far rather have remained silent and won. The actual vote was never in doubt, as the Tories, inexplicably, lined up with the Government. The central issue was whether Blair would carry the majority of the Labour Party. To have proceeded to war without the majority of the Government benches would have been unthinkable. In the end, 139 Labour MPs voted against the war, well over half the non-Government members. Blair and the war party were saved by the hugely inflated 'payroll vote' that the Government had created and which is discussed elsewhere in this book.

Within hours the war had started and the theories of St Augustine were visited upon Baghdad. In a further application of the Augustinian theory, cities which refused to capitulate were devastated. Within months, Fallujah was effectively sacked. Because the city was completely isolated and ring-fenced before it was attacked, there has never been any count of casualties. Certainly there were thousands. It is now also widely accepted that white phosphorus was used against a defenceless civilian population.

After the attack on that city, I was invited on to the BBC News and expressed the view that the day would come when Fallujah and Guernica were spoken of in the same breath. That day has already arrived. The assessment of Iraqi deaths occasioned by the war varies according to method and analysis. There is a *Lancet* survey which places the deaths at 100,000. A wider survey by the

Johns Hopkins University based upon mortality rates before and after the invasion, put the figure at 600,000. In addition to the deaths and injuries, the priceless treasures of Mesopotamia were looted – the equivalent of ransacking the British Museum.

The Americans besieged themselves in the Green Zone while their soldiers painted on their tanks revenge slogans for 9/11. They thereby displayed the grotesque political illiteracy that was deliberately encouraged by both Bush and Blair. As Tam Dalyell repeatedly told the Commons, the only link between al-Qaeda and Saddam Hussein was that al-Qaeda tried to assassinate him, twice.

There were, of course, no weapons of mass destruction *at all*. Small findings would have undoubtedly been manipulated and spun. But there were literally *none*. For five years, British troops were isolated and besieged in their encampment at Basra. It was to this piece of ground that British Prime Ministers were limited. Wider journeys into the country they had 'liberated' were unthinkable, whatever the degree of military protection, in view of the extreme danger in which they would be placed.

At the time of writing, the extent of the disaster has provoked four inquiries, all deliberately calculated to be inadequate. The Intelligence and Security Committee sat in secret and was the creature of the Prime Minister. The Foreign Affairs Committee had no power to call witnesses. The Hutton Inquiry was restricted to the circumstances of the death of Dr David Kelly and Lord Butler reported only on the failings of the intelligence community. Nearly six years elapsed before an inquiry was set up by the Government to consider the political culpability that led us to war. The only inquiry which purported to exonerate any of the political decisions was the Hutton Inquiry, which had neither the mandate nor the evidence or brief to do so.

Curiously, the Hutton Inquiry produced the most satisfactory result for those who wished to see wider justice. His finding that the first dossier had not been 'sexed up' was received with disbelief. Almost universally, the media and the people proclaimed a whitewash. The verdict was entirely justified. As John Kampfner forcibly points out in *Blair's Wars*, there is no mention of Alastair Campbell's undoubted suggestion to Jonathan Powell that the dossier should be the subject of a 'substantial rewrite'. Also overlooked is the observation by Powell that 'the dossier was a bit of a problem because it included "nothing to demonstrate a threat, let alone an imminent threat from Saddam unless Iraq was attacked"'.

Andrew Gilligan, the BBC reporter responsible for the assertion that the dossier had been 'sexed up', was a witness at the Inquiry. His treatment by Hutton left no doubt as to both the nature and the tone of the final report. On the day before publication, a number of journalists, including Peter Oborne, organised a dinner for Gilligan at the Garrick. Both Peter Kilfoyle and I attended, in order to show solidarity from the Labour benches. Gilligan was, understandably, apprehensive, but was among friends. At the end of the evening, my parting words to Andrew were that he should be confident of final and total vindication.

In one sense, that came faster than anticipated. Alastair Campbell famously used the Hutton Report to stage a press conference at the Foreign Correspondents' Club. For a man with his media reputation, he committed an error of unbelievable crassness by entering down the grand staircase and calling for mass resignations from the BBC. ('Like a cross between Fred Astaire and Ronnie Kray', as one journalist told me.) In due course, Greg Dyke, the highly respected and much liked Director of the BBC, duly resigned. It was one of Campbell's last acts on behalf of Blair and it was a vainglorious disaster, ensuring lasting opprobrium and derision beside which Andrew Gilligan's temporary discomfiture was, in Campbell's words on another subject, 'a fucking gnat bite'.

The Butler Report suffered from two obvious deficiencies. The first was that the extent of its brief, enjoined as it was only to consider intelligence failures. Scrupulously (unlike Hutton), Butler avoided political strictures. The second disadvantage was the language in which it was written. Lord Butler, one of the most distinguished civil servants of his generation, speaks Mandarin. This is a language known to fellow high-ranking civil servants but wholly unknown to the political hacks or editors who received his report (an honourable exception was David Hughes on the *Daily Mail*). Accordingly, it was hailed as another vindication/whitewash. It was, in fact, no such thing and Lord Butler has publicly, on a number of occasions, expressed astonishment that his report should have been taken as any kind of approbation or vindication of either the Government or the Security Services. This can be sharply illustrated in one important passage. In paragraph 472 of the Butler Report, he observes:

> 'We have also recorded our surprise that policy makers and the intelligence community did not, as the generally negative results of UNMOVIC [the United Nations Monitoring, Verification and Inspection Commission] became increasingly apparent, re-evaluate the early 2003 quality of the intelligence.'

Lord Butler, as I subsequently pointed out to the House of Commons, was speaking Mandarin, a language in which he was fluent. In Mandarin, the word 'surprised' does not mean 'good lord, is that the time?' It means 'we are absolutely astonished and dumbfounded that this occurred'. In this particular instance, the Butler Committee were expressing just such astonishment that the Hans Blix reports on Iraqi cooperation were effectively ignored during the latter part of 2002 and the approach to the war. That is not a vindication. It is, as Lord Butler intended it to be, a damning indictment. You need to speak Mandarin to understand that.

Finally, after repeated attempts in the House of Commons to obtain a proper inquiry into the Iraq disaster, the Government conceded; and on 24 June 2009, the Chilcot Inquiry was born. In giving cautious welcome to the very existence of an inquiry, I drew attention, as did others, to the manifest and deliberate deficiencies in its composition. The Chilcot Inquiry contains, within its members, not a single man or woman with any experience, let alone expertise, in the forensic process. None of them has any court experience. None of them have ever cross-examined anybody and they have no counsel to do it for them. The results of this have, inevitably, in some cases, been quite deplorable.

By far the worst example has been the treatment of the former Prime Minister and the former Attorney General on the subject of the legal opinion for war. The facts of this political and legal iniquity were not revealed until the election campaign of 2005 when, finally, through gritted teeth, the Government provided the Attorney General's written opinion on the legality of the war. This document is dated 7 March 2003. It is a careful and studied piece of work, set about with serious reservations. Crucially, it dealt with the 'revival argument' which maintained, in short, that the recent UN resolution (1441) which threatened 'serious consequences' if Saddam Hussein did not cooperate, was capable of reviving resolution 678, which brought an end to the Kuwait War on the basis of just such cooperation. In short, non-cooperation, it was argued, revived the state of war. This argument was, to say the least, highly doubtful, a fact which is acknowledged in the course of the Attorney General's opinion:

'But a reasonable case does not mean that if the matter ever came before a court I would be confident that the court would agree with that view.'

In view of that doubt, he advises that:

'The safest legal course would be to secure the adoption of a further resolution to authorise the use of force.'

The clear and inevitable consequence of that opinion is that no British soldier or commander fighting in Iraq could be certain or even reasonably sure that the cause was legal. Military commanders of the highest rank have since expressed the view to me that no British Chief of Defence Staff could possibly have agreed to consign his men to war on the basis of that legal opinion. Blair must have known this very well.

On 14 March, precisely seven days later, Lord Goldsmith produced a written statement for the House of Lords. The statement is completely unequivocal. It expresses the view that resolution 1441 is sufficient to revive resolution 678, as Saddam Hussein is in material breach of his obligations to disarm. The doubts and reservations expressed in writing a week previously totally disappeared. On the same day the Attorney General attended Cabinet.

The Cabinet was informed verbally that, in his view, the war was legal. No equivocation was advanced and no doubts were expressed. Critically, no one in the Cabinet was informed of the existence of written opinion which had been produced for the Prime Minister seven days previously. Not one minister asked if the opinion they were then receiving in Cabinet had been produced in writing. In the Commons' debate, when the Chilcot Inquiry was set up, I said that this issue, more than any other, should be the subject of robust investigation. It was of transcendent importance and significance for two reasons. First, had the Cabinet or Parliament known of the original opinion it would have had a devastating effect on the case for war. Secondly, which was the only safe inference, Goldsmith's opinion had changed as a result of conversations with the Prime Minister. It spoke volumes for Blair's determination to proceed to war at all costs.

Tony Blair was called to give evidence to the Chilcot Inquiry on 27 January 2010. At half-past seven on the Monday preceding his appearance, I presented myself at the offices of the Chilcot Inquiry with a letter and an extract of a question I had put to the Prime Minister. The Parliamentary Question simply asked the Prime Minister to say whether the Cabinet had been *made aware not of the content but of the existence of the Attorney General's opinion*. The answer he gave at the dispatch box was transparent avoidance.

In my letter I invited the Inquiry specifically to deal with this issue and relentlessly to pursue the failure of the Attorney General to provide his opinion to the Cabinet and to Parliament.

I duly watched the evidence and 'cross-examination' of both Blair and Goldsmith. When this issue failed to be investigated, I found myself unconsciously kicking an innocent piece of furniture. No enquiry was made as to the conversations between the Prime Minister and the Attorney General. No attempt was made to investigate their meetings, whether these were minuted or what had occurred. No attempt was made to elicit the Prime Minister's view of the opinion with which he had been faced. No investigation was made as to the silence at the Cabinet meeting attended by both the Attorney General and the Prime Minister. No investigation was made of the Attorney General as to his view of his duty to the Cabinet and Parliament and as to why he had, effectively, buried the opinion of 7 March. In forensic terms, it was a deplorable exhibition. The Chilcot Inquiry is only partly to blame. None of its members have the requisite forensic skills to cross-examine on these issues but, equally, they are partly to blame. They had the information. Goldsmith's conduct is neither technical nor legal. It is entirely obvious and required the most detailed investigation, including a demand for all surrounding and supporting documents. The explanation given by Goldsmith for the change in his view is that he had met the Chief of Defence Staff and the head of the Civil Service and had been asked, effectively, to firm up his opinion. Legal training is wholly unnecessary to understand the proposition that being asked to 'firm up' an opinion is no justification for changing it.

I immediately presented an article to the *Guardian*, which was published online in their 'Comment is Free' section. The extract (below), which was printed in the main paper, cogently reflected the rest of the article and was the subject of a considerable postbag from those who had seen the evidence and who, by the tenor of their letters, had also been kicking the furniture:

> 'Whether by accident or design, Tony Blair has precisely the tribunal he would have devised. An Inquiry has been created that is devoid of the forensic tools properly to inquire. It is a tribunal without teeth, providing trial without tribulation. And, of course, evidence is not on oath. The results were predictable. In the main areas of controversy the Inquiry has proved itself totally ill-equipped to test or challenge testimony that demands the most rigorous and forensic examination.'

I also wrote to John Chilcot and, in reply, received an invitation to a personal meeting. It was a remarkably open and candid meeting, the price of which was an undertaking I willingly gave that its content would not be published until the publication of the report. It is an undertaking that I will honour, but in doing so I can simply state that the trenchant basis of my criticism remains unaltered.

Iraq was Blair's last war. In view of the extent of the disaster, Labour, remarkably, returned to Government. My own majority was reduced to 213 in circumstances which I discuss elsewhere in this book. But I did survive. In the neighbouring, nearly identical constituency of Gravesham, my colleague, Chris Pond, was not so lucky. It is reasonable to suppose that his support for the Iraq War was one of the deciding factors in his defeat. At the first meeting of the Labour PLP after the election, I braved the triumphalist mood to point out to the Prime Minister that his leadership and the Iraq War had cost us sixty parliamentary seats and a massive fall in the popular vote. For this contribution I was duly and roundly booed.

Blair's final war had not only destroyed large parts of Iraq, it had also destroyed large areas of public political faith. The Cabinet had been revealed as the most supine in history, a verdict from Peter Hennessy, whose adherence to the principle of Cabinet government has been one of the longest and most distinguished parts of his long and distinguished career. John Prescott, a member of that Cabinet as the Deputy Prime Minister, also gave evidence to the Chilcot Inquiry and I record it here and refrain from comment. The reader will make his or her own judgement on this contribution from a man who once sat in the second most powerful seat in the land:

Sir Roderic Lyne: 'Okay. Shall we move on to the intelligence then, the JIC assessments?'
Rt Hon The Lord Prescott: 'Yes. That's interesting, because when I kept reading them, I kept thinking to myself, "Is this intelligence?" It is basically what you have heard somewhere and what somebody else has told everybody. That's presumably how intelligence is brought to bear. So I got the feeling it wasn't very substantial but it clearly was robust. As we move more and more whether there was evidence about – involved in the weapons of mass destruction, the conclusions were a little ahead I think of the evidence we had, but perhaps that's the way it is. So I am curious to have then read the evidence provided I think in 2004 by JIC, if we look at their recommendations they made to us, they were frankly wrong and built too much on too little information. I think that was made by a number of the witnesses to you.

'That was my impression at the time, but, you know, I just thought, "This is the intelligence document. This is what you have." It seemed robust but not enough to justify that you could do that. What you do in intelligence is a bit of tittle-tattle here and a bit more information there and a judgment made, isn't it, to be fair.'

Curiously, the effect on Parliament was partly beneficial. One hundred and thirty-nine Labour Members of Parliament found the political will to oppose this disaster, irrespective of the Whip or the withdrawal of their own patronage. A number of ministers, including John Denham, honourably resigned, and it remains one of the tragic ironies of the Parliament that Robin Cook did not live to see his total and sad vindication.

Forty per cent of British people believe that Blair should be tried as a war criminal. I am one of that number. The political realities of power will ensure that this particular piece of criminal justice is never done. There is an infinitely more important verdict and that lies with the people. At the end of his speech to the American Congress, Blair expressed confidence that 'history would forgive us'. Possibly. Millions of his own citizens are unlikely to do so.

CHAPTER 21

OF NEMESIS

*In which we remember Galaxy man and the damage he has caused
– Remember the inequities of the block vote revealed in Yates's Wine
Lodge and reflect on the doubtful future of the Labour Party and the
meaning of the Millennium Dome.*

In the mid 1990s, Tony Blair, then simply a Member of Parliament for Sedgefield and Opposition front-bench spokesman, went on a routine canvass in his constituency. While doing so, he came upon a man in the front driveway of his purchased and refurbished council house. The man was polishing his Ford Galaxy and, in the conversation that followed, expressed his admiration for Margaret Thatcher and her contribution to the body politic. The meeting was to have a profound impact on Tony Blair, which he conveyed on a number of occasions to Labour Party Conferences and associated meetings. It was his Damascus moment. History, of course, is littered with such moments that have changed the course of science, art, or the fate of nations. Archimedes famously leapt from his bath, Robert the Bruce liberated Scotland on the basis of his observations of a spider, and Sir Alastair Pilkington observed hot fat lying on the surface of the water in which he was washing a frying pan. This last led to the invention of float glass which has revolutionised architecture and the face of towns and cities throughout the world. The Sedgefield meeting was such a moment. The identity of the man with the Galaxy remains unknown, but he bears an awesome responsibility. On his gravestone may well be marked, 'Here lies Mr Galaxy, who destroyed the Labour Party, the greatest international engine for social change in the twentieth century'.

One must not libel or defame this unknown (and possibly even fictitious) gentleman. His true character is unknown to us. What we do know is the view that Tony Blair formed of it. It was this perception, more than any other, which was to found the New Labour Project. Mr Galaxy loves his car. He has a family and his aspirations for himself and for them are, essentially, selfish. He does not belong to a union or institutions based upon either class or charity. As a result of his education, he knows little history and virtually nothing of its political dimensions. His source of culture, information and amusement is the commercial mass media. He can sing or hum popular songs and a number of the more infectious jingles which advertise all manner of products from cars to cosmetics. He has a wary belief in an Almighty of some kind stimulated by horror films such as *The Omen*. He does not attend church and is more involved in the cult of the celebrity than the celestial.

Mr Galaxy does not exist, but his perception has dominated the electoral ambitions of New Labour. The working class is no more. The horny hand of toil now carries the chamois leather. The obeisance to Galaxy man, ultimately, involved the rejection of principle and this, inevitably, corrodes any political movement. For the Left, it is deadly. In order to understand why, a very short tour of Labour's political history is necessary.

Two great progenitive forces created the British Labour Party at the start of the twentieth century. The first was the trade union movement, newly emancipated and thrusting towards political power. The second was the unique intellectual weight of British socialism, to be found in the works of Bentham, Morris, Cobbett, Wilde, Shaw and in the poetry of Percy Bysshe Shelley. Karl Marx, who had gloomily predicted the British revolution, was fully cognisant of the first, and totally indifferent to the second. In their search for political power and influence, the trade unions had made overtures to the Liberal Party. Meetings had taken place and their overtures had been quietly and firmly refused. The Liberal Party, inheritors of the Whig tradition, perceived themselves to be the custodians of individual liberty and of democratic reform. For them, the collective industrial and economic power of the organised working class was a matter for social rather than political history. The trade unions famously formed their own party, which swiftly attracted the radical and reforming intelligentsia into a formidable coalition, unique in political history. The Cooperative movement, the campaigners for universal suffrage, the Fabian Societies and a raft of non-conformists all signed up to Labour and, in the course of a quarter of a century, the Liberal Party was left in ruins. No political movement in history has achieved more for the social condition of any nation than Labour. The principles of collective bargaining, universal education, the creation of the welfare state and the universal provision of housing were established in barely half a century. This was achieved by the inspired use of a free democratic process against a background of global totalitarian conflict.

By the 1980s, the Party was gripped by a crisis of both identity and purpose. Because of the democratic nature of its institutions, the crisis was publicly and dramatically revealed on a daily basis. It was ruthlessly exploited by a hostile press and the cumulative effect was electoral disaster. The two reasons for the crisis were not difficult to analyse. First, the Party was a victim of its own success. The public services which it had fought for and created were now a matter of established fact. The universal provision of health, education and social welfare were no longer matters of conflicting theology.

'The National Health Service,' said Margaret Thatcher, 'is safe in our hands.' For David Cameron, the improvement of the Health Service was the central thrust of his General Election campaign. On public service, the political divisions were now, crudely, over management and efficiency – which may be an important campaign issue but is hardly, as Austin Mitchell once observed, the battle hymn of the republic.

Mass education had also ensured that the class system was dissolving, and with it the guaranteed support of a tribal working class. In addition, by the 1980s the power of the trade union movement was in steep decline; a process accelerated rather than created by the rule of Margaret Thatcher. The exponential growth of industrial technology had ensured the end of the mass workforce. The inevitable march of multi-national corporations within a globalised context destroyed the main sanctions behind collective bargaining, and multi-national trade unionism remained part of the mythology of songs such as the 'Internationale'. Finally, their rigid relationship with the Labour Party had also become democratically corrupt. The manipulation of the block vote at Conference was a repellent annual spectacle, calculated only to alienate the voting public. One of my earliest memories of a Labour Party Conference in Blackpool in 1974 is sitting in Yates's Wine Lodge over lunch on the first day of Conference. A number of union barons, which included Hugh Scanlon, Clive Jenkins and Ray Buckton, formed the hub of an admiring crowd. They were seated at a table behind a number of bottles of Yates's champagne and the remains of the splendid steak sandwiches which are, to this day, available at its carvery. The Conference agenda, consisting of interminable and often unintelligible composite resolutions, was open on the table before them and they were quite publicly and volubly fixing the vote. Embedded in my memory is Ray Buckton inspecting his

with celebrity and wealth. Thus the Labour Party was drawn, without protest, into the bed of market capital and produced a political deformity known as the New Labour Project. This strutting infant Caliban enjoyed a number of midwives. In no particular order, these were John Major and a Tory Party doomed by exhaustion and faction, a Labour Party collectively desperate to obtain power, a Parliamentary Party packed with professional politicians clamouring for patronage, a remarkable number of financial backers who could sense a political wind heavy with the scent of ermine and, finally, Rupert Murdoch, always anxious to appear as the handmaiden of inevitable political change.

This political mutant required not only life but a philosophy which was duly supplied in the form of the Third Way. This pretentious nonsense was the brainchild of Mr (rapidly Lord) Philip Gould. Such was the euphoria of the time, that it briefly attracted serious consideration before being (rightly) consigned to the book of political jokes where it now resides. There was, however, one aspect of the Third Way which was positively dangerous and ultimately destructive. In postulating a relatively benign pluralist society, the Third Way was unoriginal in thought and irrelevant in practice. What made it dangerous as a political credo was not the policy of government but the nature and form that the government was to take. Implicit in the Third Way was the growth of 'consensus' politics. This found its early embodiment in the proliferation of focus groups, forums and parliamentary road shows, attempting to create ad hoc impromptu representatives of 'the people's views'. One excruciating experiment in which I declined to participate was the Big Conversation. This odious piece of populism provided a national opportunity for special interest groups to commit their well-known views into formulaic submissions which were, ultimately, ignored. It also fulfilled the purpose of distracting large numbers of Labour backbenchers from their parliamentary duties and any scrutiny of executive power. Blair's contempt for

Parliament was well known, and was reinforced by the behaviour of the Government Whips. Far more dangerous, however, was the attempt to create a substitute government involving a direct dialogue with 'the people' through the agency of the media and its manipulation by Alastair Campbell.

In 1998 the *New Statesman* invited me to assess the risk of what I had termed a Tyranny of Enlightenment. After barely one year of Labour Government I wrote:

> 'Dangerous paradoxes exist. If Government is to be conducted upon the basis of populist forums and Soviet consensus then the House of Commons faces ultimate redundancy. Similarly if its policy and raison d'être shift to the centre ground then the legitimacy of the whip ultimately gives way to the dictates of conscience. To support a government simply on the basis of its brand name is barren and dishonest politics.
>
> 'And yet, of course, the acquiescence of the House of Commons is essential. The result of this paradox is potentially disastrous as Parliament is simultaneously ignored and rigorously controlled. If one superimposes the proclivity of this executive to invest vast power and influence in our unelected administrators and appointees, in and outside the Cabinet, then the potential for grave constitutional conflict should be obvious.'

I ended with Oscar Wilde's great observation:

> 'There are three kinds of despots. There is the despot who tyrannises over the body. There is the despot who tyrannises over the soul. There is the despot who tyrannises over the body and soul alike. The first is called the Prince. The second is called the Pope. The third is called the People.'

In addition to a philosophy, New Labour required a symbol.

This was conveniently supplied by historical coincidence as the Millennium Dome was re-born.

The Dome is not strictly a New Labour phenomenon. In 1996, Greenwich had been chosen as the site for a new national exhibition centre inspired by the 1951 Festival of Britain. In January 1997, the New Millennium Experience Company (NMEC) was awarded £399 million from the Lottery (the Millennium Commission) on the basis that it would, itself, raise a further £194 million from tickets, food, sales and merchandising. The development of the project, however, remained doubtful until the election of New Labour in May 1997. For Tony Blair, the project was a magnificent opportunity to mark New Labour and the new Millennium at the same time. Peter Mandelson was put in charge – and created an economic and cultural disaster.

From the beginning there was no parliamentary control. When revealed, the nature of the Dome evoked in Parliament a mixture of derision and concern. At the beginning of 1998, with two years to go, no decision whatsoever had been taken about the content of this massive project.

As the excavators commenced work, it became clear that one benefit to the Greenwich Peninsula would be the excavation and removal of vast tons of toxic waste. Unhappily, much of it was dumped in my constituency on the Isle of Grain. This simply added to a sense of growing frustration.

I began a long series of Parliamentary Questions, attempting to obtain the accounts of the Dome company (NMEC). One of the five objectives for the Millennium Experience was that there should be no call on public expenditure as a result of the project. Showing the accounts to Parliament seemed a reasonable request. On the extraordinary ground that the money being expended was not 'public expenditure' but was taken from the Millennium Fund (the Lottery) administered by the Millennium Commission and with no accountability to Parliament, no accounts were forthcoming.

Since there was no parliamentary route to question ministers, it became necessary to enlist the media. On 1 February 1998, the *Sunday Times* was good enough to carry an article by me entitled 'A Joke Monument to the Ills of our Age' describing the Dome as 'a cosmic joke of vast proportions'. I continued:

'At worst it is a millennial metaphor for the twentieth century. An age in which all things, like the Dome itself, became disposable. A century in which forest and cities, marriages, animal species, races, religions and even the Earth itself, became ephemeral. What more cynical monument can there be for this totalitarian cocksure fragile age than a vast temporary plastic bowl, erected from the aggregate contributions of the poor through the National Lottery. Despite the spin, it remains a massive pantheon to the human ego, the Ozymandias of its time.'

The Press, sensing a cover-up, joined in:

MANDELSON RAPPED OVER 'SECRET' £450m DEALS
Evening Standard
MP 'STONEWALLED' ON DOME PROJECT
Independent
MP CALLS MANDELSON TO ACCOUNT OVER DOME
Independent

None of this endeared me to Peter Mandelson.

In the ensuing two years, expenditure moved from chaos to catastrophe. In November 1999, the Millennium Commission donated an extra £50 million. When the event opened, attendance was so poor that a further £60 million was allocated to meet day-to-day running costs. Jenny Page, the Chief Executive, was sacked. In May, the Millennium Commission (the Lottery) donated another £29 million and demanded the sacking of Bob Ayling as the Chairman. In August 2000, the Millennium Commission provided a further 'loan' of £43 million and on 5 September this was increased by a further £47 million by way of grant, making a grand total from the Lottery fund of £628 million. This figure equated neatly to £1 million per constituency. I indulged in a daily fantasy of the expenditure of £1 million on worthy projects within Medway or, indeed, £3 million within the Medway Towns. Sometimes my fantasies drifted into other parts of Britain that I knew and loved and reflected on the schools, hospitals, woodlands, canals, bridges, universities or grand and permanent buildings that could have absorbed over half a billion pounds at 1998 prices. When finally the accounts were obtained from Price Waterhouse, it transpired that the project was broke and, worse still, was trading while insolvent – an offence under the Companies Act.

By the end of 1998, Mandelson had departed from Government and, perforce, the Dome Project, as a result of his failure to declare a 'loan' from Geoffrey Robinson by way of a mortgage of £300,000 in order to purchase a house in London suitable for his status.

Mandelson was replaced by Lord 'Charlie' Falconer, who became the sole shareholder in the Dome company and, thereby, responsible for debts wrongfully incurred. Happily ensconced in the Lords, Charlie was, of course, immune from the rougher questioning in the House of Commons. Unexpectedly, I had the opportunity to question him when he was being interviewed on 5 Live. Exercising a degree of mischief, the director of the programme telephoned me and invited me to 'phone in' to ask a question, which I duly did. It was, I suppose, a low blow, but nothing compared to the pummelling being handed out to the Lottery Fund. I asked Charlie whether he was concerned about his personal liability as a director and shareholder of a company which was trading whilst insolvent and accruing millions of pounds' worth of debts. He provided an extraordinary answer which, at least, scored highly for candour.

'You know, Bob,' he said, 'we regard the Millennium Fund as a bank.'

Michael Heseltine was, at the time, one of the trustees of the Millennium Fund, and when I informed him, during the course of a parliamentary debate, that Charlie Falconer regarded him as a bank, I was delighted to see his expression of shocked disbelief.

By the end of 2000, the Auditors' report revealed a startlingly hitherto unknown fact. After the observation that the company was insolvent, the report revealed that the Government had provided the directors of the Dome company with an indemnity, in the following terms:

'In consideration of their continuing to act as directors, the Government will indemnify the directors of NMEC in respect of any personal civil liability including, without limitation, wrongful trading or similar misfeasance by reason of the company's insolvency.'

In other words, the Government had secretly undertaken a debt liability for the insolvency of NMEC which was being happily paid off by the Lottery Fund.

The contents of the Dome were finally auctioned in the 'sale of the century'. (No bidder, apparently, was found for the centrepiece – a hermaphrodite colossus which could be entered and exited from every orifice at no extra charge. The face of this colossal figure was barely human and resembled no member of the NMEC or the New Labour Project.)

Vast public expenditure has since been turned into satisfactory private profit for the company which, at the end of 2000, relieved the Government of the £1 million a month for the building's maintenance. The O2 now provides the venue for pop concerts and there are recurring applications for a mega-casino which, I suppose, constitutes the 'enduring legacy' which was the Government's precondition for the Millennium experience.

The whole ghastly business had a passably amusing sequel in 2007. One of the main financiers of O2 is Philip Anschutz, the 126th richest man in America, who possesses a fine business brain and a large ranch in Kansas. In 2007, he had expressed an interest in creating a mega-casino within the O2 area. In the same year, he was visited at his Kansas ranch by John Prescott, the Deputy Prime Minister. The visit was not declared in the Members' Book of Interests on the basis that it was 'official business'. Given the position of both the Deputy Prime Minister and Mr Anschutz, this may have appeared, at least, unwise. The visit was (inevitably) revealed, and John Prescott announced that he would certainly make a declaration in the register even though he was not, technically, bound to do so. The scandal failed to diminish and the Deputy Prime Minister duly appeared on the *Today* programme to be cross-examined by John Humphrys. In a comparatively mild interview he was asked the obvious question, namely what Government business was being transacted on Mr Anschutz's ranch in Kansas. In a splendidly long and multi-functional answer, the Deputy Prime Minister indicated that the visit was, in some way, associated with the 'Doha Round'. This international trade mechanism is a means by which poor countries may obtain access to rich markets for their primary produce. John Humphrys indicated, rather than expressed, a measure of disbelief, whereupon John Prescott added the secondary explanation that he had always been a huge fan of cowboy films and wanted to see a 'real ranch'. The interview was not a happy one for the Deputy Prime Minister and illustrated the rule, well known to barristers, that it is always best to run one defence rather than two. If you attempt the second course there is always a possibility that both will be disbelieved.

In the great scheme of things, the Dome was not of the greatest political significance and the sums lost to the public were dwarfed by the massive subsidy handed to unregulated banks in the crash of 2009. It did, however, provide a coruscating insight into the nature of government and, with it, the Third Way. This was intended to be the 'People's Dome'. This was bread and circuses, millennium style. At one level, democratic politics has always represented struggle between the mores of Greece and Rome. On this occasion Rome won hands down and, in so doing, had leached the public subscriptions of the poor.

In the final Labour Parliament, the New Labour Project became soiled gaberdine. Its nemesis finally came when it was revealed that its one claim to sound government, prudent management of the economy, was built on the sand of toxic debt.

The New Labour Project and the Third Way were, essentially, domestic phenomena, but it is impossible not to reflect on the might-have-beens. Would the Labour Party of Clem Attlee, Nye Bevan, Harold Wilson, Jim Callaghan or (tragically) John Smith have joyfully endorsed George W. Bush, Donald Rumsfeld or Dick Cheney? Would they have signed up to the Project for a New American Century? Would they have produced the dodgy dossiers to mislead the people and Parliament into war? Would these denizens of old Labour have sought the private hospitality of Silvio Berlusconi or posed and postured on billionaires' yachts in Corfu? Is it possible to conceive of John Smith, Clem Attlee or Harold Wilson supplicating behind George W. Bush, offering to run errands to the Middle East, and being received with the humiliating 'Yo Smith/Attlee/Wilson'?

In writing this memoir I am conscious of the accusation of ingratitude. I came to Parliament at a comparatively late age on the crest of a Labour surge. Did I owe that to New Labour? Were the assaults on both civil liberties and on three different countries of the world the price I should pay quietly for my own fortune and the years of immense pleasure and satisfaction that I have enjoyed? I have thought hard on this. I am not, I think, a curmudgeon by nature, nor do I possess the hair shirt of socialist orthodoxy. I owe my time in Parliament to the Labour Party itself, to which I still belong and to which the civilised world owes a debt beyond reckoning.

The pleasures of radical politics are still readily available outside Parliament. I have always taken great pleasure in the works of British socialists: eccentric, iconoclastic and benign. In particular, I regularly revisit Oscar Wilde's 'Study of the Soul of Man Under Socialism' in which he writes:

> 'But the best amongst the poor are never grateful. They are ungrateful, discontented, disobedient, and rebellious. They are quite right to be so. Charity they feel to be a ridiculously inadequate mode of partial restitution, or a sentimental dole usually accompanied by some impertinent attempt on the part of the sentimentalist to tyrannise over their private lives. Why should they be grateful for the crumbs that fall from the rich man's table? They should be seated at the board, and are beginning to know it.'

And again:

> 'Socialism itself will be of value simply because it will lead to Individualism.'

Amen to that.

A POSTSCRIPT

The Labour Party continues to exist. Just. After the collapse of the Labour vote in 2010, commentators expressed amazement at the surge of new members who applied to join. It did not surprise me. Many of those will be taken from the tens of thousands who destroyed their Party cards but now perceive once again the future possibility of a democratic socialist government. But, contrary to partisan punditry from commentators such as Polly Toynbee, the present Coalition Government is not a hope for Labour, it is a potential political grave. The nation wanted a Conservative Government on probation and that is precisely what it has unwittingly achieved. For the first time since Lloyd George, a Liberal stands at the dispatch box and deals with Prime Minister's Questions (not at all badly at that). Liberal Democrats sit at the Cabinet table. The Party that was reduced to six Members of Parliament has returned from the political abyss and is no longer a freely available joke. Their own, once mocked, brand of environmentalism and their steadfast adherence to the principles of civil liberty throughout the last thirteen years, now chime perfectly with a substantial part of the public mood.

It is Labour which has lost its essential raison d'être, its identity and its purpose. Recovery is still possible, but to achieve it we must return to the bedrock of our beliefs. The watchword of New Labour was 'modernisation'. The most elementary etymology tells us that the radical owes its name to radix (the root). The moderniser to modus (fashion).

The challenges of modern politics are not obscure. They are to rescue the domestic and global under-classes and to ensure their willing rewarded participation in free societies which inhabit an improving and secure environment. For these we require international peace and rationality, the essential Fabian virtues of the true Labour Party. We must cease to be a tiny strutting figure in the giant shadow of unstable friends. The Romans always encouraged their satraps to rush first headlong into battle in the vainglorious pursuit of influence and near certainty of death, so let us learn and, whilst learning, revisit the Book of David and attempt to avoid the fate of Uriah the Hittite, thrust into the front line for the convenience and gratification of his cuckolding king.

Tony Blair departed the Parliament he disliked at the very moment he ceased to be Prime Minister. His assiduous cultivation of the American Right now brings its own financial rewards. It also brought him the office of Peace Envoy to the Middle East. On *Have I Got News for You,* I was asked for my reaction to this appointment. I replied that there are approximately 6.5 billion people on earth and I could only think of one less suited to the job. He has held that post for three years. Before the atrocious assault on Gaza by Israeli Forces in 2008 he had not once visited that besieged and beleaguered strip of land.

On *Have I Got News for You* I was wrong, but only just.

EPILOGUE

This memoir was first published in June 2011. Twelve months have since passed – time enough to reflect on the political landscape and observe some significant and welcome change. Coalition government has proved surprisingly stable. Those who wanted a Tory government on probation have achieved something very close. It is possible to celebrate at least a pause in the relentless, populist assault on civil liberty which formed the cultural identity of New Labour. At the time of writing intrusive surveillance powers are included in the legislative program. Defeating them will form a test of parliamentary will. There has been only one new military adventure – Libya – which enjoyed international legitimacy and, to date, a measure of success.

Otherwise two epic developments demand renewed consideration – the continuing banking crisis, centred on the uncertain destiny of Europe and the fall of the House of Murdoch. With the benefit of hindsight they can be seen to possess a clear political nexus.

The character of the New Labour administration (discussed in chapter twenty-one) both encouraged and encompassed the simultaneous growth of the financial tower of Babel and the political power of the Murdoch Empire. It is no accident that these toxic and corrosive mutants rose, prospered and collapsed in virtual tandem. Both were fed and nurtured by a government and a political ethic steeped in populist presentation and the adulation of money. The one became the handmaiden of the other. Banks provided profligate borrowing and the pantomime profits that sustained the illusion of sound and prosperous government. In return they were rewarded with purblind regulation and implicit approval. The Murdoch press provided florid, near fanatical support for illegal foreign wars and the erosion of liberty which included the repeated excoriation of liberal opposition. In return they were rewarded with extraordinary access, influence and obsequious flattery.

The effect for both was the same. A vaunting arrogance founded on a perception of uncontrolled, untrammelled power. The result was the near collapse of the economy and a pusillanimous, delinquent form journalism directly derived from the culture of a family clique.

The banking disaster will receive no formal public scrutiny. It is in truth unnecessary, since public opinion has reached its verdict. For decades, it will be impossible to engineer such grotesque private enrichment based on public risk.

The fall of Murdoch provoked the Leveson Enquiry. Daily it reveals and dissects a strutting gangster world of patronage, corruption and casual intimidation. Thankfully, unlike Chilcot, this is a proper enquiry. It is chaired by a fine judge and conducted with a forensic precision which resembles the meticulous peeling of protective hide. The analogy with the fall of Al Capone is irresistible. Phone hacking, like Capone's tax evasion, was the least of the political and ethical damage inflicted by Murdoch. As with Capone it was the belief in untouchable power which contained its own nemesis.

Rebekah Brooks, former Chief Executive of News International, has just concluded her evidence to Leveson. It began with a saccharine appeal for press freedom and was followed by the unwillingly extracted details of her cloying relationships with Blair and Cameron. A feeling of nausea was inevitable but it is swiftly followed by a sense of universal relief at the passing of a putrid age.

Bob Marshall-Andrews
May 2012

LIST OF ILLUSTRATIONS

1. Gill in Africa
2. Neil Kinnock
3. Author at Parliamentary Palace of Varieties charity event
4. Author in constituency
5. Author with Ian Hislop, Cancer Research fundraiser
6. Brian Sedgemore
7. Alan Simpson
8. Lynne Jones
9. Alice Mahon
10. Hilary Armstrong
11. David Blunkett
12. David Davis
13. Boris Johnson
14. Martin Rowson cartoon, 'Lazarus Not Failing to Rise from the Dead'
15. Martin Rowson cartoon, calling for the resignation of the Speaker
16. Author speaking in the House of Commons
17. Author speaking in Westminster Hall
18. Author on first day as MP for Medway
19. Author with Fred Bacon and Peter Hennessey

Cover versos: The Cartoonist's Calendar, Nos. 7 and 133. Both reproduced with kind permission of Martin Rowson.

Credits for the photographs
Author 1, 2, 3, 4, 5, 16, 17, 18, 19; David Mansell/Guardian News & Media Ltd 6, 7, 8, 9, 10, 11, 12, 13; Martin Rowson 14, 15

ACKNOWLEDGEMENTS

With love and thanks to my family, Gill, Laura, Will, Tom and Anna for their constant support and laughter, to the Medway Labour party especially Derek and Joyce Esterson; to John Davey and the Profile team and to Old Testament Prophets wherever they are.

INDEX